Jean Manco took a broad interdisciplinary approach in her work, integrating the very latest research in DNA studies with archaeology, history and linguistics to delve into the deep history of Europe and its peoples and bring new and often controversial conclusions to a wide audience. She had a particular interest in archaeogenetics and what they can tell us about migrations of people in the past, which came to fruition in this, her last book. She was the author of *Ancestral Journeys* and *Blood of the Celts*, both published by Thames & Hudson.

JEAN MANCO

The Origins of the Anglo-Saxons

DECODING THE ANCESTRY OF THE ENGLISH

137 illustrations

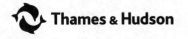

In memory of Sir Terry Pratchett,
with the assurance that this book
has maps and runes in it

JEAN MANCO 1946–2018

Frontispiece *An early 6th-century square-headed brooch
from a grave in Chessell Down, Isle of Wight, decorated
in Anglo-Saxon Style I; 13.8 cm (5½ inches) long.*

The Origins of the Anglo-Saxons © 2018 and 2019
Thames & Hudson Ltd, London

Text by Jean Manco

First published in 2018 in the United States of America by
Thames & Hudson Inc., 500 Fifth Avenue, New York, New York 10110

www.thamesandhudsonusa.com

This compact paperback edition first published in 2020

Library of Congress Control Number 2019940662

ISBN 978-0-500-29543-4

Printed and bound in Slovenia by DZS-Grafik d.o.o.

Contents

Prologue

Who are the English? Their language and culture have had an impact on the modern world out of all proportion to the size of their homeland. This is a people familiar around the globe. Yet what do we really know about their ancestry? Traditionally they have been seen as the descendants of the Germanic peoples, known to the Romans as Germani, who poured into post-Roman Britain: mainly Angles, Saxons and Jutes. [1] Today we call these arrivals Anglo-Saxons, a composite term unknown at the time, but which became convenient when realms of Angles and Saxons were combined under Alfred the Great.

The English certainly speak a Germanic language. [2] Yet it would be folly to assert that the modern English possess no other ancestry. The previous

1 Germanic raiding before Britain left the Roman empire turned into settlement by Angles, Saxons and Jutes in the period afterwards.

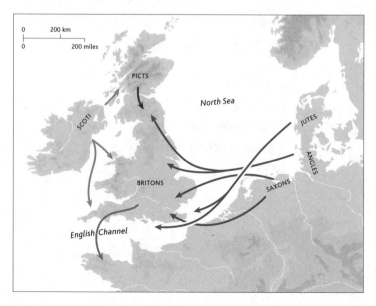

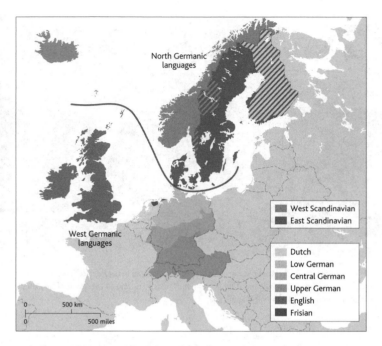

2 *The Germanic languages are divided into three groups, North, East and West, but no East Germanic languages survive today.*

Celtic population was not swept out of every corner of Britain, never to return. Subsequent invasions and immigrations are well known. So the real question is of degree. Two world wars in which Britain fought Germany tainted the concept of a common heritage. Biases against invasion led to a view of the Anglo-Saxon advent as no more than a veneer over a Romano-British population. Conversely, some authors have argued that Germanic people could have arrived in Britain long before the Anglo-Saxons. At last, such theories can be tested empirically through ancient DNA. This new technology can also shed light on deeper ancestry. Where were the Germani formed? Who were their ancestors? The process has barely begun, yet already the sprawling bush of conjecture is being pruned to a few strong propositions. Blending these with new research from archaeology and linguistics reveals a long and adventurous journey before a word of English was spoken.

3 *The violent end of the Anglo-Saxon era is graphically depicted in the Bayeux Tapestry, created a few years after William, Duke of Normandy, was victorious at the Battle of Hastings in 1066 and so won the throne of England.*

Books on the Anglo-Saxons traditionally start with the arrival in post-Roman Britain of Germanic-speaking people and progress chronologically to that famous date of 1066. [3] This book is different in structure and scope. We start with the vision that Anglo-Saxons had of themselves and their ancestors. Then we follow the trail backwards in time to the limits of human memory and far beyond. By Chapter 3 our detective work has led us so deep into the past that we reach mammoth hunters of Siberia, a key group for understanding the origins not only of the Germani, but also of the whole family of languages to which Germanic belongs, before we turn forward again to trek across time and territory to Copper Age Scandinavia.

In Chapter 4 we consider the Nordic Bronze Age as part of an interconnected Europe. The following two chapters examine the ways in which the Germanic people emerged into history as distinctly different from their distant cousins the Celts and Italics, who developed in a kinder climate. The desperate drive towards better land brought the Germani into conflict with both Celts and Romans long before the entry into Britain. The Anglo-Saxon advent can thus be seen as one episode of an epic.

In recent times, it has become popular to assure readers that the Anglo-Saxon period was not really a 'Dark Age'. This ignores the inconvenient fact that no historian ever said that it was. Since written evidence is the source material for historians, they traditionally use the term 'dark age' to mean the obscurity created by gaps in the written record. For example, the Greek Dark Age lasted from about 1100 BC, when writing in Greek stopped, to about 730 BC, when it began again. In Britain the term 'Dark Ages' reflected the shortage of surviving writing from the end of Roman control until the Anglo-Saxons emerged into literacy. It never referred to the entire six centuries of the Anglo-Saxon period. Since literacy is one of the attributes of civilization, one can understand how 'Dark Ages' has come to mean 'barbaric' in popular usage. So what is really under attack is the vision of the Roman world as more civilized than what preceded or followed it in Britain. This idea lost popularity among the British as their own empire disintegrated. It was more comforting to claim parity of sophistication between Celt and Roman, and between Romano-British and incoming Angles and Saxons.

It would be truer to say that in the Anglo-Saxon period we see the emergence of a modern state from the wreckage of an antique empire. Transplanted into the milder climate of Britain, which made possible the agricultural surpluses that underpin a complex society, a Germanic way of life adapted itself to new circumstances. This took time. Farmers with no interest in urban life, and recognizing no leader except a local one, took centuries to adopt towns and the apparatus of a nation state. Only then can we truly speak of an English nation. This implies no value judgment. We can admire the art and ingenuity of our long-gone forefathers, who hunted mammoth and survived an Ice Age, as much as the art and ingenuity of film-makers who bring that deep past back to life today. The gap between the Anglo-Saxons and their modern descendants is far shorter, and much in their lifestyle still seems familiar to us today.

It is convenient for the historian to chop our past into digestible chunks, such as 'Anglo-Saxon' or 'Norman'. Naturally, there were significant changes that divide these periods. Yet we should beware the misperception that change *only* happened at these dividing lines. Anglo-Saxon studies in the 20th century began with the assumption that the very earliest Germanic arrivals in Britain brought with them the concept of the village and its open fields, the foundation of the medieval landscape of middle England. As archaeologists began to unearth evidence against this, some assumed that the village must, in that case, have been the work of the Normans. Much subsequent research has revealed the complex reality of developments *within* the Anglo-Saxon period, rather than at its beginning or end.

The abandonment of the gods of the north in favour of Christianity was a major social change, which is covered in Chapter 8. This was tested by later waves of pagan Germanic settlers – the Vikings. Yet the struggle against them was to unite the peoples of England, as we see in Chapter 9. Our tale ends with reflections in Chapter 10 on how English became the lingua franca of the world, while paradoxically the culture of the Anglo-Saxons was almost lost to sight for centuries.

A note on spelling and terminology

Germanic languages were first written in a runic alphabet, which included signs for sounds not represented in the Latin alphabet. [see 57] Later, the Anglo-Saxons used the Latin alphabet with the addition of a few characters to express certain English sounds. The letter 'w' was not present in the original Latin alphabet, but was needed for Old English. It was initially written as 'uu' (double-u), but Anglo-Saxon scribes soon borrowed the rune called wynn (Ƿ) for this purpose. Wynn only fell out of use during the Middle English period, when it was replaced with double-u once again, from which the modern 'w' developed. For simplicity, the modern 'w' is usually used in modern printed versions of Old English texts. Three other non-Roman letters are always used in modern printed versions of Old English texts: the diphthong 'æ' and two signs which represented the English sound of 'th', the runic letter thorn (Þ), and the letter eth (Ð or ð), derived from Irish writing.[1] So, for example, there is an Anglo-Saxon poem which had no title in the original, but is generally known now by its first word, a name pronounced 'Widsith'. The original was written in capital letters, using a decorative initial wynn and the upper-case form of eth at the end. [4] All quotations in this book from texts in Old English are given in translation to Modern English and use the modern Latin alphabet. However, the Anglo-Saxon diphthong æ is used in this book for proper names, such as Æthelred. It represents the 'short a', in 'cat'. Otherwise the modern Latin alphabet is used.

4 *The start of the poem* Widsith *in the* Exeter Book, *a 10th-century anthology of Anglo-Saxon poetry donated by Leofric, the first bishop of Exeter, to Exeter Cathedral in 1072. It is the largest known collection of Old English literature still in existence.*

Also, the terms 'Britons' and 'Brittonic' rather than 'British' are used here in relation to the Celtic-speaking descendants of the Romano-British, to avoid confusion with the modern British, meaning the citizens of the United Kingdom.

Archaeological ages of Europe

Name	Alternative name	Description
Old Stone Age	Palaeolithic	From the earliest stone tool use to the end of the Ice Age
Middle Stone Age	Mesolithic	Hunter-gatherers re-colonized northern Europe after the glaciers retreated
New Stone Age	Neolithic	Farmers arrived in Europe
Copper Age	Chalcolithic	The earliest metal-working in Europe
Bronze Age		Bronze was the favoured metal
Iron Age		Iron was the favoured metal

Deduced timeline for the prehistory of the Germani

Approximate date BC	Material culture	Deduced language
3400	Yamnaya culture began on the European steppe	Proto-Indo-European
2800	Corded Ware/Single Grave/Battle Axe culture	Northwest Indo-European
2350	Bell Beaker culture entered northern Jutland, Funen and Zealand	Northwest Indo-European
1700–550	Nordic Bronze Age	Pre-Germanic
600–1	Iron Age Jastorf culture	Proto-Germanic

Timeline for the historical Anglo-Saxons

Date AD	Historical event
43	Roman conquest of Britain began
411	Death of Constantine III marked the end of Roman rule in Britain
430s	Anglo-Saxon arrivals are apparent in archaeological remains in eastern England
560	Æthelberht I came to the throne of Kent
597	Augustine arrived in Kent on a mission from Pope Gregory to convert the English
c. 625	Death of Rædwald, the earliest-known ruler of the East Angles
627	Baptism of Edwin, king of Northumbria
641	Penda, king of Mercia, killed Oswald, king of Northumbria
664	Synod of Whitby on the dating of Easter
731	*The Ecclesiastical History of the English People* was finished by Bede
871	Alfred the Great became king of the West Saxons
899	Edward the Elder became king of Wessex on the death of his father Alfred
925	Æthelstan crowned king of Mercia and Wessex at Kingston upon Thames
973	Edgar was crowned king of England in Bath Abbey
1013	King Sweyn Forkbeard of Denmark conquered England from Æthelred the Unready
1016	Sweyn's son Cnut became king of Denmark, England and Norway
1042	Edward the Confessor, son of Æthelred the Unready, became king of England
1066	The Norman Conquest of England
1100	Henry I married Matilda of Scotland, daughter of St Margaret of the English royal house

CHAPTER ONE

How the Anglo-Saxons Saw Themselves

Songs of long ago and far away

'Round the dead-mound rode then the doughty-in-battle,
Bairns of all twelve of the chiefs of the people.
More would they mourn, lament for their ruler,
Speak in measure, mention him with pleasure,
Weighed his worth, and his warlike achievements
Mightily commended, as 'tis meet one praise his
Liegelord in words and love him in spirit,
When forth from his body he fares to destruction.
So lamented mourning the men of the Geats,
Fond-loving vassals, the fall of their lord,
Said he was kindest of kings under heaven,
Gentlest of men, most winning of manner,
Friendliest to folk-troops and fondest of honour.[1]

This is the lament at the funeral of Beowulf, which ends the long poem of the same name. [5] In this stirring saga the hero battles mythic monsters, yet in a recognizable historical setting. *Beowulf* was composed in Old English, the language spoken in Anglo-Saxon England. Yet it tells of a Scandinavian world. [6] It bridges the old homeland and the new of the people who became known as Anglo-Saxons. For them, the past lay literally in another country.

The story begins with the lineage of one of its central characters, Hrothgar, king of the Danes. A pedigree, real or invented, could act as an anchor in time to hold fast a kindred. We are told that Hrothgar was descended from a mighty king called Scyld, which means 'shield'. What better symbol of the power of a strong king to shelter his people?[2] The keynote of the poem is sounded. Hrothgar was so successful in war that he ordered the building of a magnificent mead-hall. There he would preside, dispensing riches to his

5 *The first page of the* Beowulf *manuscript, which was written in Old English.*

6 *The geography of Beowulf. The Geats of the poem appear to be the people of southern Sweden known as Gautar in Old Norse. Present-day Sweden is named after the people living further north, known in the poem as Sweona, and in Swedish as Svear. The petty kingdom of the Wulfings was located between the two, according to Norse sagas.*

loyal followers. He called it Heorot, 'Hall of the Hart', from its antler finials.[3] The noble stag with its crown of antlers was an appropriate emblem for royalty. We shall see later in this chapter (p. 24) how a stag statuette crops up in an important East Anglian grave.

A hall in which to feast and house warriors was crucial for a Germanic leader, who needed a war-band as his personal guard and the core of his fighting force. According to Thietmar of Merseburg, writing in AD 1013–18, the royal seat of the Danes was at Lejre, on the island of Zealand.[4] Archaeological excavations there have revealed a series of seven successive timber halls. The first dates to about AD 500, and may be that described in *Beowulf*. It was 47 metres (154 feet) long and had gently curved walls, increasing from 5 metres wide at each end to 7 metres (23 feet) in the middle. Such a massive hall would have been among the largest buildings in northern Europe at this time. The debris of feasting there gives a good idea of the menu: suckling pigs, cattle, sheep, goats, deer, chicken, geese, ducks and fish.[5] This does not mean that every detail of *Beowulf* should be taken as

7 This poster for the 2007 film version of Beowulf depicts a muscular Ray Winstone in the title role, clad in leather armour and wielding a sword, reflecting our modern image of a Scandinavian hero in the misty past.

straightforward history. Fact and fiction were subtly blended. The character of Beowulf himself seems to be loosely based on a folk tale, which has been re-interpreted to fit into an historical setting.[6]

The poem tells us that Danish rejoicing in Heorot, the sweet sound of the harp and song of the minstrel, aroused the anger of brutish Grendel, skulking in the moors and marshes nearby. Grendel harassed Hrothgar's people for years, dragging off and devouring sleeping warriors at night. Meanwhile Beowulf, a cousin of Hrothgar, had been brought up in the court of his maternal grandfather, the king of the Geats. [see 6] When he grew to manhood he became a liege man of his uncle Hygelac, now king of the Geats. Beowulf was already famed for his heroic exploits when he first appears in the poem. [7] Hrothgar's woes presented him with a worthy challenge. He boldly crossed the sea to Hrothgar's aid. Resolving on unarmed combat as a fairer fight unless his opponent bore a weapon, Beowulf met the terrifying Grendel on the very night of his arrival. He held the monster's right arm in so steely a grip that Grendel had to snap his own sinews and rip his arm out of its socket in order to escape. The bleeding brute slunk home to die, while his severed arm became a trophy in the rejoicing Heorot.

Alas for the relieved Danes, Grendel's massive mother wreaked a rapid revenge. Taking advantage of the absence of Beowulf from Heorot, she seized Hrothgar's dearest friend from the hall the following night. When dawn broke, her footsteps were tracked across wild countryside to a desolate mere. Beowulf dared to descend into the water in full armour and discovered a water-free cavern, the lair of Grendel and his mother. There, in an ironic touch, he beheaded her with an ancient sword seized from their own hoard of weapons.

The poem concludes with another trial of Beowulf in his old age. By then his uncle Hygelac was long dead. Hygelac's son having also died, Beowulf acceded to the throne of the Geats. After fifty years, his realm was threatened by a dragon, roused by a theft from the treasure-hoard it had been guarding within an old burial mound. The idea of a dragon guarding treasure in a prehistoric barrow is not unique to *Beowulf*. It also appears in a set of Anglo-Saxon maxims,[7] and the *Völsunga Saga*, written in Iceland in the 13th century.[8] It seems akin to the concept of the Mummy's Curse. Beware disturbing the dead![9] Beowulf braved the fire-spewing dragon and slaughtered it, but was fatally wounded in this final struggle. It was foreseen that the death of this strong king would leave the Geats vulnerable to attack from the Franks, Frisians and Swedes.

Central to the poem are these three conflicts, in which Beowulf triumphs in single combat over a fearsome foe, a savage symbol of all that threatens the settled order of society. It was J. R. R. Tolkien who first pointed this out, but in lovelier language:

> [A]s in a little circle of light about their halls, men with courage
> as their stay went forward to that battle with the hostile world
> and the offspring of the dark which ends for all, even the kings
> and champions, in defeat.[10]

Yet *Beowulf* is not just one long paean in praise of heroism. Weaving its way through the poem is another thread: the qualities of good kingship. First and foremost a king must be able to protect his people. That requires more than courage. Close to the poem's centre is a crucial speech. Hrothgar, distilling the wisdom of many winters, warns Beowulf of the dangers of arrogance in a leader. Taking one's power for granted can leave one unprepared for danger and death. Quarrelling with one's own kin is foolhardy.

Loyalty to one's lord wins praise, but it should be rewarded generously by that lord. Hrothgar set a good example by bestowing treasures on Beowulf; Beowulf loyally handed this treasure to his lord, Hygelac; the latter recompensed Beowulf with the grant of a large estate, a hall and a chieftain's throne. The poet commented approvingly that thus should all kinsmen behave.

The qualities of a good queen are also considered. Both Hrothgar and Hygelac are blessed with gracious hostesses in the feasting hall. Wealhtheow, a princess of the Wulfing dynasty, was married to Hrothgar as a pledge of peace between their peoples, and weaves peace with tactful words and actions. Yet the poet is far from optimistic about such marriage politics. A side-story in *Beowulf* is the tragedy of Hildeburgh, a Danish princess married to the Frisian king Finn. A visit to her by her brother and his men ends in tragic violence. The battle leaves many dead, including Hildeburgh's brother and her son by Finn. Though a truce follows, it does not last. In a second conflict the Danes kill Finn and carry off Hildeburgh to her own people. No wonder, then, that Beowulf predicts no successful outcome to the proposed marriage between Hrothgar's daughter Freawaru and Ingeld, head of an enemy dynasty. That it would end in battle and the burning of Heorot is foreshadowed earlier in the poem.

Beowulf survives in a single medieval manuscript, probably written around AD 1000. [see 5] No one knows for certain when the poem was first composed. The action of the poem includes the death of Beowulf's uncle Hygelac in an attack on the Franks. This corresponds to a battle around AD 520 recorded by a historian of the Franks.[11] Could an early version of the poem have been composed in the 6th century? How then would we explain its Christian elements? For example, the poet describes Hrothgar's people as heathen and without knowledge of the true God,[12] while Beowulf's triumphs are credited to God's aid. Whatever the historic setting of the poem, the version known to us was clearly composed from a later perspective. But how much later? Could the poem be no earlier than the surviving manuscript? Surely not, for the text has errors arising from copying. There are clues that the original was composed in the Anglian dialect, while the existing copy was written by speakers of the West Saxon dialect. Errors in the proper names reveal that the scribes of AD 1000 were unfamiliar with the characters of *Beowulf*, suggesting that they were copying a centuries-old poem, in an age when much of the tradition on which it was based had been lost.[13]

Beowulf itself takes for granted an audience immersed in that tradition. Though the poem is the work of a single mind, it did not spring out of a vacuum. The author could draw on a wealth of material so familiar to his audience that he need only make a glancing allusion to a character to create an effect. His genius lay in the selection, modification and presentation of his sources to create a cohesive whole.[14] It has been argued that a theme glorifying the Danes could fit the 10th-century mixture of Anglo-Saxon and Scandinavian culture after Viking settlements in England.[15] Yet the poem lacks any Norse loanwords; nor are the names of its characters written in the Norse form. The linguistic evidence points to a time somewhere between AD 700 and 750.[16] A West Saxon version might have appealed to King Alfred in the 890s.[17] By that time tales of warrior heroes had gained a Christian overlay.

The story of the conversion of the Anglo-Saxons is told in *The Ecclesiastical History of the English People*, [8] finished in 731 in the monastery at Jarrow in Northumberland. Its monastic author Bede relates how, at the feasts of laymen, a harp would pass from hand to hand as each person sang to entertain the rest.[18] We can imagine *Beowulf* sung around the fire in the halls of

8 *The beautifully illuminated opening of a 9th-century copy of Bede's* The Ecclesiastical History of the English People. *Though Bede's mother-tongue was Old English, he wrote in Latin, the language of the Church.*

Anglo-Saxon lords. The Anglo-Saxon poem *Widsith*, [see 4] composed probably even earlier than *Beowulf*,[19] describes the life of a wandering minstrel, going from hall to hall to laud great men. The list of his supposed travels reads like a lesson in geography and history, extending not only over the Germanic peoples of continental Europe in the 4th to 6th centuries, but also to peoples known from the Bible and Roman history. Initially Widsith is treated as a real person. Yet as the text goes on, Widsith speaks on behalf of all minstrels, as a poetic introduction to peoples far away and long ago: 'I was with the Israelites and with the Assyrians, with the Hebrews and the Indians and with the Egyptians.' Like *Beowulf*, the poem would make a suitable part of the education of princes. Like *Beowulf*, it moralizes on the role of kings:

> I have heard tell about many men ruling over nations. Every prince
> ought to live ethically – one man governing the land in succession
> to the other – who presumes to receive its princely throne.[20]

Much of *Widsith* would be a tedious list of kings and their peoples if not enlivened by alliteration and metre and set to music as an aid to memory. Battle scenes are brief, but one includes some of the characters found in *Beowulf*. Hrothgar defeats Ingeld at Heorot.

The clash of such heroic values with the tenets of a religion which urges us to love our neighbours was summed up in one phrase. The great Anglo-Saxon scholar Alcuin of York (d. 804) admonished the bishop of Leicester in 797 for permitting harps and pagan songs in a house of God. He asked bluntly, 'What has Ingeld to do with Christ?'[21] By contrast, the Church approved of Cædmon, the first poet to compose religious verse in English. A farm worker at the Abbey of Whitby, he was encouraged by Hild, the abbess there from 657 to 680.[22]

A great king of the Angles

Presumably *Beowulf* was written originally for an audience of Angles, the people who gave their name to East Anglia. [9] They brought more from their homeland than stories. One of the best-known of all archaeological discoveries on English soil is the magnificent ship burial in Mound 1 at Sutton Hoo, Suffolk. Here we see the honour given to a warrior and leader

DEIRA	kingdom ruled by Anglo-Saxons
Elmet	kingdom ruled by Celts
	swamp or alluvium

9 *Britain in the time of Bede (c. AD 700) was a patchwork of kingdoms. The division between a largely Anglo-Saxon lowland and a largely Celtic highland was already advanced, though two Celtic kingdoms still survived within what would become England.*

of his people. A ship, the long labour of many men, would not be sacrificed for any lesser person.

The closest comparisons with the burial at Sutton Hoo Mound 1 are the spectacular ship burials at Vendel and Valsgärde in the Uppland region of

10 A replica made by the Royal Armouries of the helmet of the warrior buried in his ship at Sutton Hoo in the early 7th century. Above the eye holes are two plates depicting horned weapon dancers, related to the cult of Odin/Woden.

east central Sweden, the territory of the Svear (Swedes). The Sutton Hoo helmet is in a Germanic tradition, based originally on a Late Roman cavalry helmet. [10] Similar ones were found at Valsgärde and Vendel. [11] This is not proof that the royal dynasty of the East Angles came from Sweden specifically, but that they shared a common Germanic culture.[23] Few other ship or boat burials in Scandinavia can be dated before the Viking Age, but fascinating 5th-century boat burials have been discovered in Fallward, Lower Saxony (Germany), which we shall meet in the next chapter.[24]

Although the timber of the Sutton Hoo ship had rotted away, an impression of it was left in the sand, along with metal rivets. It was clear that it had been clinker-built, a technique also called lap-strake. This method, in which overlapping planks were fastened together with clench-nails, developed in Scandinavia. One clinker-built boat dated to AD 310–20 is astonishingly well preserved because it sank into a lake which silted up to create Nydam bog in southeastern Denmark. So we can place the construction of the Sutton Hoo ship in a Nordic tradition.[25]

Whoever this remarkable Sutton Hoo man was in life, in death he took riches to his grave. Though the body itself dissolved in the acidic soil, here were left the trappings of a successful warrior: a valuable pattern-welded sword with gold fittings, and an exceptionally fine mail shirt, as well as the magnificent helmet. The wood of his shield had disintegrated, but fine fittings remained to show where it had been propped against the wall of the chamber, along with spears. Glittering shoulder clasps may have been part of his armour. [Pl. xi] Though in the same Germanic style as other straps and buckles in the grave, these are without known parallel. This was a warrior with an eye for the finest workmanship.[26]

He was also fond of music and song, to judge by the remnants of a lyre suspended from the burial chamber wall.[27] It would have been similar to the earlier and better-preserved example in a warrior's grave in Germany. [see 17]

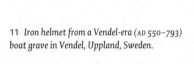

11 *Iron helmet from a Vendel-era* (AD 550–793) *boat grave in Vendel, Uppland, Sweden.*

Another object has been interpreted as a sceptre; it is a stone rod sur-mounted by the figure of a stag. [Pl. viii] No one could doubt this man's high status who saw him bedecked in his great gold belt buckle and the finely decorated purse that hung from his belt. [Pls ix, x] The coins in the purse provide some of the best dating evidence for the burial. They were minted by Frankish kings and fit a period between about 610 and 635. So the burial was probably that of Rædwald, the earliest-known ruler of the East Angles, who died around 625. There are other possibilities, such as Rædwald's son and successor Eorpwald, who died in around 627, and Eorpwald's successor Sigeberht, who died around 636.[28] Since Eorpwald had become a Christian, and Sigeberht was so devout that he entered a monastery,[29] they seem less likely candidates for so pagan a burial.

In addition to the coins, other objects in this remarkable ship burial had their origins overseas. There were eleven Byzantine silver bowls and a Byzantine silver platter which carries a stamp of the emperor Anastasius I (r. 491–518). There were textiles which could be traced to Italy and the Middle East, and a 'Coptic' bowl from Egypt.[30] The eastern Roman empire, with its capital at Byzantium (Constantinople, now Istanbul), included Italy, the Levant and Egypt. The glowing red garnet so popular for Anglo-Saxon jewelry had mainly travelled from India, though some came from Bohemia.[31]

Was Rædwald sending ships to such distant shores? It seems unlikely. Traffic from the Byzantine empire would have brought prestigious objects within much easier reach. The wealthy empire of the Franks was just across the Channel from Britain and possessed of Byzantine goods and ample garnets.[32] Frankish goods might have arrived in East Anglia via Kent, a kingdom which seems to have built its own wealth from trade with Francia.[33] Rædwald had a connection to Kent, for he had been baptized there, though his attachment to the faith proved half-hearted.[34] There was also a family connection to Francia, for Rædwald's son or stepson Sigeberht had fled there after incurring Rædwald's displeasure.[35] This opens up the possibility that Rædwald had married a Frankish princess, whose family gave her son refuge.[36] The gold-and-garnet jewelry from Sutton Hoo is sty-listically linked to both Kent and Francia, but a little mushroom-shaped garnet type seems confined to the Sutton Hoo grave goods, which suggests a local workshop.[37]

Some objects from Sutton Hoo point to contact with Britons. There were three bronze hanging bowls. These finely worked bowls, designed to be suspended, were prized possessions. Although the great majority are found in high-status Anglo-Saxon graves, the decorative style is Late La Tène (Celtic), with a few exceptions which seem a Celtic-Germanic hybrid. Were they acquired as booty, as diplomatic gifts, or in trade or tribute? The largest of the three at Sutton Hoo is one of the most elaborate known. The bowl was already old when it was buried and showed signs of repair in a Germanic manner, so it appears that Rædwald had no Celtic craftsman at his own court.[38]

We would expect Rædwald to have a great hall from which to govern his kingdom. Bede mentions the East Anglian royal centre of Rendlesham.[39] This village today lies about 8 kilometres (5 miles) from the Sutton Hoo burial site and nearly 10 kilometres (6 miles) from Snape, where there were other ship burials. Frustratingly, the Anglo-Saxon settlement proved elusive, until in 2007 reports of illegal metal-detecting alerted archaeologists to a possible site. Subsequently, plentiful clues emerged of an elite Anglo-Saxon residence. No details were released to the press, to avoid attracting more illegal activity. So when the news finally broke in 2016, it came in one dramatic package. Not only was there high-quality metalwork and jewelry, but also an outline in the ground of a large timber building, possibly a royal hall. There are remains of raptors, horses and large, well-fed dogs. Hawking, riding and hunting were certainly beloved by later monarchs. Some objects found at Rendlesham display the same exotic links as the Sutton Hoo burial. There were Frankish gold coins and Byzantine copper coins, fragments of Byzantine vessels and parts of hanging bowls from Celtic Britain. The peak of Rendlesham's importance came in the 6th to 8th centuries, when its material wealth was unparalleled among the Anglo-Saxons of the era.[40]

Anglo-Saxons writing about themselves

By the time Alfred the Great died in 899, a literate Anglo-Saxon could delve into a prose chronicle of his people in Old English. Alfred encouraged literacy and the translation of key works from Latin into English to make them more accessible to his people. He recruited learned men to that end and indeed personally translated some texts.[41] [Pl. xiv] As he said in his preface to the translation of the *Consolation of Philosophy* by Boethius, sometimes he translated word for word, and sometimes sense for sense.

12 *The sophisticated Fuller Brooch, 11.4 cm (4½ inches) in diameter, belongs in the same period and milieu of intellectual enquiry as the writing pointer made for Alfred. [Pl. xiii] In the central roundel are personifications of the five senses, while smaller roundels contain human, bird, animal and plant motifs, perhaps symbolizing the natural world open to our senses.*

It is telling that where Boethius referred to a once-renowned Roman, Alfred substituted instead a Germanic figure. 'Where now are the bones of the famous and wise goldsmith, Weland?'[42] The legendary smith Weland appears in *Beowulf* as the maker of the hero's fine chain mail,[43] and in two other surviving Old English poems.[44] Weland is depicted on a fine Anglo-Saxon casket.[45] [Pl. xiii]

Alfred also commissioned his own biography in Latin from the Welsh cleric Asser, the *Life of Alfred*. It begins in traditional fashion with a pedigree of Alfred. As with other Anglo-Saxon royal pedigrees, the further back in time it goes, the less reliable it gets. Portions were simply borrowed from other available family trees. What is fascinating about this one is the inclusion of Scyld, supposed king of the Danes (p. 13).[46] Old songs had left their traces. Indeed, Asser tells us that Alfred as a child listened to English poems being recited day and night.[47]

Alfred may have encouraged the creation of the *Anglo-Saxon Chronicle*, which was apparently begun in his time and territory. Copies then circulated, which were continued independently by monastic scribes.[48] The anonymous annalists of the *Chronicle* had earlier sources to draw upon for the period before Alfred, notably Bede's great work (p. 19). Bede in turn relied heavily on the 6th-century text by the Briton Gildas for an account of the arrival of Germanic-speaking peoples in Britain. Gildas tells us that after Britain was stripped of its Roman legions, the wretched Britons lay open to predatory Irish and Picts, who butchered them like sheep. Eventually a Brittonic leader, Vortigern, decided to call in Saxon mercenaries for protection. Fierce and impious Saxons arrived in eastern Britain in three ships of war. Gildas bewailed this folly, for the result was not protection of the Britons, but war on them, once the incomers were no longer satisfied with the provisions granted to them.

> Their mother-land, finding her first brood thus successful, sends forth a larger company of her wolfish offspring, which sailing over, join themselves to their bastard-born comrades.[49]

Bede inserted Angles into this picture of the earliest arrivals, removed the derogatory epithets about his own ancestors and added a description of the larger wave of forces:

> They came from three very powerful Germanic tribes,
> the Saxons, Angles and Jutes. The people of Kent and the
> inhabitants of the Isle of Wight are of Jutish origin and also
> those opposite the Isle of Wight, that part of the kingdom
> of Wessex which is still today called the nation of the Jutes.
> From the Saxon country, that is the district now known as
> Old Saxony, came the East Saxons, the South Saxons, and the
> West Saxons. Besides this, from the country of the Angles, that
> is, the land between the kingdoms of the Jutes and the Saxons,
> which is called *Angulus*, came the East Angles, the Middle
> Angles, the Mercians and all the Northumbrian race (that is the
> people who dwell north of the river Humber) as well as the other
> Anglian tribes. Angulus is said to have remained deserted from
> that day to this.[50]

This passage was accepted by generations of historians, but in the revisionist zeal of the 1970s–1990s, it was dismissed as little more than fable.[51] It is true that Bede was writing long after these events, but he lived all his life in Anglian Northumbria. We receive here the sense that he was reporting on an oral tradition of a mass movement from the homeland he calls *Angulus*, which later Anglo-Saxon accounts locate as the district known today as Angeln in eastern Schleswig-Holstein, Germany.[52]

Another passage in the *Ecclesiastical History* has been much misunderstood. It comes in the chapter in which Bede describes the life of the Anglo-Saxon St Ecgberht (639–729), who planned to go to continental Europe, but never actually did:

> He planned to bring blessing to many peoples by ... carrying the word of God ... to some of those nations who had not yet heard it. He knew that there were very many peoples in *Germania*, from whom the Angles and Saxons, who now live in Britain, derive their origin; hence even to this day they are by a corruption called *Garmani* by their neighbours the Britons. Now these people are the Frisians, Rugians, Danes, Huns, Old Saxons and Boruhtware [Bructeri]; there are also many other nations in the same land who are still practising heathen rites to whom this soldier of Christ proposed to go.[53]

Several authors have assumed this passage to provide a list of the peoples who came to Britain.[54] The phraseology is ambiguous. Bede clumsily interrupted his story of Ecgberht, probably taken from a now-lost life of the saint, with a digression to explain to his readers that the Angles and Saxons were Germanic. The list that follows is of the pagan peoples in Germania that Ecgberht hoped to convert. *Germania* is generally translated from Bede's Latin as 'Germany', but this is misleading. The Roman concept of Germania included the known parts of Scandinavia. [see 13] This explains the inclusion of the Danes in this list. The inclusion of the Huns is more surprising, as they were neither Germani nor in Germania in Ecgberht's day. Attila the Hun had controlled large parts of Europe, but his forces disintegrated after his death in 453. Perhaps the 'Hunni' in question were not the well-known followers of Attila, but a more obscure Germanic group. (A Germanic etymology for such a name would not be hard to find.)

By the time Bede was writing, Anglo-Saxon missionaries were actually working on the continent. Willibrord had been in Frisia since the 690s. He was joined in 716 by Wynfreth of Wessex. In 719 Wynfreth arrived in Rome, where Pope Gregory II gave him the name Boniface and a commission to preach to the pagans.[55] In 738 Boniface, by then an archbishop, appealed to 'all God-fearing Catholics sprung from the English race' for their prayers in his mission to bring Christianity to their kin on the continent, the pagan Saxons. 'Have pity on them, for even they themselves are wont to say: "We are of one blood and one bone."'[56]

Notice that Boniface here uses the term 'English' to refer to the Anglo-Saxons. Britons generally used the name 'Saxon' for all the Germani in Britain and this has passed into modern Welsh as *Saeson* and Irish as *Sasanaigh*, whence comes the derisive Scottish Gaelic *Sassenach*. Bede, an Angle himself, preferred 'Angle' as the collective term for the Germanic peoples in Britain. We can credit his influence for the fact that we use the names England (Angle-land) and English today.

So to sum up this chapter so far, the Anglo-Saxons themselves pictured a past in what is now Germany and Scandinavia.[57] The same picture emerges from the archaeological record. How large was this migration? This has been a highly contentious topic. In 1966, influential Cambridge archaeologist Grahame Clark attacked the vision of Britain's past as wave after wave of invasion.[58] His ideas fell on fertile ground. British archaeologists gradually turned against the whole concept of migration; continuity of populations from the Stone Age onwards was assumed. Any Germanic migration was presumed to be minimal; much of the Romano-British population of what is now England was pictured as simply adopting the Anglo-Saxon way of life.[59] Can genetics resolve the issue?

Genetics of the English

The first attempts to work out what proportion of Germanic blood runs in the veins of the modern English were based on DNA from the living. They certainly showed some genetic difference between the English and the Welsh, which we might deduce reflects a different post-Roman history.[60]

A much more comprehensive study by the People of the British Isles (PoBI) project has drawn similar conclusions more recently. The researchers sampled 2,039 individuals from rural areas within the United Kingdom, each of whom had all four grandparents born within 80 kilometres (50 miles) of each other. The aim was to sample any regional genetic differences that existed before the high tide of geographical mobility in the 20th century. It seemed like the last chance to do this before regional differences were too diluted to detect.

It may seem to some readers that a Welshman or Scotsman cannot be remotely similar to an Englishman. These are nations with a strong sense of separate identity. Surely their DNA should positively shout their differences? The reality is that any genetic differences today are more of a murmur. We should not be too surprised. First, the incoming Angles and Saxons were northern Europeans with much genetic heritage in common with the Celts. They had not arrived from Mars. Secondly, even if Britons and Saxons initially tended to keep each to their own communities, any such segregation was not sustained over the many centuries that have passed since. People have moved in droves from the Celtic fringe into England and vice versa. The PoBI study could detect only relatively subtle differences, but one result was striking. A single genetic cluster predominated over most of England. This was equated with the Anglo-Saxons. Yet the PoBI researchers admit that it may be impossible to distinguish genetically between the descendants of Anglo-Saxons and the later Danish Vikings.[61] Both the Angles and Danes came from Jutland. Given the ample evidence of Viking settlement in England (see Chapter 9), it seems likely that what PoBI interpreted as the Anglo-Saxon genetic signal includes that of Vikings.[62]

Even the best of such studies can present us only with the end result – the modern genetic mixture of a people whose ancestors could have arrived in many waves.[63] To discover what genetic impact the incoming Angles and Saxons made on the population of Britain at the time, we need to probe the remains of people who lived before and after the Anglo-Saxon advent. At last the answer lies within our grasp. We now have DNA from at least a handful of the people who lived in Britain in pre-Roman and Roman times and from those buried in Anglo-Saxon cemeteries.[64] These results endorse the view that the Anglo-Saxons had of themselves. They had origins outside Britain. Yet we can already see that they absorbed some descendants of the Romano-British. We will return to the details in later chapters. For the moment we follow where Beowulf and Bede point us – to the Germanic heartlands in the days when Rome ruled most of Europe.

The vocabulary of our DNA

Within each cell of your body is a nucleus in which the DNA is stored, which acts as the instruction book to make you. It forms twenty-three pairs of chromosomes. One of each pair is inherited from each parent. Twenty-two pairs of your chromosomes are gender-neutral. The other pair dictates whether you are born male or female: two X chromosomes and you are a girl, but an X and a Y make a boy. Together these twenty-three pairs of chromosomes are known as the genome.

Each chromosome is made up of two strands of DNA that coil around each other in the famous spiral staircase or double helix. The DNA is made up of sequences composed of just four nucleobases, written as A, T, C and G. Most of our DNA is shared with all other human beings, but there are locations where the genetic code varies between individuals: for example, I might have a T where you have a C. Such a location is known as a Single Nucleotide Polymorphism (SNP, pronounced 'snip').

In the female body, each pair of chromosomes combines in the ovary to produce a single DNA strand in each egg. In the male body, the same process produces single strands in each sperm, except for the Y chromosome. That was inherited from the male's father and less than 10 per cent of it can combine with the X from his mother. The non-recombining portion (NRY) is passed on from father to son. For simplicity the shorthand 'Y-DNA' is used in this book to mean NRY.

Another type of DNA also does not recombine. Mitochondrial DNA (mtDNA) codes for the production of energy. There are many mitochondria (sing. mitochondrion) in each cell of our bodies, but not within the nucleus. Mitochondrial DNA is passed down from mother to child.[65]

Y-DNA and mitochondrial DNA, therefore, provide a particularly clear way to trace ancestry. Your mtDNA should be exactly the same as your mother's and maternal grandmother's, unless there has been an error in replication along the way. Such errors, sometimes known as mutations, can crop up in any type of DNA and are hugely informative. By comparing the mtDNA of millions of people around the world, geneticists have been able to detect the sequences of these changes, and draw up a worldwide phylogeny (genetic family tree). Each person today carries a particular collection of these mutations, called a haplogroup, which can be fitted on to the family tree. The same applies to Y-DNA.[66] [See Box: Y-DNA, pp. 54–55] Much genetic research on migrations in the deep past has made use of these two parts of our DNA that are inherited from just one parent, and so known as uniparental.

Overview

- Early Anglo-Saxon literature, archaeology and genetics all paint a picture of a transplanted people.

- The earliest literature in any form of English describes people and events in Scandinavia and northern Germany.

- The Briton Gildas, writing probably in the 540s, describes the coming of the Saxons, initially as mercenaries, but soon seizing land for themselves.

- The earliest history of the English written by an Englishman, Bede's *Ecclesiastical History of the English People* (731), declares them to be descended from Angles, Saxons and Jutes who arrived from northern Germany and Jutland.

- Archaeological evidence is in accord with such an arrival. Nevertheless, British archaeologists in the latter part of the 20th century minimized the role of migration, presuming widespread continuity from the Romano-British.

- Genetics, in particular ancient DNA, has the potential to resolve the issue of degree of migration.

- So far, a small sample of individuals from before and after the Anglo-Saxon advent has been tested for ancient DNA. The results confirm that the people buried in early Anglo-Saxon cemeteries were mainly descended from incomers. But there is some evidence of intermarriage with the Romano-British.

CHAPTER TWO

The Germani

In their ancient songs, their only form of recorded history,
the Germani celebrate the earth-born god Tuisto. They assign
to him a son, Mannus, the author and founder of their race,
and to Mannus three sons, after whom the people nearest the
ocean are named Ingaevones, those of the centre Herminones,
the remainder Istvaeones. Some authorities, since the remote
past invites guesswork, record more sons of the god and more
national names, such as Marsi, Gambrivii, Suevi, Vandilii, and
those names are indeed genuine and ancient.[1]

Thus wrote the Roman writer Tacitus in AD 98. Civilization is defined by, among other things, its literacy. The 'barbarians' beyond the Rhine boundary of the Roman empire were illiterate in his day. By around AD 150, after contact with the Romans, Germanic-speakers had devised a runic alphabet, [see 57] but still had only a limited use for it. Theirs was not a society which required bureaucratic records. So to learn about them, we long relied on Latin writers. Yet how accurate could they be? The Romans were outsiders, observing a people that they may not have fully understood. The relationship between the Romans and the Germani took many twists and turns over the centuries; Germani could be seen as enemies, trading partners or useful recruits into the Roman army. Some sort of bias is almost inevitable. So in this chapter we shall compare the Classical writers not only with each other, but with the evidence of archaeology, linguistics and genetics.

Today 'Germans' refers to the people of present-day Germany. The tribes known to the Romans as Germani covered a far wider territory. [13] The Graeco-Roman geographer Ptolemy, writing in around AD 150, described Germania as bordered on the west by the Rhine, on the east by the Vistula and on the south by the Danube. That included what is now the Czech Republic and a large part of Poland. He also included in Germania 'the Cimbrian peninsula' (Jutland) and 'a very large island called Scandia'.[2]

The ancient Greeks and Romans did not penetrate deep enough into the Gulf of Bothnia to realize that Scandia (or Scandinavia, as Pliny called it),[3] was actually a peninsula. The concept of Jutland as part of Scandinavia does not crop up in surviving sources until about AD 700.[4]

The River Rhine was regarded as the border between Gaul and Germania at the time that Julius Caesar conquered Gaul in the 50s BC. The Lower Rhine runs broad and deep, making a good boundary, though not an impassable one. The Belgic tribes on its Gaulish bank had a constant struggle to keep the Germani out.[5] The Upper Rhine was all too easily crossed. By the time of Tacitus, the Romans had constructed a chain of forts along a frontier (the *Limes Germanicus*) designed to link the Rhine and Danube, protecting

13 *Germania as described by Tacitus in AD 98. Those tribes that he mentions which cannot be securely located are omitted. Not all the tribes in Germania were Germanic in his day. The Celtic Lugii are shown here. Other Celtic tribes had already been displaced from Germania. Tacitus gives the example of the Boii, who left behind the name of their territory, Boihaemum, between the rivers Vltava and Danube, now Bohemia in the Czech Republic.*

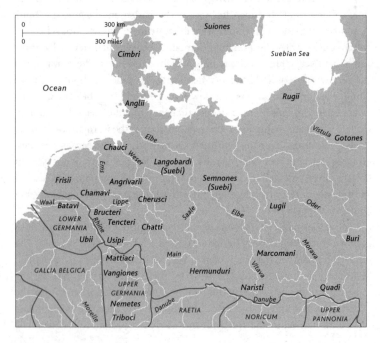

the upper reaches of these rivers. After these works, the Roman empire included Upper Germania, around the upper Rhine, and Lower Germania on the western bank of the Rhine, within which lived several Germanic tribes.[6] [13]

Ethnicity

Tacitus speculated that the Germani were an unmixed race.[7] This simplistic thinking was to have deeply unfortunate repercussions long after his time (see Chapter 5, pp. 96–98). Ethnicity need not involve biological distinctions so radical as to denote a separate race. The more we learn about our own genetic code, the less sense we can see in old ideas of race.[8] Yet kinship, real or imagined, is crucial to the sense of belonging to an ethnic group. Anthony D. S. Smith, one of the founders of the field of nationalism studies, considered that the most essential attribute of a pre-modern ethnicity was a myth of common ancestry.[9] The quotation that heads this chapter embodies exactly that. Tacitus recorded Germanic legends of descent from a common ancestor, Mannus. This idea of kinship, represented in a fictional family tree, signals an ethnic consciousness. It appears in the origin stories of other peoples who shared a language and culture, but were divided into tribes or subgroups. For example, in Greek myth the main divisions of the Greek-speaking people all shared a common ancestor in the supposed king Hellen.[10]

Another key feature is a distinctive shared culture, most particularly a shared language and/or religion.[11] Roman authors took for granted the role of language in perceived ethnicity. For example, Tacitus comments that two tribes in southern Germania were not Germanic, as proved by their languages, Gallic in one case and Pannonian in the other.[12] The Iron Age Germani were split into many tribes, but they did have a language in common. Linguists have reconstructed that language, Proto-Germanic, the parent of a family of languages which includes Danish, Dutch, English, German, Icelandic, Norwegian and Swedish. [see 2] Modern linguists named the branch after the Roman name for the people.

The earliest surviving written record of the name comes in a fragment from a lost text of the 70s or 60s BC by the Greek author Posidonius of Rhodes. It simply refers to a drink favoured by the Germani.[13] Julius Caesar's account of his conquest of Gaul in the 50s BC uses 'Germani' without explanation, which suggests that this ethnonym was in common use by then. Where had it come from? When Tacitus enquired of Germani the origin of their name, he was informed that it just happened to be the name of the tribe who first crossed the Rhine and pushed into Gaul. While the tribe had since renamed themselves the Tungri, the terror-inducing name Germani had stuck in the minds of their enemies, and had been recently adopted by the Germani themselves as the collective name for all their tribes.[14] This sounds plausible enough. We know of other Germanic tribal names formed with the -mani ending, meaning 'men' or 'people'.

Tribes

A bewildering number of Germanic tribes were noted by Roman authors. Over fifty were named by Claudius Ptolemy.[15] There are several differences between his list and earlier ones from Tacitus and Pliny. Tribes could move, splinter or merge with another tribe. For example, Tacitus tells us that the brave Batavi, who lived mainly on an island in the Rhine, were once part of the Chatti. They had broken away from them in a civil war.[16] As he explains, the large island on which they lived was formed by the split of the Rhine into the Rhine and Waal,[17] in what is now the Netherlands. [see 13] This district today is called Betuwe in Dutch, which was long assumed to reflect the name of the tribe. Yet there is a straightforward etymology from Germanic words for 'good' and 'island'. So the group of Chatti who moved there had acquired a new tribal name from their location.[18] The Marcomani ('border-men') took their name from their position at the forefront of the Germani as they moved southward, evicting the Celts. In a tribal society what mattered in identification were the people, not a fixed set of borders.

Some Germanic tribes or federations did give their names to territories. For example, modern-day Swabia (Schwaben) in southwestern Germany recalls the Suebi, yet Swabia was far from their original home. The Baltic was known as the Suebian Sea in the time of Tacitus, [see 13] a clue that the Suebi expanded southwest from a homeland in the north. The name 'Suebi' is derived from a Proto-Germanic root *s(w)e, meaning 'kindred', which is also found in the Old Norse name Svíar (Swedes). Any word denoting kinship was well suited to the production of tribal names.[19] Caesar described the Suebi as the largest and most warlike of the Germanic nations. Already in 55 BC people of the Usipi and Tencteri tribes had been driven from their lands by the Suebi.[20] Tacitus recorded later tensions between the Suebi and the Cherusci. He shrewdly commented that the Germani, when freed from external fear, habitually turned their weapons upon each other.[21] In his day the Suebi occupied more than half of Germania, and were divided into tribes, each with its own name, but all alike called Suebi. They could be recognized by their habit of combing their hair sideways and fastening it tight with a knot.[22] Tacitus appears to class the Anglii (Angles) among the Suebi.[23] Startling support for this comes from an Iron Age skull preserved in a bog, whose hair survives complete with its Suebian knot. It was found at Osterby, which lies within Angeln.[24] Two other confederations, the Franks and the Saxons, were to rise to importance as they snatched control of parts of the western Roman empire (see Chapter 6).

The Jutes are remembered today in the name of the peninsula of Jutland, but 'Jute' is a modern version of the tribal name, which is differently spelled in early sources. Tacitus mentioned a tribe called the Eudoses.[25] Eote was the standard Anglian form of the name, which appears in the Old English poem *Beowulf*.[26] In the West Saxon dialect it became Yte, as in the poem *Widsith*.[27] Bede tells us that land opposite the Isle of Wight was still in his day named for the Jutes (see p. 27). In the Norman period it became the New Forest, but was still called Ytene in English.[28]

Way of life

Caesar gives us the first account of Germanic customs. He claimed that the Germani spent all their lives in hunting and warlike pursuits, and lived principally on milk, cheese and meat, not being agriculturalists.[29] Tacitus was better informed. He agreed that Germani had no taste for peace. They chose their leaders for their valour. Fiery youths sought renown through battle. A successful war-leader would attract a body of companions, who pledged allegiance to him. As we saw in *Beowulf*, such a following had to be feasted and lavishly rewarded (see p. 18). Tacitus remarks that such open-handedness could only be supported from the spoils of war. He did not spell out that an economy of subsistence farming generates little surplus to support a specialist class of full-time soldiers, but we can read between the lines. Warriors, when not engaged in warfare, might spend a little time hunting, but more idling away their days in sleep and gluttony, Tacitus tells us. The care of house, hearth and field was left to women and old or frail men.

Though declaring that the country 'either bristles with woods or festers with swamps', Tacitus admitted that it was fertile in grain crops and rich in flocks, though he despised their cattle as under-sized, and their horses as notable for neither beauty nor speed.[30]

Archaeological evidence supports him. The cattle raised in northern Europe were generally smaller than those of the southern Roman provinces. Cattle provided milk as well as meat, so Caesar was not completely wrong. Sheep, goats and pigs were also kept. Horses were not plentiful. Contrary to Caesar's account, there is little sign of hunting for wild animals. Barley was the dominant grain crop, but oats, wheat, rye and millet also appear in pollen and seeds surviving from the period. Flax was grown for its oil-bearing seeds, but also for its fibres, to spin and weave into linen.[31]

Any Roman passing through Free Germania would notice the absence of towns and brick or stone buildings. The Germani built in unworked wood. These striking differences from Roman life would leap to the eye. Tacitus did not miss them.[32] Thanks to archaeology, we now have other evidence. Normally timber houses simply rot in the soil, leaving little trace, but the waterlogged conditions along flood-prone coasts can create the perfect conditions for preservation. Here Iron Age houses were built on an artificial mound of turf and dung, known as a *Wurt* in German or *terp* in Dutch. As floods encroached, the mound was built higher, preserving within it the remains of houses. Excavation of the *Wurt* village at Feddersen Wierde on the marshes of the Cuxhaven district in Lower Saxony, Germany, uncovered outstandingly well-preserved buildings with walls surviving over 1 metre (3 feet) in height. This was a site settled in the 1st century BC and then abruptly abandoned in the 5th century AD, due to flooding.[33]

Even without such special conditions, archaeologists can detect the post-holes left in the ground after a timber building has rotted. The holes have a different fill from the soil around them. So we now have a considerable body of knowledge of how the Germani lived. From the Bronze Age to at least the 7th century AD, the focal building of most farmsteads, from Scandinavia southwards through northern Germany to the Lower Rhine, was the timber longhouse. This was usually an east–west-oriented building with living quarters at the west end and a byre at the east end. Other houses had no internal byre, either because they belonged to craft-workers who owned no cattle, or because they functioned as a princely hall, such as that at Lejre (see p. 15). In all cases, though, two rows of massive internal posts supported the weight of the roof and divided the interior into three aisles.[34] Although the peoples to the east of the Germani also built with timber, there are no three-aisled houses in Finland or other countries bordering the east side of the Baltic Sea. The Iron Age house tradition is different there.[35] Among the lesser Germanic structures, a common type is the *Grubenhäuser* (pit house) or sunken-featured building, built over a shallow pit. [see 66] They were unlikely to serve as dwellings, but could have had a variety of other uses, including weaving or grain storage.[36]

Furniture from this period seldom survives. So it was exciting in the 1990s to discover a treasure trove of remarkably well-preserved items of the 4th and 5th centuries AD in the deep layers of the marsh at Fallward near Wremen, just a few kilometres south of Feddersen Wierde. At the edge of a cemetery was a well-preserved boat grave, which contained the metal fittings of a Late Roman military belt. This is not unusual in graves of this region and period. The Roman army evidently recruited here. The quality of the metalwork, however, suggests that this man reached a high rank before returning home. His grave also contained a small table with elaborately turned legs. It fits the claim by Tacitus that the Germani ate each at his or her own table.[37]

There was also a footstool dated around AD 425, decorated with a scene of elk hunting and a runic inscription. It would have been used in conjunction with the remarkable object, unique in Europe, that was too large to fit into the boat and therefore set beside it, the 'marsh throne'. [14] Thrones would

14 *A ceremonial chair, carved from a tree-trunk and dendro-dated to* AD 431, *found beside a boat-burial at Fallward, Germany. The carvings are in a Roman army style known as* Militärkerbschnitt *and incorporate swastikas.*

normally be inherited, not buried. Perhaps the man buried with it was the last of his line.[38] A *gifstol* (literally 'gift-seat') within the mead-hall Heorot is mentioned in *Beowulf* as a poetic word for a throne. It was the ceremonial chair from which a lord dispensed gifts. Beowulf himself was granted a *bregostol* (ruler-seat).[39]

Swastika carvings can be seen on the throne back. This symbol has a long history. It has been found in ancient art around the world, and had a variety of names in different languages. The modern name comes from the Sanskrit word *svastika*, a symbol of good fortune, from *svasti* ('it is well'). Where its use pre-dates writing, the original meaning may be uncertain, but in Romano-Celtic iconography it represents the sun and in ancient Greece the sun-god Apollo.[40] It was popular in the Germanic Iron Age, and also appears on pagan Anglo-Saxon artefacts. Unfortunately, the motif was appropriated by Adolf Hitler as a symbol of the Nazi party (see Chapter 5, p. 98). The sign now has such unsavoury connotations that we need to wrench our minds away from its modern use in order to recognize that for the Germani it was religious. It can be seen on a gold disc pendant (bracteate) depicting Odin. [see Pl. v]

Another cache of astonishingly well-preserved grave goods was uncovered in an emergency rescue excavation in the snow and ice of the winter of 2001/2. It was in grave 58, the deepest and richest in the Allemanic cemetery in Trossingen, in southwest Germany. The burial was that of a warrior, complete with a shield, lance, sword and riding equipment. So we can picture a horseman. He was about thirty to forty years old when he died in the late summer of AD 580. His personal furniture was buried with him, including a lathe-turned chair. [15] His bed was used as his coffin. [16] As if this were not enough to make this burial extraordinary, the warrior was also a musician. Held in his left arm, as if to indicate that he played it himself rather than just owning it, was a lyre typical of the period. [17] It was decorated with figures of warriors facing one another.[41]

Tacitus, a man blessed from birth with azure skies, public buildings gleaming with marble, and houses warmed by central heating, wrote frankly of the unlovely scenery, bitter climate and ugly houses of Germania. In fact, his chief reason for thinking the Germani to be an unmixed race was that he found it impossible to picture anyone from elsewhere wanting to move to Germania. He saw the Germani as reckless in their drinking and dicing. When all else was lost, they would gamble themselves into bondage. Yet

15 (above) A lathe-turned chair from the 6th-century burial of a warrior in grave 58 at Trossingen, Germany, recognizably the ancestor of a common type of medieval (and later) chair.

16 (below) The bed of the warrior of Trossingen was cut down to use as his coffin.

17 (above right) This lyre was also found in the warrior's grave at Trossingen. The strings had decayed, but it was otherwise remarkably well preserved.

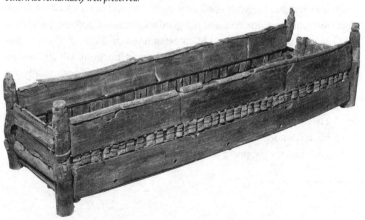

he admired those aspects of Germanic life which he saw as reminiscent of the Roman Republican virtues, abandoned in the decadent days under the Caesars. Most importantly for him, the Germani practised strict monogamy. 'No one there finds vice amusing.'[42] Centuries later, in the 440s, the continental Saxons were still being commended for their chastity, while condemned for their cruelty.[43]

The Germani favoured a form of democracy, as the Romans had done in the time of their Republic. Leaders would debate minor matters, but the whole community would gather to make major decisions. Caesar and Tacitus noted that land was not private property among the Germani. Chiefs would annually allot holdings to clans or groups of kinsmen. Slaves were not given roles in their master's household, in the Roman way. Each had control of his own house and home, and provided a fixed amount of grain, cattle or clothing to his master.[44] It was a hardier and more self-sufficient way of life than the civilization built by the Romans on the fruits of empire.

Pantheon and prophetesses

Caesar was curious about the religion of the Germani:

> The only beings they recognize as gods are things that they can see, and by which they are obviously benefited, such as Sun, Moon and Fire; the other gods they have never even heard of.[45]

Veneration for the sun and moon appears ancient and widespread.[46] The Romans themselves worshipped a solar god, Sol, and moon-goddess, Luna. The Germanic versions reversed the genders. Sól was a goddess personifying the sun, while her brother Máni personified the moon.[47] The Romans also had a pantheon of deities expressing human functions, which Caesar's informants failed to detect in the Germani, but Tacitus, writing only 150 years after Caesar, had no difficulty:

> They worship Mercury above all, and consider it proper to win his favour on certain days even by human sacrifices; Hercules and Mars they appease with the beasts normally allowed.[48]

The Romans equated foreign gods and goddesses with the most similar in their own pantheon. One example of this deity-matching left a lasting legacy. Whereas the early Germani reckoned the passing of time by nights, rather than days,[49] contact with the Roman world led to the adoption of the Roman seven-day week. Each day of the week in the Roman calendar commemorated a planetary deity. For English-speakers 'Saturday' (Saturn's-day) retains the Roman god, 'Sunday' is a literal translation of the Latin *dies Solis*, while Monday (Moon-day) translates the Latin *dies Lunae*.[50] Germanic-speakers replaced the rest of the Roman day names with the equivalent deity of their own.

The Roman god of war, Mars, was replaced with the Old English Tiw to make *Tiwesdæg*, becoming Tuesday in modern English. The name of this god in Proto-Germanic can be reconstructed as **tîwaz*, which could just mean 'god'. He was probably a sky-god initially, regarded as the father-figure of the Nordic pantheon. He became Týr in Old Norse.[51] The story of how Týr lost a hand is told in the *Prose Edda*, written by Icelandic historian Snorri Sturluson around the year 1220, but it was known much earlier, for it is depicted on a bracteate of around AD 500.[52] [18] Týr placed his hand in the mouth of the monstrous wolf Fenrir as a pledge of good faith, so that the wolf would allow himself to be bound. When Fenrir realized that he had been tricked, he bit off that hand of false faith.[53]

By the time Tacitus was writing, Týr had been supplanted as chief of the Germanic gods by Woden, commemorated in the weekday name Wednesday, equivalent to *dies Mercurii* in Latin. Modern Swedish makes the day *Onsdag* (Odin's day). The Norse Odin and West Germanic Woden were the same figure, as recognized in the *Prose Edda*: 'Voten, whom we call Odin'.

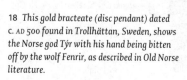

18 *This gold bracteate (disc pendant) dated c. AD 500 found in Trollhättan, Sweden, shows the Norse god Týr with his hand being bitten off by the wolf Fenrir, as described in Old Norse literature.*

It names Odin as the father of the gods.[54] Odin also appears in the *Ynglinga Saga*, compiled in around 1230, probably also by Snorri Sturluson. This tale rationalizes Odin as a great ruler who was deified. It tells us that Odin became exalted for many reasons. He had a fair and noble countenance that rejoiced the hearts of all who saw it. He was ferocious in battle. He was so eloquent and poetic that all who heard him were swayed to believe his every word. Another prized quality was the wisdom he acquired by wide travel and his own curious form of intelligence gathering. He was able to enter the minds of birds, animals, fish and snakes, and travel far with them, while his own body lay as if asleep or dead. He had two ravens, whom he had trained to speak. They flew over distant countries and returned with news. He was also attended by two wolves.[55] Thus Odin had features of a shaman, who could enter a trance to communicate with the spirit world. The Saami, neighbours to the Norse, practised shamanism.[56]

Snorri wrote of many sons of Odin, 'from whom are sprung many great houses'.[57] One was said to have lived at Lejre,[58] the seat of Danish royalty (see p. 15). A silver seated figurine thought to represent Odin has been found there. [19]

A particular type of bracteate, known as the C Type, showing a man's head over a four-legged animal, has long been supposed to depict Odin. [Pl. v] One example carries a runic inscription *Houaz*, interpreted as 'The High One', a by-name of Odin. If so, the inclusion of bird and animal suggests that he is shown as a shaman. More recently it has been proposed

19 *Silver figurine thought to represent Odin on his throne, flanked by his two ravens, Huginn and Muninn, representing thought and memory. Behind are his two wolves. It was found at Lejre, Denmark, in 2009; 1.75 cm (³⁄₄ inch) high.*

that this type of bracteate was a sun amulet. Certainly the radiating border design on some examples gives them a sun symbolism.[59]

This is only a partial match for Mercury, Roman messenger of the gods. Mercury was an appropriate patron of travellers, commerce, messengers and eloquence, as well as thieves and tricksters, but not seen as a war god. Odin/Woden is the embodiment of the qualities of a great leader within Germanic society, in whom wisdom was coupled with belligerence. Indeed, there is a clue in the structure of the name itself that leadership was the key feature. The 'din/den' element indicates a ruler.[60]

The third of the Germanic war-gods is remembered in the weekday name Thursday (Thor's-day). Thor's day replaced the Roman *dies Iovis* (Jove's day). Jove or Jupiter, being a sky-god in origin, could bring down thunder-bolts as a sign of his wrath. Thor, too, was a thunder-god. He was regarded as the strongest of gods and men, and wielded a hammer as his weapon.[61] His great strength would also invite a Roman comparison with Hercules, which would explain why Tacitus thought that the three chief Germanic gods were Mercury, Hercules and Mars.[62]

Friday celebrates Frige (*Frigg* in Old Norse), the wife of Odin/Woden.[63] She replaced Venus, Roman goddess of love, as the patroness of this day.[64] Frigg had prophetic abilities: 'The fate of all does Frigg know well.'[65] The Germanic reliance on female divination was noted by the Romans from their first clash with these peoples. In 113 BC the Cimbri and Teutones swept south in quest of a new homeland and came up against the resistance of Rome. Later historians could draw on contemporary sources describing the encounter. Strabo says:

> Writers report a custom of the Cimbri to this effect: their wives, who would accompany them on their expeditions, were attended by priestesses who were seers; these were grey-haired, clad in white, with flaxen cloaks fastened on with clasps, girt with girdles of bronze, and bare-footed.

He goes on to describe their grisly method of divination by the inspec-tion of the blood or entrails of executed prisoners.[66] When Caesar was fighting Ariovistus, a Germanic leader who had arrived in Gaul as a mercenary and decided to stay as a colonist, he found him elusive. Seeking the reason from Germanic prisoners, he was told that Germanic matrons had divined that Ariovistus was not destined to win if he fought before the new moon.[67] Tacitus generalized that the Germani 'believe that there resides in women something holy and prophetic'. Yet his evidence suggests that only specific women were so honoured. He cites the case of Veleda, who had encouraged the revolt of the Bructeri against Roman rule by prophecies of Germanic victory.[68] The use of divination before battle perhaps explains why such a woman could even travel with Germani serving in the Roman army. A list of officers and servants from a Roman camp at Elephantine in Egypt in the 2nd century AD includes Walburg, sibyl of the Semnones.[69] By the time that the Norse were writing about their mythology, a female seer was know as a *völva*.[70]

Pseudo-history

Whence came the Germani? One widespread type of origin story for Christian Europeans was based on biblical genealogy from Noah. The Romano-Jewish historian Josephus saw Japheth, one of the three sons of Noah, as the founding father of European peoples.[71] Isidore, bishop of Seville (d. 636) took the idea further. He was involved in the conversion of the Visigothic royal family to Catholicism. This Germanic people had founded the Visigothic kingdom in Spain in the 5th century AD. A diligent scholar, Isidore compiled an encyclopaedia of knowledge using extracts from Classical sources. It became one of the best-known works in medieval libraries. He expanded on Josephus to derive an origin for the Goths from Magog, son of Japheth, because of the similarity of the last syllable of Magog with the name 'Goth'.[72] A scholarly play on words filled the gap in real knowledge. In England, Alfred the Great seems to have promoted the idea of descent from biblical figures. It was in his reign that the first Anglo-Saxon genealogies appear which lead back to Noah and even beyond to Adam. In the *Anglo-Saxon Chronicle*, Alfred's father Æthelwulf of Wessex was given a genealogy from Noah, which omits Japheth in favour of Sceaf (suggested in *Beowulf* to be the father of Scyld, legendary king of the Danes) as an apocryphal fourth son of Noah. Such cavalier treatment of the Old Testament found no favour with the dedicated churchman Ælfric, Abbot of Eynsham (d. *c.* 1010), who was careful in his writings to state that Noah had three sons, and to elaborate that Japheth was the ancestor of the 'northern people' by the 'north sea'.[73]

A second popular belief drew on Classical learning. Between the 6th and 12th centuries AD, one European nation after another claimed Trojan ancestry: Goths, Franks, Venetians, Normans, British and finally Scandinavians. The Greek *Iliad*, written in the 8th century BC, tells the epic tale of the Trojan War. One of the oldest surviving works of European literature, the *Iliad* had a huge influence upon later origin stories. As the Romans rose to eclipse the Greeks, they chose to concoct a genesis in Troy for themselves. In Virgil's epic *Aeneid*, Aeneas, a Trojan hero and therefore an enemy of the Greeks, travelled to Italy. After the fall of the western Roman empire, those who had seized the spoils were eager to present themselves as legitimate inheritors. Scandinavia had never been within the Roman empire, but origin stories there could have drawn on earlier Germanic pseudo-history. A common feature of these tales was a fanciful genealogy, based on the naïve equation of names.[74] The *Prose Edda* gives Odin a descent from King Priam of Troy, in 'Turkland' (Turkey). Priam was imagined to have a daughter Troan, who had a son Tror 'whom we call Thor'. A lengthy genealogy follows, which makes Odin the eighteenth in descent from Thor. This inconsistency with the statement in the same source that Odin was the father of the gods betrays the patchwork stitched together here. Odin's journeys with his people are described. 'Many glorious things were spoken of them, so that they were held more like gods than men.' In the midst of this make-believe, Snorri Sturluson shrewdly commented that those names of Nordic forefathers that were written down were all in the language still spoken in the region. Whereas in England, he knew, there were ancient lists of land-names and place-names which appear to be in another tongue.[75] Here indeed was proof that the English had supplanted another people (the Romano-British) at a time recent enough to leave clues, whereas the origins of the Germani were too deep in the past to leave written traces.

In the *Ynglinga Saga* Snorri Sturluson elaborated on the travels of Odin after he left 'Turkland'. He became chief of a country called Ásaland, east of the River Don. The Don was regarded in antiquity as the boundary between Europe and Asia. So Snorri or his source used a similarity of names to equate Asia with the mythological Ásaland, home of the Æsir, the chief family of Nordic gods. We are told that Odin left his domain and wandered to Russia, then to Saxony. Leaving some of his sons to rule that country, Odin took up residence on the island of Fyn in Denmark and from there moved to Sweden. The story is unconvincingly set in Roman times.[76] As it

The European genetic mixture

The last few years have seen a great leap forward in studies of ancient DNA. It is now possible to obtain entire genomes from ancient individuals. From comparison of these to each other and modern Europeans, a pattern has emerged. The modern European gene pool was formed from three main source populations. The earliest in Europe were the western hunter-gatherers (WHG). At the height of the last Ice Age, small groups of foragers were trapped in habitable havens in southern Europe. As the glaciers retreated, their descendants spread northwards to re-colonize most of Europe, though thinly. The foragers mainly lived in small, mobile bands. Their genetic signature prevailed in most of Europe until the arrival of early European farmers (EEF) from Anatolia. Farmers could outbreed foragers and created a population explosion, though occupation density was still far lower than today. Meanwhile, Siberian hunter-gatherers trickled westwards once the climate warmed, entering the eastern fringes of Europe. They have been labelled the ancient north Eurasians (ANE). Gradually their descendants adopted herding and metalwork from their neighbours. In the process they mixed genetically with peoples who had been in Europe earlier and also acquired a fourth genetic signature found in a hunter-gatherer of the Caucasus and so labelled Caucasus hunter-gatherer (CHG).

It was in the Copper Age (see Chapter 3) that the diluted ANE plus CHG genetic signature spread west and north in Europe. Modern European populations are mixtures of the three components, in varying amounts. The Sardinians today are genetically the closest people in Europe to the farmers of the Neolithic period.[77]

20 *Graph to show the relationship of samples from various nations to the three main sources of present-day European populations: western hunter-gatherers (WHG), early European farmers (EEF) and ancient north Eurasians (ANE).*

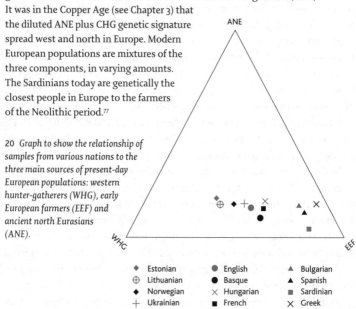

◆ Estonian	● English	▲ Bulgarian
⊕ Lithuanian	● Basque	▲ Spanish
◆ Norwegian	✕ Hungarian	■ Sardinian
✛ Ukrainian	■ French	✕ Greek

chances, an origin on the European steppe, which the River Don divides, is deduced by modern scholars for the speakers of the whole language family to which Germanic belongs, but in an era too distant for human recall, as we shall see in the next chapter.

Overview

- The Romans encountered Germani in a region of northern Europe bounded by the rivers Rhine, Vistula and Danube on the mainland, and including Scandinavia. They labelled the region Germania.

- The Germani were tribal, but had a language and culture in common and a myth of common origin.

- The Germani were subsistence farmers who organized themselves democratically, yet had some degree of hierarchy. A war-leader would maintain a band of warriors.

- The Germani built in wood. Their competent joinery is revealed by examples of furniture preserved in bog.

- They had a polytheistic religion similar to that of the Romans, Greeks and Celts of the time. It included a goddess of the sun, a god of the moon and deities personifying human attributes.

- After Germanic peoples were converted to Christianity, which went hand-in-hand with literacy, they concocted pseudo-histories of their prehistoric origins, based on the Bible or the Greek *Iliad*. The true origin of the Germani lay too deep in the past for human recollection.

CHAPTER THREE

The Long and Winding Road

> One must need travel on foot in ways remote and carry his
> provisions with him and tread the spray-flung track and the
> dangerous territory of alien peoples.[1]

S o says an Anglo-Saxon poem on the fortunes of men, or misfortunes
in this case. The author was thinking of a single, friendless wanderer.
Here we trace the ancestry of a language, which could not survive if only
one person spoke it. So the travels of a language are the travels of a community. It should leave clues in archaeology and genetics, as well as in
language itself.

The Indo-European family

Germanic belongs to a larger family, Indo-European, [21] which today
dominates Europe and also has millions of speakers in Asia. [22] In the
days before modern communications, any language had to be spoken by a
community face to face on a daily basis. It would gradually change with
time. If a section of the community moved so far away that they could not
talk constantly to the parent group, then they would not be part of the
parental linguistic process any more. Instead, they would develop their
own dialect. Eventually the parent and child communities would speak
different languages. That is how language families are created.

Once 'child' languages have separated to the point of mutual unintel-
ligibility, how do we detect that they descend from a common parent? As
travellers versed in the Classical languages of Europe came in contact with
the ancient Sanskrit language of India, they noticed similarities in vocabulary. For example, the word for 'father' in Latin and Greek is *pater* and in
Sanskrit is *pitar*. Likewise the word for 'mother' in Latin is *mater*, in ancient
Greek is *meter* and in Sanskrit is *matar*. Yet words can be borrowed between
languages, or appear similar by coincidence. It is only if linguists can marry
such correspondences to similarities in grammar that they can be sure that

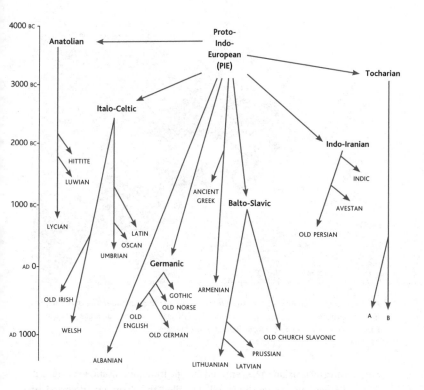

21 A tree of Indo-European languages, showing the estimated time period at which a group broke away from the Proto-Indo-European parent, so that its speech developed independently and became a daughter language, and then the estimated time of any splits in that daughter language. The first appearance of a language in writing is indicated by the names in small capitals, such as HITTITE. The names in bold, such as **Balto-Slavic**, are the creation of linguists; these languages were not recorded in writing.

languages are related. By 1813, linguists had formulated a model of a language family which they labelled Indo-European.[2] It has been intensively studied since.

The parent language of the Indo-European family did not survive long enough to be written down. Linguists call it Proto-Indo-European (PIE). Its homeland has long been deduced on linguistic grounds to be the Copper Age European steppe, north of the Black and Caspian seas.[3] Ancient DNA is now reinforcing the conclusions of linguists. A genetic signature labelled

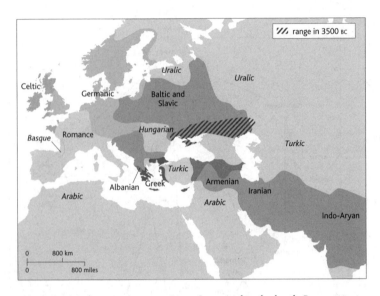

22 Indo-European languages in AD 1500. From a Copper Age homeland on the European steppe, Indo-European languages spread far and wide. This is now the dominant language family in Europe. Names of non-Indo-European languages are in italics.

ancient north Eurasian (ANE) entered Europe from Siberia and was present in the Copper Age steppe pastoralists called the Yamnaya, deduced to be the speakers of PIE. It is now found in almost all people of European descent.[4] [see Box p. 48]

Mammoth hunters

Where had the ANE genetic signature come from? The earliest sample of it so far found comes from a four-year-old boy buried 24,000 years ago in central Siberia. His remains were discovered in the late 1920s by Russian archaeologists near the village of Mal'ta. The climate was harsh in his day. It was the height of the Ice Age. Human life was delicately balanced on the edge of extinction. Mal'ta may not have been a permanent settlement; hunters often moved seasonally. It has been suggested that the site lay on a reindeer migration route. If so, the family of Mal'ta Boy would have camped there in spring and autumn, to capture reindeer coming and going.

In winter they might have retreated into the sheltered Yenisei River basin to the west, which was the chief refuge for Siberian hunter-gatherers of the time. In summer they could pursue the woolly mammoth which grazed the Siberian steppe. Every part of these massive animals could be used by hunters. The walls of semi-subterranean huts at Mal'ta were made from mammoth bones, and the roof from reindeer antlers, probably covered with animal skins and sod to keep out the biting winds.[5]

Mal'ta Boy's people carved figurines from mammoth tusk. These may be the oldest known images anywhere in the world of sewn fur clothing.[6] [23] Carvings of birds have also been found there. The artistic flowering at Mal'ta has been something of a puzzle. It is not commonplace in Palaeolithic Siberia. So where did these people come from and where did they go? A similar site at Buret', in the same region, is earlier at around 25,000 years old. Going back further in time, some mammoth hunters had roamed north of the Arctic Circle to Yenisei Bay by 45,000 years ago.[7] It was an astonishing feat of human endurance. They had learned to live in very cold climates even before the Ice Age gripped the Earth. About 28,000 years ago such hardy hunters left their detritus at the Yana Rhinoceros Horn Sites (RHS), in northeast Siberia. Like Mal'ta, the Yana RHS are exceptional in the items found there, including ornaments, decorated ivory vessels, engraved mammoth tusks and needles. Significantly, there was also a foreshaft made from the horn of a woolly rhinoceros, which is remarkably similar to the Clovis points that appear later in the Americas.[8]

The ANE genetic cluster discovered in Mal'ta Boy is found today in both Europeans and Native Americans. So some relatives of Mal'ta Boy must have been among those who travelled across the now-submerged Bering land bridge to people the Americas, though a greater contribution to the ancestral Native American gene pool was made by relatives of present-day East Asians.[9] A mammoth hunter living about 17,000 years ago at Afontova Gora, on the bank of the Yenisei River, also had the ANE genetic component. He carried Y-DNA

23 *A small figurine, less than 4 cm (1½ inches) high, from Mal'ta depicting a child wrapped in furs against the icy cold.*

53

Y-DNA

Only males carry a Y chromosome. So the pattern of DNA on this chromosome enables us to track descent from father to son. Sometimes there are faults in replication, often known as mutations. You could see it as a typing error in the chains of letters along the DNA. For example, somewhere along the line from your paternal great-great-grandfather to your father, a T might have mutated into a C at a particular point. The pattern of mutations in an individual's Y-DNA places him in a haplogroup, which can be fitted on to a tree showing the male-line relationships of all mankind. [24] For example, R1 descends from R; R1a and R1b are subclades (genetic lineages) under R1, and so on. Since these 'relative' names change as new mutations are discovered and the tree changes, it is common to identify a haplogroup also by the mutation which defines it, which is unchanging. So you may see R1a1a1 written as R1a1a1 (M417) or R-M417 for short.

Haplogroup I2a is the most common so far found in European Mesolithic hunter-gatherers, except on the eastern fringes of Europe, where R appears among arrivals from Siberia. The most common haplogroup among farmers arriving in Europe from the Near East was G2a. It took a major population turnover in the Copper and Bronze Ages to bring haplogroup R to its present prominence in Europe.[10] [see 29]

haplogroup Q. Today Q is still found in North Eurasia, [25] but one large subclade is almost exclusive to Native Americans. Mal'ta Boy carried the brother haplogroup R.[11] Subclades of R are strongly represented today in most Indo-European-speaking countries. [see 29]

How did relatives of Mal'ta Boy arrive on the European steppe? Dwellings made of mammoth bone were erected between 15,000 and 14,000 years ago along the upper and middle Dnieper basin in what is now Ukraine. The sheltered river valley would provide winter quarters for those who hunted mammoth on the steppe in summer.[12] Since no DNA has been obtained from any of these sites, we cannot say whether or not they were made by relatives of Mal'ta Boy. Yet an incursion into Europe from Siberia around this time might explain why a man who died at Villabruna, Italy, about 14,000 years ago carried a now-extinct lineage of Y-DNA R1b1a, while another example of R appears in France as the climate warmed, around 10,000 BC.[13] Three men in a group of fishermen living by the Iron Gates on the Danube in about 9000 BC carried R1b1a and yet were otherwise genetically typical

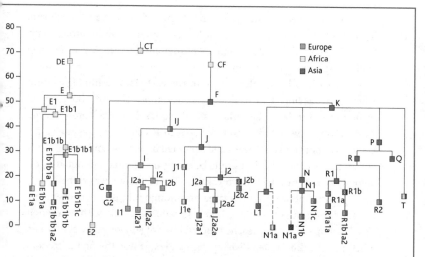

24 A section of the phylogeny (genetic family tree) of Y-DNA chiefly showing the haplogroups common in Europe and their estimated age. Geneticists have given capital letters to main branches of the tree. Then subclades within the branches are numbered and lettered in order of descent.

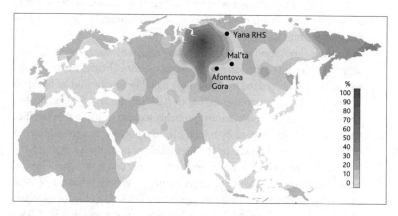

25 The modern distribution of Y-DNA haplogroup Q in Eurasia and sites mentioned in the text.

of western European hunter-gatherers.[14] If the earliest arrivals from Siberia had once been genetic matches for Mal'ta Boy, then intermarriage with locals had diluted their ANE component to non-existence. It was not they who contributed ANE to Yamnaya.

So we look to later influences from the east. Two technologies from Siberia can be linked to new arrivals in Europe. The first pottery was made in the Far East. The earliest sherds so far discovered are from the Xianrendong Cave in China, and are between 20,000 and 19,000 years old.[15] Early Asian pots had thick walls and a pointed base, ideal for heating foods within an open fire. The heat would be evenly distributed through the pot, helping to prevent cracks and breakages. The technique was carried westwards across Siberia by hunter-gatherers. Around Lake Baikal in Siberia the favoured form of pot combined the pointed-base shape with an everted rim. This type of pottery reached the middle Volga river valley close to its junction with the Samara River by 7000 BC. [26] It was the first pottery in Europe. From there pottery of the same type had spread to the Baltic and Scandinavia by about 5500 BC, before any sign of contact with farming.[16] [27] A pottery-using hunter-gatherer of the Samara region carried ANE and the Y-DNA haplogroup R1b1a.[17] In the Baltic, the Narva culture continued the pottery-making hunter-gatherer tradition. Two Narva men in Latvia carried Y-DNA haplogroup R1b1a1a, while two others in Lithuania carried variants of the I2a1 haplogroup typical of more western European foragers.[18] Two foraging peoples had met.

Another innovation in much the same region at much the same time as pottery resulted in long, thin, regular stone blades with parallel edges. They were created by clamping a suitable core of flint or obsidian and then applying indirect pressure to flake off the sharp-edged blades. This complex technique was most probably handed down within families and so would have spread by migration. Like pottery, it arrived between the Urals and the Caspian in the Mesolithic period. It also reached the Baltic and Lapland by a more northerly route and from there spread across Scandinavia. The newcomers carried a genetic mixture of ANE and WHG, labelled eastern hunter-gatherer (EHG). EHG has been found in some Mesolithic hunters in Sweden, who carried variants of Y-DNA haplogroup I2. This could be explained by mixture between western and eastern foragers.[19] [28]

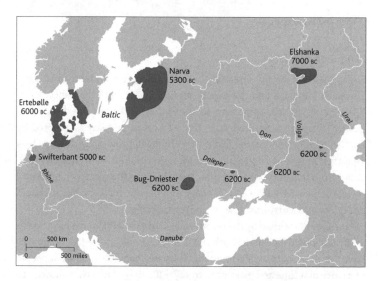

26 (left) The first pottery in Europe. A vessel from Staraya Elshanka on the River Samara, Russia. It was designed for cooking. The pointed base distributed the heat of the fire evenly.

27 (above) The earliest pottery in Europe was made by hunter-gatherers. It spread up the Volga from the Elshanka culture to the Baltic, where it appears in the Narva culture and then west along the coast to southern Scandinavia, where it is known as Ertebølle, and the Netherlands, where it is known as Swifterbant. Meanwhile this pottery spread west along the steppe.

28 Hunter-gatherer groups from western Europe (WHG) and eastern Europe (EHG) mixed in Scandinavia in the Mesolithic period. The ice sheet covering Scandinavia is shown around 8000 BC – both the most credible (solid line) and maximum extent (dashed line).

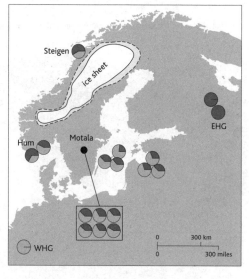

Language and DNA

Today there is a strong correlation between the native speaking of an Indo-European language and the genetic signals of ANE and the subclades of Y-DNA R1.[20] [29] It is important to stress that DNA does not dictate language. Language is learned. If a child of Korean ancestry is adopted by English-speakers soon after birth, that child will grow up with English as a mother tongue. As a general rule, though, children learn their first language from their biological parents. That produces the greater-than-chance correlations we see between language and genetic markers, but it should not be seen as a cast-iron, one-to-one relationship.

Nor should we imagine that Proto-Indo-European (PIE) must have begun at the calculated date of the birth of Y-DNA R1 28,200 years ago.[21] Languages have their own pace of development. They are shaped around what people of a particular time and place need to say. PIE can be dated by its lexicon to no earlier than 4000 BC. Scholars have painstakingly reconstructed as much as possible of its vocabulary, which reveals a great deal about the lifestyle of its speakers. They were familiar with agriculture. That alone proves that this language was not spoken by ancient hunter-gatherers.[22] Moreover, PIE-speakers were familiar with the plough. The earliest farmers used digging sticks. The idea of using oxen to pull a plough came later. It was part of a Copper Age wave of realization that some animals could be used not just as food, but to lessen human labour. Oxen could drag a sledge.

29 *Distribution of the subclades of Y-DNA R today in Europe, Asia and Africa.*

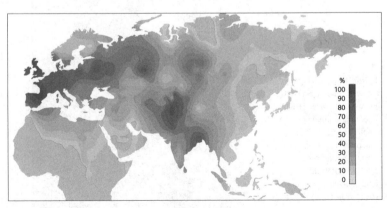

With the invention of the wheel around 3500 BC came the wagon. There are PIE words for both. PIE-speakers were also familiar with metallurgy. They had a concept of social ranking, but few words for specific occupations and none for urban life. The lexicon reveals a Copper Age society, though not an urbanized state.[23]

The European steppe

PIE can be located geographically by its linguistic contacts. Where one language borrows several words from another at a time before writing, that suggests that they were neighbours. PIE-speakers had contact with the Proto-Uralic language, probably spoken around the junction of the Volga and Kama rivers (see p. 71). PIE also had contacts with the languages of the north Caucasus.[24] So we can picture PIE north of the Caspian and west of the Ural mountains, on the European steppe.[25] [30]

Naturally this language did not come out of nothing. There must have been a pre-PIE language, or rather a gradual linguistic development as pottery-making foragers on the steppe adopted stock-raising, and then copper-working and wagons. Hunter-gatherers often camped close to a fresh water source, preferably one which would also provide fish. The rivers Dniester, South Bug, Dnieper and Donets all run south across the steppe to the Black Sea. Archaeologists have identified two groups of pottery-making fisher-foragers making use of these rivers: the Bug-Dniester culture and Dnieper-Donets I. Both gained by contact with farming cultures to the west. The most heavily populated part of the Pontic-Caspian steppe at the time was around the Dnieper Rapids, a stretch of the river with ten major cascades. Fish migrating upstream could be caught here in vast quantities. It was here that Dnieper-Donets I foragers transformed themselves into Dnieper-Donets II cattle-farmers about 5200 BC.[26]

Ancient DNA reveals Dnieper-Donets II to be a mixed people. Prior to the arrival of pottery-makers, there were foragers in the vicinity who were genetically almost typical of hunter-gatherers across most of Europe, to judge by the single sample so far published. He was a man buried at Vasylivka, Ukraine, about 11,000 years ago. His Y-DNA haplogroup was I2a2a (P220). [see Box pp. 54–55] Taking a sweep across the whole genome, his ancestry was almost all western hunter-gatherer (WHG). Yet he carried a small amount of the ANE signature, associated with ancient

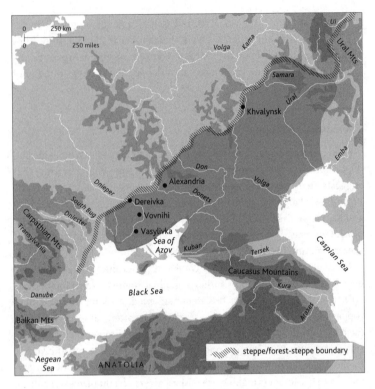

30 *The Pontic-Caspian steppe, with sites mentioned in the text.*

northern Eurasians.[27] [see Box p. 48] Was that ANE from the people who made the mammoth-bone dwellings along the Dnieper millennia earlier? (p. 54). A man of the Dnieper-Donets II culture, buried at Vovnihi, Ukraine, proved to be similar genetically, but with slightly more ANE, and the Y-DNA haplogroup R1a (L146).[28] This is as we would expect if pottery-making people intermixed with local foragers.

By around 4700–4600 BC, stock-breeding had spread as far east as the Volga, creating the Khvalynsk culture, which is particularly interesting for its copper-working, hints of horse domestication and social structure. Copper-working began in the Near East, but around 5000 BC smelting and cast-copper objects appeared in the Balkans.[29] The oldest copper objects in the Volga–Ural steppes had been traded from what is now Bulgaria all the way to Khvalynsk, on the west bank of the Volga River, in what is now Russia. [see 30] Locals took up the idea. Using copper from the Balkans, they crudely imitated the technology. By contrast, horse-breeding began on the steppe. At Khvalynsk horses were grouped with cattle and sheep in funeral sacrifices, as though they too were domesticated. The funeral ritual was significant, for it indicates a hierarchy in this community. Only about one in five people were buried with sacrificed animals. Another distinction was individual graves for certain people, rather than the group burial found in earlier cultures, and a distinctive burial posture, on the back with knees raised, with heads to the north or east. These funeral customs later became widespread on the European steppe.[30]

The men of Copper Age Khvalynsk were genetically similar to the early pottery-maker on the Volga (p. 56) with his ANE input, but also carried the CHG component, perhaps from the nearby Caucasus. [see Box p. 48] One young man aged between twenty and thirty was buried with 293 copper artefacts (mostly beads), which suggests a high status in his small community. He carried Y-DNA haplogroup R1b1 (M415). Another man aged thirty to thirty-five, buried with a copper ring and a copper bead, carried R1a1 (M459). Here is proof that both branches of R1 were present in the culture.[31]

The traffic of ideas and goods across the European steppe was not all in one direction. Influences from the Volga or nearby moved west to the Dnieper Rapids to become an element in the Sredni Stog culture about 4400 BC. One of the best-known sites of this culture is at Dereivka, on the Dnieper River, but the culture stretched eastwards as far as the Lower Don.[32] Near the village of Alexandria in the Kupyansk district of Ukraine, a man carrying Y-DNA R1a1a1 (M417) was buried in a Sredni Stog cemetery.[33] Almost all the early Sredni Stog pottery had the round or pointed bases and flaring, everted rims that had been a feature of pottery at the eastern end of the European steppe since its first arrival. Some was decorated by pressing cord into the surface while the clay was wet, a technique used earlier at many sites around the Volga and Don rivers. The typical Sredni Stog burial posture was copied from that of Khvalynsk; all the burials were individual and some were covered with a small mound.[34]

So archaeology gives us evidence of contact between the pockets of people along the European steppe that we can imagine speaking a pre-PIE language. Linguistic developments would probably be shared. So when the Yamnaya cultural horizon rolled across the European steppe from around 3300 BC, putting its mark on local cultures, this would not bring a complete change of language everywhere. Evolving between the rivers Volga and Don, mainly from the Khvalynsk culture via the Repin culture (3900–3300 BC, sometimes labelled Early Yamnaya), this was a more mobile society, living in tents and ox-drawn carts.[35] The earliest evidence of the wheel comes from the Cucuteni-Tripolye farming culture on the western edge of the European steppe, in the form of wheeled toys. Around 3600 BC this culture produced models of sledges harnessed with oxen. By the inventive stroke of adding wheels, it seems that the sledge became the cart. [31] Normally a new invention is named by the inventor, so it is significant that PIE-speakers coined their own words for wheels and wagons, derived from PIE roots. This suggests that PIE-speakers were close to the heart of the invention. Archaeology shows that steppe pastoralists had begun to infiltrate the Cucuteni-Tripolye farmers by this time.[36]

The Yamnaya cultural package is distinctive. The most visible element of their culture today are the mounds (called 'kurgans') which mark their

31 *This wagon was unearthed at Lchasen in Armenia. It dates from c. 2000 BC, long after the earliest wagons, but its preservation is remarkable. It had heavy, solid wheels. A superstructure of bent withies could have been covered with hide.*

graves. The kurgan placed a new emphasis on the individual by being a single grave, rather than the collective graves common among Neolithic farmers. As we saw above, the process of burial change had begun in previous steppe cultures at Khvalynsk and Sredni Stog. The difference is perhaps more one of initial intent, since many house secondary burials. We can guess that those few with rich grave goods, especially wheeled vehicles, were for honoured leaders of the community. Burial with tool-kits marked the special status of metal-workers. The Kargaly copper ore deposits were discovered in the foothills of the southern Urals, and exploited by Yamnaya people.[37] New weapon designs included the tanged dagger and the shaft-hole axe. The Yamnaya people wore woven clothes, gold or silver spiral hair rings (lockenringe), distinctive bone toggles and decorated bone discs.[38] The hair binders are found in pairs with both men and women, and would have been worn on the end of braids to keep them from unwinding. Cord decoration was common on pottery.[39]

As the European steppe became colder and drier after 3200 BC, Yamnaya people were tempted further afield.[40] [see 32] The technical innovations of horse-riding, wheeled transport and metal-working were gradually adopted across a wider territory. Often they are accompanied by other Yamnaya characteristics which consolidate the link to the cultural progenitor. Several archaeological cultures derived from Yamnaya have been identified as plausible vectors for PIE.[41]

Two of these cultures, Bell Beaker and Corded Ware, are so wide-ranging that they could account for the spread of Indo-European into the regions in which we later find the Celtic, Italic, Germanic, Baltic and Slavic language families spoken. This does not mean that the parent languages of all these families developed in the Copper Age. Most arose far later. [see 22] So what language would the people of Corded Ware and Bell Beaker have spoken? The Celtic, Italic, Germanic, Baltic and Slavic language families have enough linguistic links not shared with other Indo-European languages that the term 'Northwest Indo-European' was suggested to describe an early stage in their mutual development.[42] For example, the PIE word for 'one' was dropped in Germanic, Italic, Celtic and possibly Balto-Slavic in favour of derivatives of PIE *óynos, originally meaning 'single'.[43] Certainly there are river-names across Europe that appear to be derived from a form of Indo-European earlier than any of its known branches.[44]

The Corded Ware culture

From around 2800 to 2750 BC a new way of life spread over the North European Plain and into southern Fennoscandia.[45] [32] This vast archaeological culture is commonly called Corded Ware after its most characteristic pottery, which was decorated with cord-impressions. [33] As we have seen, this decoration was common on Yamnaya and earlier steppe pottery. Other names used, such as Single Grave and Battle Axe, reflect other notable features of the culture. It dotted the landscape with round mounds, under each of which was typically buried a single individual in a crouched position with grave goods. This was a visible sign of a new emphasis on the individual, an echo of Yamnaya thinking. The new type of burial respected gender. Male graves evoke a warrior ideal with their stone axes, while female graves have personal ornaments. The graves of metal-workers are distinctive. These are clues to a new social structure. Among dress items are bone toggles and discs identical to those from the steppes. Specialized cattle herding increased the pastoral component in the economy.[46]

Indeed, at one time the Corded Ware people were considered entirely pastoral and nomadic, since their burials were far easier to find in most areas than their settlements. Closer analysis has revealed that Corded Ware lifestyle varied by region.[47] Fortuitously, some Corded Ware houses survived far better than timber usually does. They were built on stilts in the marshes beside Lake Zürich in Switzerland, and were preserved as the water rose over them. Elsewhere, painstaking excavation has greatly enlarged the number of known Corded Ware settlements.

At Wattendorf-Motzenstein in Germany, about 20 kilometres (12½ miles) northeast of the city of Bamberg, a small farming community of about thirty-five people lived in log-built huts beside a stone pathway. While most of the land surrounding the settlement was given over to pasture, mainly for cattle, one plot was used for growing crops, including barley and einkorn wheat. Stone querns were used to grind grain into flour. The inhabitants kept horses. Perhaps they hunted on horseback, as venison was plentiful in their diet.[48]

By contrast, at a small settlement in Mortens Sande in Denmark, only one arrowhead was found, suggesting that hunting was not a major activity. Barley was grown. The most interesting feature, though, was a workshop for turning amber into beads.[49] We shall see in the next chapter how important the amber trade became in the Nordic Bronze Age.

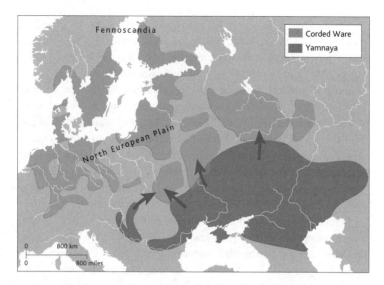

32 *The Corded Ware culture is found over a massive stretch of northeast Europe, from eastern France to Russia and from Scandinavia to the Alpine foothills and Carpathian Mountains.*

Farming had reached central Europe long before this period, but it was not until around 4000 BC that the Funnel Beaker culture brought farming to the southern parts of Scandinavia. These farmers later acquired wheeled vehicles, the plough and wool-spinning from their more advanced southern neighbour, the Late Cucuteni-Tripolye culture.[50] Then in north and west Jutland 'stone heap graves' were created between 3100 and 2800 BC, which contained the corpses of cattle in one part and humans in another.

33 *Corded Ware pottery was named for a common form of decoration found on it, made by pressing cord into the wet clay. The pottery comes in a variety of shapes; these examples are from Sweden.*

The deceased could have been borne to burial by an ox-drawn cart and the oxen then slaughtered. Burials with pairs of cattle have also been found in northern Germany, but are known earlier in the Carpathian Basin.[51] This suggests that ideas were filtering northward along with technology.

South of Jutland, between the Elbe and the Vistula, the Globular Amphora culture, named for its characteristic pots, acted as another chronological bridge between Funnel Beaker and Corded Ware. DNA samples from the people of this stock-breeding culture show no steppe component. They appear typical of the European Neolithic.[52] Yet the culture draws some traits from the steppe, such as a preference for single graves. Like the 'stone heap graves' in Jutland, a Globular Amphora grave could contain a human burial in one section and a pair of oxen in an adjoining section.[53] So Corded Ware penetration northwards could have followed existing trade or migration routes. By contrast, the heavily forested region east of the Baltic, rich in game, beside a sea teeming with fish, was more attractive to those happy to live by fishing and hunting. The Corded Ware culture was the first to bring herding and milk-drinking to the region that is now Finland, Estonia, Latvia and Lithuania. Even so, agriculture as an everyday way of life developed there no earlier than 1000 BC.[54] Northern Scandinavia remained untouched even by Corded Ware.

The relationship between Corded Ware and the cultures of the steppe had long been discussed by archaeologists, with both similarities and differences pointed out. From the 1970s there was a preference for interpretations stressing local continuity. Swedish prehistorian Kristian Kristiansen was almost a lone voice in 1989 pointing out that a purely local genesis for Corded Ware was untenable, but even he did not propose massive migration from the steppe.[55] A decade later migration routes upriver from the steppe were under discussion.[56] Yet it took ancient DNA to clarify who was related to whom. The first shock to continuity theories came in papers published in 2009, showing that neither the earliest farmers of central Europe nor the Funnel Beaker farmers in Scandinavia were descended from local hunter-gatherers.[57] That deduction was based on ancient mitochondrial DNA alone. As techniques for extracting ancient DNA improved, genome-wide results were obtained, which supported those conclusions and added another.

A third component of the European gene pool had spread from the steppe in the Copper Age. [see Box p. 48] A sample of Corded Ware people from Germany was modelled as approximately three-quarters Yamnaya, basing this on the only Yamnaya samples available at the time, which were from the eastern end of the European steppe.[58] We now know that further west on the steppe, Yamnaya absorbed some early farming DNA, making western Corded Ware people more similar to western Yamnaya,[59] while some Corded Ware individuals in Latvia and Lithuania were very close genetically to the eastern Yamnaya samples.[60]

Yet we have a complication. Corded Ware spread into parts of the north where foragers of Siberian ancestry had gone before them, bringing the ANE component. Is there any way to distinguish genetically between these early arrivals and the Corded Ware people? Fortunately there is. Thirteen thousand years ago a man was buried in Satsurblia cave, on the southern side of the Caucasus Mountains, in what is now Georgia. His DNA proved to be most similar to that of another ancient individual found at the Kotias Klde rock shelter in Georgia, who lived about 9,700 years ago. They belonged to a small group that managed to survive the Ice Age in isolation from foragers in Europe, and so developed a distinct DNA signature, which has been labelled CHG. We can imagine CHG filtering north on to the steppe, for this component appeared in people of the Copper Age Khvalynsk culture by 4700–4600 BC (see p. 60), and later in Yamnaya.[61] It was missing from early pottery-makers in Latvia, first appearing there in a Corded Ware individual.[62]

Another possible confusion can also be eliminated. CHG appears in Neolithic farmers of Iran and the Armenian Bronze Age, but Corded Ware individuals genetically resemble Yamnaya rather than Bronze Age Armenians, showing that the CHG in Bronze Age Europe came from the steppe rather than direct from the southern Caucasus.[63]

Corded Ware males predominantly carried Y-DNA R1a. In particular R1a1a1b (Z645/S224) has been found both in Baltic and Scandinavian Corded Ware. It is the ancestor of the R1a1a1b1a3 (Z284/S221) that we find today in men of Scandinavian descent. R1a1a1b appears in two men buried around 2500 BC in Scandinavia. One, found at Ķyndeløse on the Danish island of Zealand, actually carried the Scandinavian subclade defined by Z284/S221.[64] The other was buried at Ölsund, Hälsingland, Sweden.[65]

The Bell Beaker culture entered central Europe later than Corded Ware, settling in patches as far east as Poland. Over much of central Europe it was succeeded by a series of cultures which become identifiable as Celtic in the Iron Age.[66] The pattern in Scandinavia was different. There, Bell Beaker arrived late and did not completely replace Corded Ware. It trickled from the northern Rhine zone to northern Jutland about 2350 BC, creating outposts on the Danish islands of Funen and Zealand and in southwest Norway. Bell Beaker people explored much of Europe in their search for valuable raw materials. North Jutland offered high-quality flint. Daggers made from it by Bell Beaker people were traded into Norway, Sweden and northern Germany. Norway was of interest for its seams of copper ore. The urge within the Bell Beaker culture to prospect, craft and trade triggered a new period in Scandinavia, labelled the Late Neolithic in the Scandinavian chronology.[67] It was a prelude to the remarkable Nordic Bronze Age, which we encounter in the next chapter. R1b-U106 has been found in a man buried at Lilla Beddinge, Sweden, between 2275 and 2032 BC. Though his grave lies in a Battle Axe (Corded Ware) cemetery, the date places it in the Late Neolithic.[68] Today haplogroup R1b-U106 shadows the spread of Germanic languages. [see 49]

Routes to the north

How did Germanic develop? On the tree of Indo-European languages [see 21], we can see a group splitting away from its parent about 3000 BC, which, millennia later, around 500 BC, had developed into Proto-Germanic, the immediate ancestor of the separate Germanic branches. So there was a long period of evolution, which we could call Pre-Germanic for short, though technically it is Pre-Proto-Germanic.[69]

Where did this happen? Linguists usually work out such things by traces of contacts with other languages – a borrowed or shared word, perhaps. It may be possible to deduce at what stage in the development of a language a particular contact occurred. Putting together these clues, it seems that Germanic has a complex history. [34] Picture a journey starting in the Indo-European homeland, in contact with the dialect that would become Balto-Slavic. Most specialists envisage Balto-Slavic developing from PIE into the Middle Dnieper region.[70] The words for 'eleven', 'twelve' and 'thousand' in Proto-Germanic have cognates only in certain Balto-Slavic languages, which suggests contact at a very early stage. It seems that Pre-Germanic lost contact with that easterly sister, still at an early stage, to come in contact with Italic and Celtic, or more likely Italo-Celtic, the parent

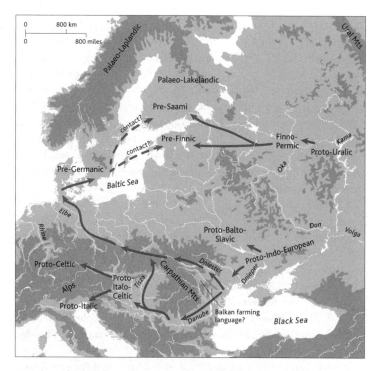

34 *A theoretical linguistic progress of the ancestors of the Germani from the Indo-European homeland, starting from the Dniester estuary and moving across the North European Plain into Scandinavia, with a possible alternative or additional route via the Danube.*

of both language branches. It was probably at this point that Pre-Germanic lost the PIE word *sem for the number 'one' and substituted the PIE word *óynos ('single'), which also provided the usual word for 'one' in Italic and Celtic.[71] The extension of Yamnaya up the Danube valley probably saw the gradual development of Italo-Celtic from Northwest Indo-European. Proto-Celtic probably developed around the heads of the rivers Danube and Rhine, north of the Alps.[72]

Archaeologist David Anthony argues for a starting point for the ancestors of the Germani in the Usatovo culture (3300–2700 BC) around the Dniester estuary, and movement upriver to form part of the Corded Ware culture. The Usatovo culture was a mixture of Yamnaya and Late

Cucuteni-Tripolye.[73] In keeping with the Yamnaya pastoral-nomadic lifestyle, only a limited vocabulary for crops and land cultivation can be reconstructed for PIE. Pre-Germanic picked up additional farming vocabulary, such as words for 'pea' and 'goat', from a now-lost language which was not part of the Indo-European family. Its speakers were evidently farmers. So the lost language could have been that of Cucuteni-Tripolye. A Balkan farming language would best explain why traces of the same language are found in Balto-Slavic, Italo-Celtic, Armenian and Greek, although linguist Guus Kroonen makes the point that this language could have spread north with Late Neolithic farmers and so be encountered by Corded Ware arrivals in southern Scandinavia.[74]

An alternative or additional route for Pre-Germanic could have followed the Yamnaya culture as it expanded up the Danube valley into the Carpathian Basin. From there one branch moved up the Tisza River and fed into Corded Ware beyond the Carpathian Mountains.[75] [see 32] There is no linguistic reason to suppose that the people who eventually came to speak Germanic were all descended from just one band that stayed together in a long trek north from the Black Sea all the way to Scandinavia. On the contrary, the complexity of Germanic would be in keeping with Indo-European-speakers arriving from several routes, who could have banded together to form the linguistic community in which Pre-Germanic evolved.

Moving further north, Corded Ware spread into southern Scandinavia around 2800 BC, where it is known as the Battle Axe culture, or Boat Axe culture from the boat-shaped axe predominant there. [35] Again, two routes are possible and not mutually exclusive.

One analysis of Corded Ware pottery, tools, weapons and ornaments found links between southern Sweden and two regions of north Germany: Schleswig-Holstein and Mecklenburg. There was also a link between

35 A boat-shaped stone battle axe from southern Norway. A hole was bored into the stone so that it could be fitted on to a wooden haft. This type of axe is generally found in southern Scandinavia, northern Germany and the Baltic.

Denmark and Sweden.[76] So a route via Jutland to Sweden is shown on the map. [see 34] Another analysis suggests that the Battle Axe pottery in Sweden most nearly resembles a Corded Ware type which seems to have evolved in southwest Finland. So some Corded Ware makers could have arrived in Sweden via the eastern Baltic.[77]

In the north, Pre-Germanic-speakers might encounter the now lost language of the early Scandinavian hunter-gatherers, labelled Palaeo-Laplandic. From them the incomers could have picked up words for local fauna and flora, just as Saami foragers did, as they entered Lapland.[78] A word for 'seal' appears in Proto-Germanic as *selhaz* and in an early form of Finnic as *šülkeš*. Saami and Finnic belong to the Uralic family of languages. So the word for seal has been seen as a loan from Uralic to Pre-Germanic.[79] But, as we shall see, new thinking places contact with any Uralic language as rather later. Following the Corded Ware people came Bell Beaker adventurers into Jutland, who probably spoke a similar dialect of Indo-European to that spoken at the time by the descendants of Corded Ware makers there. This blend of peoples developed the splendid Nordic Bronze Age. This tallies with the impression from linguistics that Germanic had a long period of development in isolation from other Indo-European languages.[80]

By contrast, Pre-Germanic was in contact with two Uralic languages. Over a hundred Pre-Germanic loanwords into Pre-Finnic have been identified, and an early layer of Germanic loans into Pre-Saami can also be detected. In recent years ideas have been changing on both the date and location of Proto-Uralic. It is now considered younger than PIE. The consensus that the parent of the Uralic family developed near the Ural mountains remains unchanged, but two possible homelands along the River Volga are under discussion: the Volga-Kama and Volga-Oka regions. Choice between the two is difficult, but the Volga-Kama option is shown on the map here. [see 34] Proto-Uralic seems to have split by 2000 BC. Its descendant Proto-Finno-Permic would be archaeologically well placed in the Volga-Oka region, where it can be linked to the expansion of the Netted Ware culture around 1900–1800 BC from that region into the East Baltic zone, where the parents of the Finnic and Saamic language families developed.[81] The influence of the Nordic Bronze Age culture can be seen on the coasts of Finland and Estonia from about 1500 BC onwards. These areas may have been bilingual at this time.[82]

Overview

- The Germanic language family is one branch of the large Indo-European language family, which today dominates Europe and has millions of speakers in Asia.

- Its parent language, Proto-Indo-European (PIE), is deduced to have been spoken on the Copper Age European steppe, north of the Black and Caspian seas.

- A genetic signature labelled ancient north Eurasian (ANE) entered eastern Europe from Siberia with foragers who brought innovations: pottery and pressure-blade-making. Today there is a strong correlation between the native speaking of an Indo-European language and the genetic signals of ANE and subclades of Y-DNA R1.

- Some of these innovatory foragers were among the first people to enter Scandinavia, where they mixed with western European foragers.

- Some of their relatives settled on the European steppe, where they mixed with local foragers and farmers. The eventual result was Copper Age steppe pastoralists called the Yamnaya, who carried ANE and are deduced to be the speakers of PIE.

- The Yamnaya are culturally and genetically related to a later culture called Corded Ware, after the cord-impressed decoration on its most typical pottery.

- Some of the Corded Ware makers entered Scandinavia, where they probably encountered descendants of the foragers who had arrived so much earlier, as foraging remained a way of life in the north, although farmers had settled in southern Scandinavia.

- People of another Yamnaya-related culture – Bell Beaker – arrived later in Denmark. Together the descendants of this fusion of peoples would create the rich Nordic Bronze Age, discussed in the next chapter.

CHAPTER FOUR

Travel, Trade and Bronze

> Zeus the Father made a third generation of mortal men, a brazen
> race ... terrible and strong ... Their armour was of bronze ... and of
> bronze were their implements: there was no black iron.[1]

So the early Greek poet Hesiod wrote of the third of the supposed five
ages of humanity. Much of his poem was based on myth. He envisaged
an Age of Gold in the deep past, followed by an Age of Silver, and viewed
his own Iron Age as degenerate by comparison. It is intriguing, though,
that he knew of a time before his own when the metal of choice was bronze.
The Roman poet Titus Lucretius Carus (*c.* 99–*c.* 55 BC) was on more solid
ground in picturing the past as a sequence in which humankind first
wrought on wood and stone, then copper and bronze and finally iron.[2] This
idea was revived in the Age of Enlightenment. Yet it took the painstaking
labours of Danish antiquarian Christian Jürgensen Thomsen (1788–1865) to

36 *Christian Jürgensen Thomsen
showing visitors around the Old
Norse Museum in 1846, while it
was housed in the Christiansborg
Palace. This was the foundation
collection for the present
National Museum of Denmark.*

turn theory into a practical chronology. The son of a wealthy Copenhagen businessman, Thomsen could indulge his hobby of collecting coins and antiquities, becoming an expert in the field. In 1816 he was appointed secretary of the Danish Royal Commission for the Collection and Preservation of Antiquities. Part of his task was to organize a national collection for display to the public. [36] He decided to classify artefacts according to whether they were made of stone, bronze or iron. Once that sequence was established, he noted what other objects had been found together with the key artefacts. Thus a broader picture could be painted of the Ages of Stone, Bronze and Iron. His three-age system was widely adopted within the developing discipline of archaeology.[3]

Marvellous metals: copper to bronze

One problem gradually emerged: an age was missing. The Copper Age might seem too insignificant to mention in Scandinavia, but it was a long and important period in the Near East and southern Europe. The first metal to be worked anywhere in the world was copper. Millennia before true metallurgy, people were attracted to blue and green copper ores and naturally occurring (native) copper. The first farmers in western Asia saw the potential for personal adornment. Copper belts run through the Taurus Mountains of Anatolia to the Zagros Mountains of Iran. In the core of this area, present-day eastern Turkey and northern Iraq, people began to cold-work native copper. As early as about 8000 BC there is evidence from sites such as Çayönü Tepesi in eastern Turkey of some application of heat to ease the production process.

Where did copper smelting start? Bewilderingly, the technique crops up at around 5000 BC in places far apart, but equally blessed with seams of copper ore. Early copper-smelting sites have been found at Tal-i Iblis in southeastern Iran and at Belovode in eastern Serbia. Given the difficulty of acquiring the technology, and its arrival in multiple places at roughly the same time, it seems likely that the knowledge of copper-working was passed on within a family or clan. We may picture them initially trading the worked objects that appear quite widely, and then members of the clan perhaps settling in societies wealthy enough to support specialists. The home of smelting was probably in eastern Anatolia, where copper had already been exploited for so long.[4]

Natural copper ores are seldom free of impurities – traces of other metals. So perhaps the earliest alloys arose by accident. Metal-workers could have noticed, for example, that certain copper ores naturally rich in arsenic made a more ductile metal. What followed was a sophisticated understanding of metal properties. A plethora of copper-working debris from two recently excavated sites, Çamlıbel Tarlası in central Turkey and Arisman in west central Iran, has been enlightening. The methodology is clear. Arsenic and copper were being intentionally alloyed by the mid-fourth millennium BC. In the Balkans almost pure copper continued in use, but where any alloy was used in the period around 4000–2500 BC, arsenical copper was predominant. Bronze, the harder, tougher copper–tin alloy, did not appear until around the middle of that period. Nor did bronze immediately become the favoured alloy, to the exclusion of all others. So it is now clear that what has been traditionally labelled the Early Bronze Age was actually an age of arsenical copper for most of its duration. It was long thought that the tin used in the earliest bronze of western Asia must have come from central Asia, but the discovery of a tin mine at Kestal in Turkey, dating from about 3170 BC, transformed our understanding of early bronze. Another source of tin has been found at Hisarcık, near ancient Kanesh, a town which attracted Assyrian traders, as we shall see later in this chapter.

In northeast Europe, foragers picked up nuggets of native copper around Lake Onega in Russia between 4000 and 2000 BC, but such copper finds are rare in Scandinavia.[5] Some Funnel Beaker farmers imported copper objects into Scandinavia, but copper metal-working arrived in the region with the Bell Beaker people. Even so, the number of pure copper objects found there is tiny by comparison to the later riches in bronze.[6]

Contact with the Únětice bronze-making culture (2300–1600 BC) of central Europe was crucial in the development of the Nordic Bronze Age. The Únětice culture seems to have sprung from a Bell Beaker foundation, and certainly traded with Late Bell Beaker Britain, but also with parts of Scandinavia (central and eastern Denmark and southern Sweden) which had not experienced Bell Beaker settlement.[7] One odd connection was unearthed in the grave of a murder victim. At an Únětice settlement in Milejowice, southwest Poland, four bodies were buried together in a shallow pit in around 1844 BC, a time of great prosperity and expansion in the Únětice culture. One was a tall man who could be traced by isotopes to an origin in Scania, in southwest Sweden. He had been shot in the back with an arrow. He was

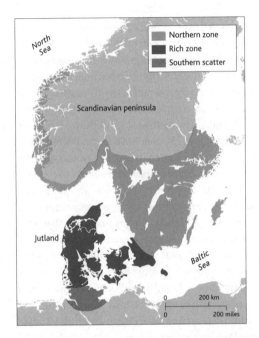

37 *The Nordic Bronze Age. The richest zone had concentrations of elaborate metalwork deposited in mounds and wetlands, with rich sources of amber and flint. To the south was a zone of more scattered metalwork depositions. The northern zone had less metalwork but thousands of rock art images.*

buried back to back with a local woman who held a local child in her arms. He held another local woman in his own arms. We may perhaps read into these positions a double sexual relationship which outraged local feeling.[8]

The discovery of tin in Cornwall gave Britain a bronze-making lead over Europe outside the Aegean, starting at around 2200 BC. Scandinavia and central Europe slipped into the Bronze Age at about 1750 BC, importing bronze objects from the Mediterranean region. Yet the period between 1600 and 1500 BC marks the true start of the Nordic Bronze Age, with not only a dramatic increase in the number of bronze objects, but also evidence of local bronze-working. The Nordic Bronze Age was unique, especially between 1500 and 1100 BC in what is now Denmark and the southern tip of Sweden. [37] The density of deposits of high-quality weapons and ornaments there is unparalleled in Europe. The technique and artistry in bronze is rivalled in Europe only by the Minoan and Mycenaean cultures, the earliest civilizations in Europe. Exceptional pieces include the Rørby scimitars [see 41 and 42] and the 'sun chariot' from Trundholm.[9] [see 46 and Pls vi and vii]

Trading networks

Bronze Age Europe was astonishingly inter-connected. Trading networks built up across the continent in part because of the demand for the precious raw materials for bronze. Although some Bell Beaker prospectors had been interested in Norwegian copper (see p. 68), this had no long-term impact. Sources of copper and tin are known today in Scandinavia, but in the Bronze Age they were ignored in favour of imports. Results of chemical analyses of some seventy bronze daggers and axes from Bronze Age Sweden were consistent with the main copper ore sources being the Iberian peninsula and Sardinia. Five objects, though, could be made from copper hewed from Cypriot copper mines.[10] Tin probably came from southwest Britain or the Ore Mountains (*Erzgebirge*), on the border between present-day Germany and the Czech Republic. What could Scandinavia offer in exchange? Its great asset was the treasured, translucent amber. [38, 39] This was a fossilized tree resin from the age of the dinosaurs. Bronze Age people did not need to mine for it, for the sea did the work for them. Amber floats on water. Storms churn pieces of it from the seabed and fling them up on the shores of the Baltic and eastern parts of the North Sea. Prehistorian Kristian Kristiansen estimates that, after a storm, an experienced amber-collector can pick up 2 kilograms (4½ pounds) of amber on the west coast of Jutland in a day. Its value in the Bronze Age Mediterranean would equal 400 kilograms

38 An insect trapped in a piece of ancient Baltic amber from Gdansk, Pomerania, Poland.

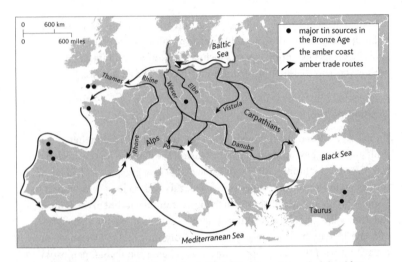

39 *The routes along which amber was traded during the Bronze Age can be deduced from discoveries of Baltic and North Sea amber far from their sources.*

(about 880 pounds) of copper.[11] The exchange of amber for copper in the Bronze Age is strongly supported by the discoveries of Nordic amber in places close to copper ores with isotopes that correspond with Scandinavian bronze artefacts: Siegerland in what is now Germany, North Tyrol, Sierra Morena in Iberia, Sardinia, Cyprus and Lavrion in Greece.[12]

We need not picture a direct shuttle between a copper mine and a northern beach. Exchanges could be made at a convenient entrepôt. Early networks were probably created by the far-flung Bell Beaker people. The Isle of Thanet on the southeastern tip of England seems to have been an early landing site for Copper Age arrivals. Separated from the bulk of the North Downs by the Wantsum Channel, Thanet was a true island at the time. [see 75] Offshore islands make convenient maritime trading posts; we shall see that traders were operating on Thanet in Anglo-Saxon times. Thanet has an outstandingly dense distribution of Bronze Age burials.[13] Overlooking Pegwell Bay is a cluster of round barrows; they stand on the highest point of the coastline, where they could be seen from far out at sea. The location was probably chosen for that very reason. In the shadow of these ancestors was a cemetery in use from the Late Bronze Age to the Middle Iron Age. Isotopic analysis has revealed where these people came from. Of the twenty-two skeletons tested, eight were local, seven were from Scandinavia and five were from southwest Iberia. Interestingly, the earliest phase was the most mixed: local, Norse and Iberian.[14] Were these members of a far-flung family or were they unrelated? Only DNA could tell us.

Amber beads were buried with their owners in certain well-furnished Bronze Age Bell Beaker graves in Britain. Though these are widely scattered, there is a particularly interesting group in Wiltshire and Dorset, long ago dubbed the 'Wessex culture'. Three burials of the Wessex group contained amber necklaces with rectangular amber spacer plates with a particular pattern bored into them.[15] [40] Spacer plates with this pattern are found in two other Bronze Age cultures of Europe, both later than the Wessex group. At the very beginning of the Mycenaean period in Greece, about 1650–1550 BC, amber from the Baltic appeared in the rich shaft-graves of the Mycenaean elite. These included the same type of spacer plates, which suggest that necklaces had arrived from the Wessex region as finished objects. These Mycenaean amber treasures in turn pre-date the earliest appearance (c. 1500 BC) of amber necklace components, including the same type of

40 *Laid out in Wiltshire Museum is a complex necklace of amber beads interspersed with amber spacer plates, which originally united the strings of beads. It came from the 'Golden Barrow' at Upton Lowell in Wiltshire, England.*

spacer plates, in the Tumulus culture of southern Germany. So it seems that amber could travel by stages, first to Britain, perhaps in exchange for tin, and then further afield as desirable manufactured objects.[16] From the Wessex region, amber could have travelled to Brittany, where there is other evidence of trade with Britain, and from there along the Atlantic and even perhaps into the Mediterranean. Both Baltic and Sicilian amber reached Iberia in the Copper and Bronze Ages. Archaeological sites with amber in Iberia generally lie close to the coast or upriver from the coast, suggesting an arrival by sea.[17] An alternative route from Britain could follow the Rhine and Rhône to the Mediterranean. [see 39]

A direct route from Jutland to central Europe would be to follow the Weser or Elbe rivers southwards. A land trek from the headwaters of either could bring amber into the Carpathian Basin, where bronze-making societies sprang up from around 1750–1700 BC, introducing new casting techniques and weapon types. Amber beads appear in burials and hoards there. The Danube connected these groups to the Black Sea and thence to the eastern Mediterranean. So this was presumably one of the earliest routes by which amber reached Mycenae. After about 1500 BC the bronze-making cultures of the Carpathian Basin declined, but amber could be routed through the expanding Tumulus culture. Moving south from there, the barrier of the Alps is daunting, but the Brenner Pass through these mountains was already in use. Amber has been found at Bronze Age sites on the route south from the Brenner Pass into the Po Valley, and densely in the Po Valley itself. Alternatively, the Alps could be skirted on the east. Either route gives access to the Adriatic. Then transport by sea would bring amber to Mycenaean Greece. The richest source of amber was the Bay of Danzig (Gdańsk). After 2000 BC, metalwork from the British Isles and the Alps appears in this region. We may guess that it was exchanged for the precious amber, which may have been transported south to join one of the other routes, and/or traded west via Jutland.[18]

The Mycenaeans traded widely, which helps to explain the amber found among the treasures of Mesopotamia. A rare and intricately carved lion-head vessel was excavated in a royal tomb in the ancient city of Qatna, in modern Syria, which flourished for several centuries before being destroyed in c. 1340 BC. [Pl. iii] Analysis showed the lion had been carved from a piece of Baltic amber.[18] In return, another luxury item wended its way north. Around 2500 BC certain craftsmen, probably in Mesopotamia, had learned how to make glass by fusing quartz or sand with fluxing agents such as potash or soda. The end result could vary in colour, depending on which natural impurities were present. Glittering glass beads were prized for jewelry. Manufacture on a larger scale started about a thousand years later in both Mesopotamia and Egypt.

Burials of the 14th–12th centuries BC in Denmark and Schleswig-Holstein in north Germany have yielded glass beads ranging from dark blue to green, white and yellow. Analysis of a selection revealed that most had come from the workshops of Nippur, Mesopotamia, about 50 kilometres (just over 30 miles) southeast of Baghdad in present-day Iraq. [Pl. i] Egyptian glass was rarer. Two cobalt blue glass beads found in Danish graves came from the Amarna workshops that also supplied the glass that Tutankhamun took to his grave. One of these cobalt beads was found in a female grave at Ølby, on the island of Zealand, dated to the 14th century BC. This woman was richly adorned with bronze ornaments. She wore the glass bead, together with two of amber, on her upper arm. The other glass bead was found in another rich female grave of similar date from Hesselager on the island of Funen.[20]

So the Nordic Bronze Age must have felt the backwash of the collapse of most of the civilizations bordering the Mediterranean around 1200 BC. Egypt was the only one of the great powers of the time to survive these upheavals. Greece was plunged into a Dark Age in which literacy vanished, along with the complex administration that had required it.[21] The postulated amber route south from the Bay of Danzig (Gdańsk) seems to have collapsed.[22]

At roughly the same time we see the beginnings of the presumably Celtic-speaking Hallstatt culture, which developed around the upper reaches of the rivers Danube and Rhine. It began as part of the wider phenomenon of the Urnfield culture, so named for the habit of cremating the dead and interring their ashes in urns. This wider culture spread north up to the southern border of the Nordic Bronze Age and reached the Baltic shore to the east of it as far as the Vistula. So Hallstatt chiefs were well placed to control long-distance trade routes linking the amber of the Baltic and Jutland to the Mediterranean. By the end of the Nordic Bronze Age, new Mediterranean civilizations had arisen with an appetite for amber: the Etruscans in northern Italy, and the resurgent city-states of Greece.

Transport and travellers

The Bronze Age was not the earliest period in which we see evidence of long-distance links, but it was a time when one could find similar imagery from north to south and east to west in Europe. Among the images are boats and ships, wagons and chariots. Travel was important in this era. Depictions of ships or boats predominate in the thousands of rock art images around the coast of southern Norway and Sweden. These can be roughly dated by their position in relation to the changing shoreline as the land gradually rose. The earliest, dating to between about 1700 and 1500 BC, tend to be the longest, with large crews, similar to that shown on the scimitar from Rørby.[23] [41, 42]

These early images share an iconographic simplicity with a ship depicted on a vase found at Kolonna in Greece. Some authors have been sufficiently impressed by the similarities to suggest that Mediterranean boat-builders were employed by Nordic chiefs, or even that Mycenaeans penetrated the Baltic.[24] Yet the differences are as marked as the similarities. None of the Nordic depictions of the time include a mast or sail, while the ship on the Kolonna vase has two masts. Sailing ships are depicted on Minoan seals by about 2000 BC. Both rowing boats and sailing ships appear on Minoan painted friezes at Akrotiri on the Greek island of Santorini, dating to before c. 1600 BC. By contrast, there is no evidence for sail in Scandinavia before the 7th century AD.[25]

With another form of transport, the link to distant places is clearer. The four-wheeled wagon pulled by a pair of oxen was invented around 3500 BC (see p. 62) and spread northwards even before the full development of the Corded Ware culture. The 'stone heap graves' in Denmark suggest that wagons were used there by about 3100 BC (see p. 65). The bogs of Denmark have preserved early wooden wheels of the solid type used for such wagons. The invention of spoked wheels around 2000 BC made possible a faster, lighter vehicle, the horse-drawn, two-wheeled chariot.

The origin of the chariot lies far from Scandinavia. The Sintashta culture of the Asian steppe, just east of the Ural Mountains, was directly or indirectly descended from the Yamnaya culture, users of wagons. In Sintashta the lighter vehicle appears. A man could be buried with his chariot. As the wood rotted it left stains in the ground, preserving the shape of the two-wheeled vehicle, including the spokes of the wheels. So far at least sixteen such graves have been found. They are dated between 2100 and 1700 BC, older than any chariots elsewhere.

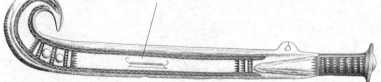

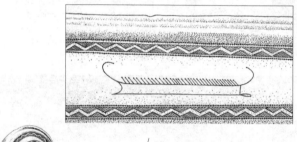

41, 42 A bronze scimitar from Rørby Mose, western Zealand, Denmark, one of two found there. Both are decorated with geometric patterns which reveal a date of c. 1600–1500 BC. The blade takes the shape of a ship, emphasized on this one by the inscribed image of a double-sterned ship, with thirty-six crew. It has stern and keel extensions, like many of the depictions of ships in rock art of the Nordic Bronze Age.

The chariot moved via the steppe into Europe. Its progress up the Danube can be tracked by cheek-pieces from horse-harnesses. While the wooden parts of chariots decayed, cheek-pieces show that chariots were present in central Europe as early as the 19th century BC. From the Carpathian Basin

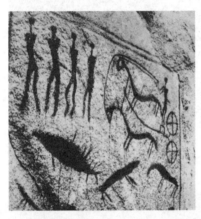

43, 44 *Decorated stones forming the sides of the cist of 'The King's Grave' at Kivik, Sweden, erected c. 1400 BC. The stone on the left of the series (no. 8) may depict a ritual scene, perhaps events at the funeral. Two men at top right are playing the curved trumpets known as lurs. Next from left (no. 7; detail left) has a clear depiction of a chariot. On the following stone (no. 6) are a pair of four-spoke wheels or sun crosses.*

it seems that a particular type of chariot with a four-spoke wheel reached Greece and Scandinavia. Such a chariot is depicted in Scandinavian rock art and on slab 7 in the tomb at Kivik in Sweden. [43, 44] The massive cairn at Kivik, on the ancient coastline of southeast Sweden, was long assumed to be that of a powerful individual, and so was named 'The King's Grave'. The unique feature of the burial is a set of eight decorated stones which formed the sides of the cist.[26] Bones in and around the cist were found in an excavation in 1931. It was only in the present century that these bones were analysed, throwing a different light upon the monument. They show that the chamber was re-used for burial several times. The earliest burials are those of two teenagers laid in the same cist between 1400 and 1300 BC.[27]

The chariot was a stripped-down vehicle without a seat, but once the technology for spoke wheels was adopted, it could be used for more work-aday transport, such as carts. Yet not every person would possess a vehicle or sailing vessel of any kind. Nor would the average farmer abandon his land to spend months jaunting abroad. Long-distance travel was still an adventure, arduous by comparison with today, and probably safest carried out in a group, guided by persons with knowledge of distant places.

The literate Bronze Age Near East may provide some insight into the process. An Assyrian merchant colony at ancient Kanesh, near the modern city of Kayseri in central Turkey, left records dating from 1934 to 1921 BC. The Assyrian traders were natives of the city state of Assur, on the west bank of the Tigris in present-day Iraq. Assyrians traded far and wide through a network of sworn agreements with local rulers. Trading families might be founded by a merchant travelling in person from Assur to the market in Kanesh, but his sons and grandsons might settle in Kanesh, acting as the local agents for the family business.[28]

Northern Europe was neither urban or literate in the Bronze Age, nor indeed until long after, so the process would not be exactly the same there. Yet a safe place in which to trade, protected by a local chief and his warriors, would attract both traders and craftspeople. This was the time in which a social elite started to emerge. It can be no coincidence that rich burials are so often associated with trade hubs. Trade was becoming a source of wealth. Those who organized it would need transport specialists: ship-builders, navigators, horse-trainers and builders of wagons and chariots. Perhaps warriors could be hired to protect goods in transit. So new social groups appeared.[29]

Trade contacts might lead to marriage alliances. Two possible cases have emerged with startling clarity. Local conditions preserved a female body buried one summer day in the year 1370 BC within a barrow outside Egtved, Denmark. [45] She was approximately sixteen to eighteen years old when she died. Analyses of the young woman's hair, teeth and nails show that she originated in a region far from Denmark, and that she had returned to that region for four to six months before coming back to Denmark about a month before she died. The woollen fabric of her clothes is not native, but seems to be from the Black Forest region of southern Germany. So Egtved Girl could have been given in marriage to a man in Jutland, to forge an alliance between two powerful families.[30]

Egtved Girl is one of a group of people of her place and time buried in oak coffins. They represented the elite of free farmers and warriors of Early Bronze Age Denmark. Skrydstrup Woman was another. She was buried under a mound at Skrydstrup around 1300 to 1200 BC. She made one long journey in her life: that was to reach Denmark when she was thirteen or fourteen years old, a marriageable age for girls at that time. She lived there until she died at a similar age to Egtved Girl. Analyses of her teeth and hair show that she came from outside Denmark, though the location is impossible to pinpoint. She would have been a striking figure, tall and dressed in beautifully embroidered clothes, with big gold earrings and long, thick hair tied up in an intricate style.[31]

45 *The burial of Egtved Girl, on display at the National Museum of Denmark. Of her body nothing is shown. Her clothes are amazingly well preserved. She wore a short skirt made of cords, a type depicted on some Nordic Bronze Age figurines. Above it is a sleeved garment. Between the two is a disc-shaped bronze belt plate, symbolizing the sun.*

The cycle of the sun

At first sight, the famous Trundholm 'sun chariot' [46, Pls vi and vii] seems to attest to the age of the Norse myth that the goddess Sól rides through the sky on a horse-drawn chariot (see p. 42). This myth finds masculine parallels in Greek myth and the Indic *Rigveda*. Helios or Apollo was the Greek personification of the sun, who drove the sun chariot across the sky each day. Several gods perform the same function in the *Rigveda*, for example Savitar, who advances through the dusky firmament in his golden chariot, decked with pearl and drawn by two bright bay horses.[32]

Yet the Trundholm 'sun chariot' is not actually a chariot, but a model of a horse pulling a sun disc, placed on a six-wheeled chassis. Other Scandinavian iconography shows the sun being pulled by a horse, without any chariot. [47] Looking from the northern hemisphere, the sun shines from the south. So the apparent movement of the sun from east to west is perceived as from left to right. Then when the sun set in the west, it was imagined to be making its way beneath the ocean to rise again at dawn. The wheels on the Trundholm model could be used to pull it first one way and then the other, to illustrate the sun's movement across the heavens by day (gold side of the disc) and through the netherworld by night (the dark side of the disc).[33] [46]

Danish prehistorian Flemming Kaul argues from the images on Nordic bronze razors and rock art that the sun's journey was envisaged as an elaborate cycle, including creatures more at home in the water, particularly for the dawn and dusk transitions. One complex depiction on a bronze razor shows a (night-time) ship moving left, while a fish draws the sun to a (daytime) ship moving right. Only ships moving to the right could be depicted in association with sun discs, reflecting the sun's daytime journey. At noon the sun-horse transports the sun to the afternoon ship. At dusk a snake could aid the sun to sink below the horizon, joining a night ship without a visible sun.[34]

So images can give us insight into a myth that developed before the concept of the chariot reached Scandinavia. In that case, the remarkable similarities in the sky-chariot myths of India, Greece and Scandinavia must reflect ideas travelling with the chariot, presumably carried by specialist chariot makers.

This clarifies the meaning of an emblem common in Scandinavian rock art, that of a cross within a circle. This cannot represent a wheel before the introduction of the chariot, for the earlier wheels were solid. It appears, therefore, to be a solar symbol. Gold discs with a cross decoration appear in the Bell Beaker period in Ireland. In Scandinavian rock art, it is clear that an actual wheel is intended where the symbol forms part of a vehicle, but in other cases the symbol is held aloft by men or transported by a boat. Where it appears on a stand, with or without wheels, it appears to be a cult object, like the bronze from Trundholm.[35]

One piece of evidence for the equivalence of solar discs and solar wheels is their appearance in a special group of female burials in Denmark. Egtved Girl was buried with a disc-shaped bronze belt plate decorated with spirals. [see 45] So were two other women, one at Hesselager on the island of Funen, and another at Ølby, though the largest of these belt plates was found at Langstrup. [Pl. iv] In shape and decoration, the belt plates have an obvious relationship with the Trundholm sun chariot. A woman buried earlier at Tobøl in south Denmark, under a huge mound to denote her status, had a bronze wheel placed in the same position, in front of her pelvis. All four have been interpreted as sun priestesses.[36] In the absence of written records, certainty eludes us. It is clear, though, that these were high-status women, wearing a sun symbol where it might be seen as a powerful protection for the womb.

A wonderful object from the Museum of Denmark draws amber into the sun-cult, as it is combined with the cross-in-circle motif. [Pl. ii] Amber 'sun discs' incised with a cross appear in the Globular Amphora culture, well before the Nordic Bronze Age.[37] The warm glow of amber makes an obvious emblem of the sun.

In the Late Bronze Age the Etruscans were eager for amber, but it is fascinating to see that they were also absorbing ideas from the north. Their capital at Tarquinia had a monumental complex from the 10th century with echoes of Scandinavian practices. The Scandinavian *lur* (curved trumpet) [see 44] has a match in the Etruscan *lituus*. A deposit of a *lituus*, axe and shield at Tarquinia finds no parallels elsewhere in the Mediterranean. The only comparisons can be made with southern Scandinavia. The cross-in-circle motif also appears in the complex at Tarquinia.[38] As we shall see, the interest in amber by the civilizations of the Mediterranean did not die with the Bronze Age, but the Etruscans moved from being a strong influence on the rising power of Rome to being absorbed into the Roman empire.

46 *The bronze 'sun chariot' from Trundholm on northwest Zealand dates to* c. *1500–1300* BC. *The disc, decorated with spirals, represents the sun, which is being drawn across the sky by a horse. One side of the disc is gold-plated, probably for the day-time sun [Pls vi and vii]; the other, seen here, is dark, for the night.*

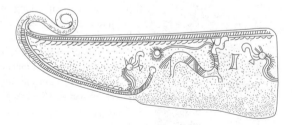

47 *A bronze razor from Neder Hvolris, Denmark,* c. *900* BC. *The sun-horse is pulling the sun to the right, just in front of the bow of a ship also moving to the right, which is decorated with a horse's head.*

Scandinavian Y-DNA mixture

Despite the relatively small number of ancient DNA samples from Scandinavia so far, by the end of the Nordic Bronze Age we can see in its people examples of the three Y-DNA haplogroups that predominate in Scandinavian men today. [48] As has been mentioned (p. 67), the R1a1a1b1a3 (Z284/S221) that we find today in men of Scandinavian descent was already present around 2500 BC in Scandinavia. Its subclade R1a1a1b1a3a (L448/S200) is the dominant type in Norway and also in Scotland, where it appears linked to Viking settlers. This is not the only form of R1a in present-day Scandinavia. The much rarer R1a1a1a (CTS7083/L664/S298) is found in all countries around the North Sea. Three males buried in a Corded Ware grave at Eulau (Saxony-Anhalt, Germany) carried a haplotype that appears to be immediately ancestral to R-L664.[39] Corded Ware was later replaced in this region by Bell Beaker, but the lineage could have survived in a limited way further north.[40]

R1b-U106 was found in a man buried about 2275–2032 BC at Lilla Beddinge in Sweden, as already mentioned (see p. 68).[41] [49] The brother of R1b-U106 is the huge R1b-P312 haplogroup, which is equally well represented in modern Scandinavia. As it dominates western Europe overall, we need to focus on particular subclades which may be specific to Scandinavia, for example R1b1a1a2a1a2d (L238/S182), and R1b1a1a2a1a2a1b2 (L165/S68), both found in Scandinavia and the Northern and Western Isles of Scotland, which suggests that these markers arrived in the Isles with Vikings.[42] Both have an estimated birth-date of around 2500 BC,[43] which would fit an arrival in Scandinavia with Bell Beaker.

With Y-DNA I1 (M253), we come to the most distinctive marker of Germanic-speakers. [50] This is a haplogroup with a long history. It formed among European hunter-gatherers, but was absorbed in a minor way by farmers entering Europe. We find it in an early farmer in Hungary about 5000 BC.[44] Yet a rapid

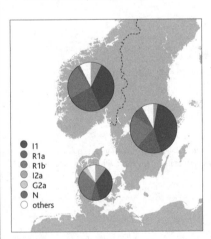

I1
R1a
R1b
I2a
G2a
N
others

48 *The percentages of different Y-DNA haplogroups found in a sample of modern men from the three Scandinavian countries. Three haplogroups predominate: I1, R1b and R1a*

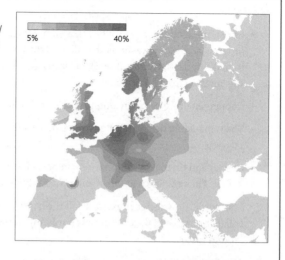

49 *Y-DNA haplogroup R1b-U106/ S21 is densest in areas that are Germanic-speaking today, and found at lower levels in places which had a Germanic elite in the post-Roman period: France, Galicia and northern Italy.*

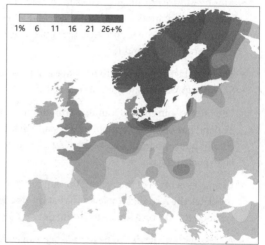

50 *Y-DNA haplogroup I1 is not predominant in any country today, but it is found wherever Germanic speakers spread.*

expansion of the lineage in the Bronze Age can be detected.[45] All modern I1 men so far tested descend from a common ancestor who lived about 2600 BC.[46] Where he lived we cannot be certain, but his haplogroup was present in the Nordic Bronze Age. One man carrying Y-DNA I1 was buried at Angmollan in Sweden about 1300 BC.[47] The haplogroup is found today wherever Germanic-speakers spread.

Overview

- Christian J. Thomsen (1788–1865) created the three-age system of ordering archaeological finds according to the raw material used to make tools: the Stone, Bronze and Iron Ages. The Copper Age was missing from his scheme.

- Copper-smelting began in around 5000 BC in Serbia and Iran.

- The remarkably rich Nordic Bronze began between 1600 and 1500 BC.

- Copper and tin to make bronze were imported in exchange for amber. Thus trading networks built up across the continent.

- The Nordic Bronze Age must have felt the backwash of the collapse of most of the civilizations bordering the Mediterranean around 1200 BC.

- Among Bronze Age images across Europe are boats and ships, wagons and chariots. Scandinavia had solid-wheeled wagons from the start of the Bronze Age; the spoke-wheeled chariot was a later arrival in around 1400 BC.

- Trade contacts might lead to marriage alliances. Egtved Girl and Skrydstrup Woman are possible examples.

- The bronze 'sun chariot' found at Trundholm on northwest Zealand has become a symbol of Denmark. In fact, it is not a chariot but a model of a horse drawing a sun disc, placed on a six-wheeled chassis.

- In images, a myth of the cycle of the sun can be detected which pre-dates the recorded Norse myth that the goddess Sól rides through the sky on a horse-drawn chariot.

- A cross within a circle seems to have been an emblem of the sun. It could be combined with amber, whose warm glow suggests the sun.

- By the end of the Nordic Bronze Age, new Mediterranean civilizations had arisen with an appetite for amber – the Etruscans in northern Italy, and the resurgent city-states of Greece.

CHAPTER FIVE

The Iron Cradle of Germanic

> Pytheas says that the Gutones, a people of Germany, inhabit the
> shores of an estuary of the ocean ... at one day's sail from this
> territory is the Isle of Abalus, upon the shores of which, amber
> is thrown up by the waves in spring ... the inhabitants ... sell it to
> their neighbours, the Teutones.[1]

The continuing interest in amber by the civilizations of the south is reflected in this snippet from Pliny the Elder, the Roman naturalist and geographer. He began his encyclopaedic work, *Natural History*, in AD 77 and had not made a final revision when he died, while trying to rescue a friend from the catastrophic eruption of Mount Vesuvius in AD 79. He trawled through many earlier authors, and was so exasperated by the nonsense too often written about amber that he titled a chapter 'Amber: the many falsehoods that have been told about it'. One of the ideas he contemptuously dismisses is the claim by the much earlier Athenian politician Nicias (*c.* 470–413 BC) that amber was produced by the rays of the sun. Yet it is interesting to see how amber could still be connected to the sun in thought as the Greeks re-entered a time of writing.

Pliny himself knew that amber came from pine resin and was a product of the islands of the 'Northern Ocean'. In his day the Germani exported amber to Pannonia, a Roman province in the northern Balkans, [see 13] whence it was traded by the Veneti, a people living on the shores of the Adriatic in what is now northeast Italy.[2] One of the few earlier authors that Pliny did not contradict on the topic was the Greek explorer Pytheas, who wrote the earliest-known account of a voyage from the Mediterranean as far as the northern source of amber. The book by Pytheas, called *On the Ocean*, does not survive, but it can be roughly dated to between 310 and 306 BC.[3] From him we see the Germani emerging into history as amber-collectors.

In the Late Bronze Age, climate change tugged Scandinavian farmers south. The deterioration of the climate was gradual, bringing increasingly wetter and colder times to Jutland, culminating in so steep a decline in the decades around 700 BC that much agricultural land was abandoned and bog built up.[4] Pollen history reveals a similar picture in southern Sweden. Around 500 BC forest encroached on areas that had long been farmland.[5] Another lure southwards lay in the amber trade. Jutland had prospered on it. Now the amber-rich Pomeranian coast beckoned. Some time in the 8th century BC a more easterly amber route was established from the Baltic to Italy and the Balkans. These long-distance trading links brought pottery styles from central Europe as far north as eastern Sweden, while Nordic Bronze Age metalwork appeared on the southern Baltic shores in western Pomerania.[6]

As Nordic Bronze Age people shifted south, they came in closer contact with Celtic-speakers already familiar from long-distance trade. The people of the central European Hallstatt culture had started to develop iron-working by this time. They had been influenced by an iron-working steppe people known to history as the Cimmerians, who had moved up the Danube and infiltrated the Urnfield zone (introduced in Chapter 4). Cimmerians settled in the Carpathian Basin with their steppe-bred horses and the habit of wagon burial. Both iron-working and wagon burial were adopted by the developing Hallstatt culture.[7]

Gradually iron overtook bronze as the metal of choice. By 460 BC iron-working Celts were expanding northwards to develop La Tène princely centres on the fringe of the Hallstatt core. Both Hallstatt and La Tène influences fed further northwards, triggering a shift from bronze to iron. [51] In what is now northern Poland, the Pomeranian culture, with its fascinating face-urns, developed in the 9th to 8th centuries BC out of the local branch of the Urnfield culture, but with distant echoes of Hallstatt, such as Late Hallstatt brooches. It seems that Celtic-speakers had forged commercial links with amber-gatherers. Significantly, the horse took on a special role. Burials include burnt horse bones, and incised images of horses are found on urns.[8] [52, 53]

Modern politics and ancient culture

The earliest Iron Age culture of northern Germany was first recognized by German archaeologist Martin Heinrich Gustav Schwantes (1881–1960), as he excavated urn cemeteries in the area around Bevensen, in Lower Saxony,

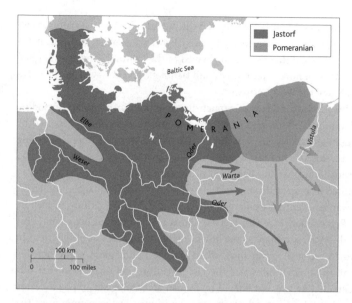

51 *The Iron Age Jastorf culture (700–1 BC) developed from the Nordic Bronze Age blended with elements of the Celtic Hallstatt culture. It expanded further eastwards over time. Meanwhile, the Pomeranian Face Urn culture (700–200 BC) developed west of the River Vistula from the local Urnfield culture, with Hallstatt influences. It moved south and had deserted Pomerania by the 5th century BC.*

52, 53 *A Pomeranian face urn from Grabowa Bobowski, with a horse-drawn wagon incised on the side. Such urns were buried containing human remains.*

the home of his youth. He named it the Jastorf culture in 1909, after a cemetery at Jastorf, near Bevensen. By 1911 he had widened his horizons. In his book published that year he conceived of this cultural zone as extending over much of northern Germany and Denmark, and he saw it as 'the headquarters of the West Germans'.[9]

This crossed a modern, and much disputed, political boundary. Including Jutland in the homeland of the West Germans was happily accepted by German archaeologists, but did not please the North Germanic-speaking Danes. This was not just a political issue. Archaeology as a discipline had developed against the backdrop of modern nation states. Each country acquired its own tradition of scholarship in its own language. Undeterred, Schwantes eventually enlarged his view of the Jastorf culture to include the Pomeranian Face Urn culture and the Scandinavian peninsula. This failed to gain acceptance, but his inclusion of Jutland was still current in German archaeology in 1998, when Wiebke Künnemann wrote her dissertation on Schwantes and the Jastorf culture and discovered that this understanding was not shared by Danish archaeologists. Today it seems clear that while south Jutland can be included in the periphery of the Jastorf culture, north Jutland cannot. The predominant cremation pit burial custom of north Jutland at the time is completely different from the typical Jastorf urn burial.[10]

Meanwhile, political tensions between Germany and the Poles went far beyond boundary disputes. At stake was the very existence of Poland. As a nation state Poland had been wiped off the map in 1795, with its lands partitioned between Austria, Russia and Prussia (the dominant power within the German empire). So before the First World War, Schwantes was working within a German empire that encompassed the territory of the Pomeranian Face Urn culture. Poland did not regain full independence until 1918. Within this new Polish state, national pride became entwined in the development of Polish archaeology. The discovery in 1933 of a fortified settlement at Biskupin in Wielkopolska fascinated the Polish public. This was the region in western central Poland in which the Polish state began to form in the 9th and 10th centuries AD. Yet the site was much earlier. It was identified as belonging to the Lusatian culture, the local variety of Urnfield, and was seen as the product of Proto-Slavic speakers, ancestors of the Poles.[11] Thus the Poles were given an illusion of territorial continuity, surely particularly gratifying for a nation so recently resurrected.

i (*top left*) Blue glass beads from Mesopotamia, found in a grave at Humlum, Denmark, dating from the 12th century BC.

ii (*top right*) When this Bronze Age 'sun-holder' from Denmark is held up to the light, a sun cross appears in the middle of the amber disc; it is 7 cm (2¾ inches) high.

iii (*above*) This lion-head vessel, *c.* 6 cm (2½ inches) wide, found in a royal tomb beneath the Bronze Age city of Qatna in Syria, was carved from a piece of Baltic amber.

iv (*above*) Detail of a spiral-decorated bronze belt plate from Langstrup, North Zealand, *c.* 1400 BC. The entire plate is 28 cm (11 inches) in diameter.

v (*below*) Scandinavian gold bracteate (disc ornament), 4.8 cm (2 inches) high, thought to depict the face of Odin above a horned quadruped. Beside him is a messenger raven; below is a swastika, a sun-symbol. The radiating border also suggests sun symbolism.

vi, vii (*opposite*) The bronze 'sun chariot' found at Trundholm on northwest Zealand has become a symbol of Denmark. It dates to the period *c.* 1500–1300 BC and is *c.* 54 cm (21 inches) long. The disc, decorated with spirals, represents the sun, which is being drawn across the sky by a horse. Only one side of the disc is gold-plated, as seen above, probably representing the day-time sun.

viii (*left*) This enigmatic object from the Sutton Hoo burial is interpreted as a sceptre. A four-sided stone bar terminates at each end with an onion-shaped knob originally painted red, immediately below which are carved human masks. It is topped with an iron ring upon which stands a bronze stag. The whole object is 82 cm (32¼ inches) long.

ix (*opposite top*) The magnificent gold belt buckle from Sutton Hoo, 13.2 cm (5 inches) long. The upper surface is covered entirely with zoomorphic interlace, influenced by the convoluted animal ornamentation developed in Scandinavia.

x (*opposite centre*) The lid of the purse from Sutton Hoo features some of the finest polychrome jewelry of the period. On a base of ivory are jewelled plaques using garnets and millefiori glass. The purse, 19 cm (7½ inches) long, contained thirty-seven Merovingian gold coins.

xi (*opposite below*) Gold shoulder clasp from Sutton Hoo, decorated with cloisonné garnets and millefiori glass, 12.7 cm (5 inches) long. There are crossed boars on the rounded end panels.

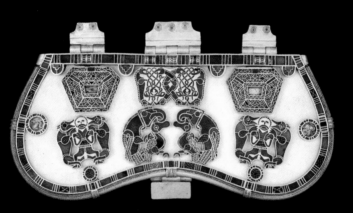

xii (*left*) This extraordinary pendant was worn by the 'Saxon Princess' in a burial from the second half of the 7th century. Cloisonné garnets surround a central gem incised to form a scallop shape; 9 cm (3½ inches) high.

xiii (*below*) The Franks or Auzon Casket, made in Northumbria *c.* 700, is a whalebone box, 30 cm (12 inches) long, carved in relief with scenes from Roman, Jewish, Christian and Germanic traditions. The accompanying texts are in Old English and Latin, mainly in a runic alphabet. Pictured here is the front panel, representing the Germanic legend of Weland the Smith (left) and the Adoration of the Magi (right). It graphically demonstrates the fusion of cultures in Middle and Late Saxon life.

xiv The Alfred Jewel is about 6.4 cm (2½ inches) long and was made of gold filigree enclosing a highly polished tear-shaped piece of clear quartz. The dragonesque head at the base of the jewel has a socket which probably held an ivory pointer. An inscription around the edge reads AELFRED MEC HEHT GEWYRCAN – 'Alfred ordered me to be made'. So this would be one of the precious pointers (*æstel*) created to accompany Alfred's translation of Pope Gregory the Great's Pastoral Rule.

xv (*left*) This appealing and strange stylized horse from the Staffordshire Hoard has the look of a sea-horse; 4.1 cm (1½ inches) high.

xvi (*right*) The pectoral cross from the Staffordshire Hoard, 6.6 cm (2½ inches) high, was made of gold with a central garnet and could have been worn by a bishop or abbot. Its shape and the central garnet are similar to the pendant cross from the grave of St Cuthbert (died AD 687).

At the same time, their German neighbours were generating far more grandiose fallacies about their own past, which were to prove deeply dangerous. The story begins quite innocuously. A number of German philologists were prominent in the field of Indo-European studies. The pioneering Franz Bopp (1791–1867) did much to put the study of historical linguistics on a sound scientific basis. Max Müller (1823–1900), a noted scholar of Sanskrit, coined the term 'Aryan', derived from Sanskrit texts, to denote the speakers of Proto-Indo-European.[12] By 1875 the German Jewish philologist Theodor Benfey (1809–1881) had reached the conclusion that their homeland lay north of the Black Sea, from the Danube delta to the Caspian. German philologist Otto Schrader (1855–1919), writing in 1883, fleshed out this theory,[13] which has been supported by so many later linguists and archaeologists that it is the standard position today (see Chapter 3). That has not prevented a host of other homeland ideas being proposed over the years. An 'Aryan homeland' proved all too tempting as fantasy, rather than sober scholarship.

Early Indo-European studies had fostered a concept of kinship between the European and Asian speakers of the massive language family, but by the end of the 19th century, western imperialism had generated a race pseudo-science which rationalized bigotry. We could see this trend partly as a reaction to the renaissance of Classical learning that had generated deep respect for ancient Greece and Rome. The level of knowledge and technology in these Mediterranean civilizations was not surpassed until the Scientific and Industrial Revolutions of the 17th and 18th centuries. Often leading the way in scientific discovery were speakers of Germanic languages, who had been classed by the Greeks and Romans as 'barbarians'. Their swelling pride demanded a different vision of the past. Racists saw the massive expansion of the Indo-European people in ancient times as evidence of Aryan superiority. They were perceived as conquerors. From the perspective of such racists, 'Aryans' (a name actually used by ancient Iranian and Indic-speakers) had to be European. Specifically, they had to have sprung from the same soil as the forefathers of the chief industrial nations of the 19th century.

So the racists settled upon the fair-skinned, light-haired people of the north as 'Aryans'. Max Müller mocked this seductive vision in 1888. By then he had lived in Britain and taught at Oxford for most of his adult life. Some scholars in both Germany and the United States were less objective.

A German philologist turned archaeologist, Gustaf Kossinna (1858–1931), proposed that the Proto-Indo-Europeans arose from the Corded Ware culture in northern Germany.[14]

This intellectual climate was exploited from the 1930s to promote both racism and pan-Germanic unity. Though Tacitus had been as critical as he was complimentary, his depiction of the Germani as fierce, free, democratic and pure in morals and bloodline was seized upon to promote unwarranted claims of racial superiority.[15] After Adolf Hitler rose to power in 1933, he initiated the National Socialist (Nazi) Party's funding for German research into prehistory. Archaeology was hijacked by the Nazi propaganda machine. Hitler even adopted the ancient swastika (p. 40) as a symbol of the party. The political context was Germany's crushing defeat in the First World War. That was a huge blow to the country's imperial ambitions. In 1918 Germany's colonies were parcelled out among the victors. Germany's economy sank into depression. The Nazi doctrine of Nordic supremacy restored the self-respect of a defeated people, but at enormous cost. Nazi Germany massacred millions of Jews, occupied Austria, Belgium, Denmark, France, Luxembourg, the Netherlands, Norway and Poland and planned the invasion of Britain.[16]

The invasion of Poland by Nazi Germany in 1939 was presented as the reclamation of land anciently Germanic, to the understandable outrage of the Poles. Germany acted in league with the Soviet Union, which annexed eastern Poland. Effectively Poland had once again been partitioned. When the Soviet Union switched sides in 1941, the eventual outcome after the Second World War was a new Poland with redrawn boundaries, operating as a Soviet satellite state. Only in 1989 did Poland achieve complete independence once more. Since then, political pressures on Polish archaeology have eased. While in the post-war period the iconic stronghold of Biskupin was put forward as proof of the ancient Slavic identity of Poland, in the 1990s Polish archaeologists began to explain that Biskupin could not have been inhabited by Proto-Slavs.[17] Polish archaeologists have now identified the Jastorf culture in parts of Poland, specifically in Wielkopolska and part of Pomerania.[18] [see 53] Yet the expansion of the Germani is only one part of a complex picture, infused by a people with no voice at all in these particular propaganda battles – the Celts.

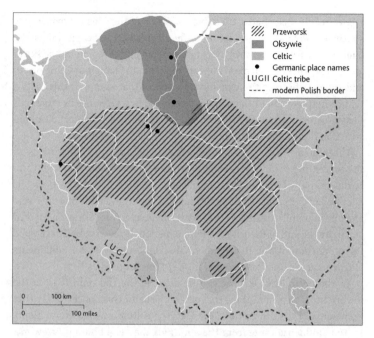

54 *Late Iron Age cultures and Germanic place-names in Poland.*

Face to face with Celts

The Jastorf culture in its earliest phase is now seen as the most probable homeland of Proto-Germanic, the immediate parent of the three main branches of the Germanic language family. [see 59] As the period opened, the people of this culture had a rural economy of scattered farmsteads. Signs of wealth or hierarchy were limited. Cremation continued to be the established burial rite, with little in the way of grave goods. Gradually this pattern changed, so that by the 1st century BC, a chieftain's house can be recognized by its size alone, so much larger than the general run of farmhouses. Villages became more common. At the same time, dress styles were adopted from the Celtic La Tène culture to the south. Rank could be proclaimed by high-status grave goods, such as crown-shaped neck-rings (*Kronenhalsringe*), which also appear in later cultures arising from Jastorf. Inhumation graves reappeared.[19]

Meanwhile, Celts had settled in enclaves on fertile soils in what is now southwest Poland (Silesia) and southern Poland.[20] A people called the Lugii, with a number of subgroups, were noted in this region by Tacitus in AD 98.[21] [54] The 'Lug' element appears widely in the names of Celtic places and tribes, reflecting the worship of a god of that name. In this case, a Celtic interpretation of the name is reinforced by a reference in Ptolemy's *Geography* to a town in the area named *Lougidounon*, an obvious Celtic construction from 'Lugi' and 'dunon' (fort).[22]

The influence of the Celts was felt widely in what are now Polish lands. In the 3rd century BC the Przeworsk culture arose in the upper Oder and Warta basins from the expanding Jastorf culture. It is marked by the enthusiastic adoption of Celtic iron-working technology. Locally available bog ores were smelted in primitive furnaces in every settlement of this culture discovered so far. By the end of the Late Pre-Roman period, Przeworsk had developed the production of iron to an industrial scale. Tools, war gear, ornaments and dress accessories were copied from La Tène prototypes.[23]

To the north, the Oksywie culture arose in the 2nd century BC in the lower Vistula basin and along that part of the Baltic coast once home to the Pomeranian Face Urn culture. The Oksywie culture was a cultural blend. La Tène influence came from the south via the neighbouring Przeworsk culture, and from the Jastorf zone in the west, though the latter had the stronger impact. Baltic Sea connections were added to the mix. A group of graves with above-standard goods, including Celtic imports, shows that the privileged classes had access to luxury goods from afar. Were they exchanged for amber? Oksywie was followed by the Wielbark culture (c. AD 30 to 400). Influences from eastern Sweden in Wielbark were thought to reflect the arrival of the Goths in mainland Europe. In recent years, archaeologists have pointed to the continuity of settlement between the Oksywie and Wielbark cultures. The change from cremation to inhumation, seen as the critical difference between the two, was gradual rather than sudden.[24] Indeed, the influence from eastern Sweden in this area dates back into the Late Bronze Age.[25] The Wielbark culture expanded into former Przeworsk territory.

Although the Celtification of Poland in this period is striking, there are clues that the Przeworsk and Oksywie/Wielbark cultures represent Germanic-speakers soaking up Celtic ideas. The first modern, scholarly study of the earliest detectable layer of place-names in Poland appeared in 2001. As in any other part of Europe, the earliest names tend to be those of watercourses. Poland has some with a Germanic etymology, such as names ending in -bok, from Early Germanic *-bak, meaning 'brook', or -awa, from Early Germanic *-ahwó meaning 'river', which became *-ahva in Gothic. One group clusters around the Vistula. Another runs along the upper Oder (Odra) River.[26] [see 54] Needless to say, no such evidence can justify a modern German invasion of Poland, any more than the Celtic etymology of the River Rhine could justify a modern Irish invasion of Germany. History has no reverse gear.

The name of the Rhine is one of a number of words borrowed into Proto-Germanic from Celtic. Just as the Germani adopted iron-working from the Celts, so they adopted the Celtic word for iron, which became *īsarną in Proto-Germanic. Two other words hint at social changes. The Celtic word for king (*rīk), similar to the Latin rex, was adopted. The Germani already had three words of their own for leaders, including the one that is familiar today as 'king', the equivalent of kuning in Old High German. Kuning seems derived from a Proto-Germanic word for 'kindred' and so means 'belonging to a kindred', or 'descending from a kindred'. Since everyone belongs to a kindred, that might seem a strange word for a king. The meaning here is more specific, something like 'a prince of the blood'. The kindred in question would be those that traditionally supplied leaders, yet not royal in the sense that we use the word today. The indications are that kuning denoted someone more like a chieftain. For example, one runic inscription refers to twenty sea-kings banded together for warlike undertakings. It seems that the Celtic word *rīk was borrowed with the meaning 'powerful' or 'authority', and incorporated into names, following Celtic practice. The Frankish King Chloderic is an example. The name Richard, meaning 'strong in rule', remains popular today. The notion of authority can be paired with the concept of subordinates. Another borrowing was a Celtic word reconstructed as *ambaktos, meaning 'member of the retinue of an important leader', which became *ambahtaz in Proto-Germanic. Military concepts adopted from the Celts are expressed in the borrowed words *brunjōn (mailshirt) and *gīslaz (hostage). Other borrowed words were *lēkijaz (physician) and *walhaz (foreigner).[27]

The word for 'foreigner' was taken from the name of a Celtic tribe, the Volcae. Linguists can date this borrowing to probably before the 3rd century BC. Derivations of *walhaz were later used to describe speakers of

Celtic and Romance languages. Old English *Wealhas* gave us the names 'Welsh' and 'Wales'.[28] Modern German *Welsch* may signify French or Italian. It would seem that the Volcae were in close contact with Germani when Proto-Germanic was developing. Since the Celts to the south of Germani in what is now Poland were called the Lugii, we may guess that the Volcae lived on the southern border of the Jastorf culture in what is now Germany. By the time that Roman authors were grappling with Celtic tribal names, the expanding Germani had ejected the Celts from a large area of Germania. Two tribes of Volcae were known in southern Gaul. Caesar tells us that a branch of the Volcae Tectosages had migrated from Gaul to the Hercynian Forest in Germania.[29] They certainly appear in both places by this time, but who can be sure of the direction of migration? Caesar was not to know that a large part of the Germania of his day had been Celtic-speaking centuries earlier. As the Roman empire engulfed former Celtic lands, the Germani found themselves dealing directly with a Mediterranean civilization once more.

Overview

- In the Late Bronze Age, climate change tugged Scandinavian farmers south, bringing them into closer contact with iron-working Celtic-speakers of the central European Hallstatt culture.

- By 460 BC iron-working Celts were expanding northwards to develop La Tène princely centres on the fringe of the Hallstatt core. Both Hallstatt and La Tène influences fed further northwards, triggering a shift from bronze to iron.

- The earliest Germanic iron-working culture was first recognized by Martin Heinrich Gustav Schwantes. He named it the Jastorf culture (700–1 BC). Though he saw it as the homeland of the West Germans, it is now recognized to be the most probable homeland of Proto-Germanic, the parent of all the Germanic branches. It extended from what is now northern Germany into southern Jutland and parts of Poland.

- In the first half of the 20th century, national pride became entwined in archaeology. Poland, newly resurrected as a nation state, was anxious to portray the soil of Poland as anciently Slavic. Meanwhile a German archaeologist proposed that the Proto-Indo-Europeans arose in northern Germany. This thinking was combined with pseudo-scientific racism to emerge in the Nazi era as the glorification of a supposed master race.

- As Proto-Germanic-speakers adopted elements of La Tène culture, so they borrowed words from Celtic.

- As the Roman empire engulfed former Celtic lands, the Germani came into direct contact with Romans.

CHAPTER SIX

The Haves and the Have-Nots

> No war remained then except against the Germans, more to
> dispel the disgrace of losing an army with Varus than from
> desire of extending the Empire or for any worthwhile prize.[1]

War and peace

Thus Tacitus summed up the state of the Roman empire at the end of the reign of Augustus in AD 14. The conquering Julius Caesar had been assassinated in 44 BC by those who resented his increasing power in the Roman Republic. His heir was his great-nephew Octavian, who joined with two other leading figures to defeat the assassins of Caesar and then divided the Republic between themselves, ruling as military dictators. The result was civil war, from which Octavian emerged the winner. It was only in 27 BC that he took the name Augustus and began to wield imperial power. Augustus greatly enlarged the empire, annexing Pannonia, Egypt, Dalmatia, Raetia and Noricum and completing the conquest of Hispania. From 12 BC his army commanders pressed across the Rhine into Germania. His stepson Drusus repulsed an alliance of restive Germanic tribes who had crossed into Gaul, chasing them back into their own territory, and then sailed down the Rhine and won over the Frisii into alliance. The following year Drusus consolidated his gains as far as the River Weser, taking advantage of strife among the tribes. A few years later it was the turn of his elder brother Tiberius to continue the struggle eastwards, pushing the Roman frontier to the Elbe. But as Roman historian Cassius Dio reports, the Romans were only holding portions of Germania, 'not entire regions, but merely such districts as happened to have been subdued'. Roman soldiers were wintering and towns were being founded in places east of the Rhine. The barbarians were adapting themselves to Roman ways and becoming accustomed to hold markets.[2]

The remnants of one such market town have been discovered on the edge of the modern village of Waldgirmes, part of Lahnau on the River Lahn in Hesse, in present-day Germany. It had a typical Roman layout, centred on a forum, within which was a gilded equestrian statue of Augustus. The stone foundations of the forum would have been alien to locals, who continued to build only in timber. Fortunately for archaeologists, timber was also used within the Roman town. Planks used to line a well survived by being waterlogged, so dendrochronology (tree-ring dating) provided a date for the start of the construction of the town. These timbers were cut in the winter of 4/3 BC. The town was never to be finished. The last Roman coins there bear the stamp of the ill-fated Publius Quinctilius Varus.[3]

In AD 7 Varus, related by marriage to Augustus, was granted command in Germania.[4] Just two years later he led three Roman legions to their deaths in the Teutoburg Forest. Cassius Dio places the blame for this humiliating defeat squarely on the shoulders of Varus. From Dio's point of view, the Germani were previously so gently weaned into Roman ways that they barely realized that they were changing. The attitude of Varus came as a rude awakening. He issued orders to them as if they were actually slaves of the Romans and exacted money as he would from subject nations. The independent Germani were not inclined to submit.[5] Yet it was another Roman policy, that of recruiting army auxiliaries from among the barbarians on their borders, which spectacularly backfired in the events that followed. One such recruit was Arminius, of the royal kin of the Cherusci, a Germanic tribe mentioned by Tacitus. [see 13] The Cherusci had been absorbed into what the Romans regarded as their territory by the advances of Tiberius. It was unfortunate for Varus that Arminius had by this time returned to the Cherusci, after acquiring wealth and an intimate knowledge of the Roman army from years of service as the leader of a force of Roman auxiliaries. He spoke Latin, understood Roman ways and was regarded as an ally. So he was a frequent dinner guest at the table of Varus. Thus he was well placed to shake off the yoke of Rome by stealth.

Pretending friendship, Arminius provided local guides for Varus when he planned a tour of the territory between the Rhine and the Elbe in the spring and summer of AD 9. Varus had with him the 17th, 18th and 19th legions, but was not expecting resistance. The army snaked along narrow tracks in a column stretching for miles, and was all too vulnerable to the harrying planned by Arminius, once the legions were far enough east of the Rhine. Roman soldiers were butchered in huge numbers and Varus committed suicide. Augustus was horrified when the news reached him. For the rest of his life he ordered punitive raids into Germania.[6]

On the death of Augustus in AD 14, he was succeeded as emperor by Tiberius, who ordered his adopted son Germanicus to avenge Rome's loss. Yet only two years later he urged Germanicus to come home to Rome. 'You can leave the Cherusci and other rebel tribes – now that Roman vengeance has been served – to internal strife.'[7] It was effectively the end of Rome's desire to expand east of the Rhine and the *Limes Germanicus*.

Historians in modern times have hailed the battle of the Teutoburg Forest as Rome's greatest defeat,[8] and a battle that changed history.[9] [55] It was certainly a major disaster for the Romans. More than a tenth of the entire Roman army had been wiped out within days.[10] The costs of war were plain to see. It was not only a matter of lives lost, but the resources needed to perpetually garrison an empire. What were the benefits? The Romans had gained enormously from the acquisition of empire, but could they have reached the point where the costs of further enlargement outweighed the gains? Tacitus implied as much in the quotation that heads this chapter, at least as far as Germania was concerned.

The Romans were interested in good agricultural land and mineral resources. Iberia had gold, silver, copper, wine and olive oil. That was an early target for Rome, as was Greece. Julius Caesar and his great-great-grandnephew Claudius added the richest of the Celtic-speaking lands to the north: Gaul and southern Britain. The Germanic economy was too poor at the time to repay the effort of conquest in either booty or taxes. It had no great agricultural surplus which could support specialists.[11] The report on Germania written by Tacitus in AD 98 might have been designed to discourage his countrymen from attempted conquest. He knew of no nodes of gold or silver in Germania. What of amber? Astonishingly, Tacitus claims that the Aestii were the *only* people to collect amber. These were the eastern neighbours of the

55 *Roman face mask from Kalkriese, Germany, the site of a key ambush in the attack by Arminius on Varus and his legions.*

Germani, understood by modern historians to be Balts. They had never prized amber themselves, and it lay unheeded on their shore until 'our luxury made its reputation'.[12] If so, the focus of the amber trade had shifted eastwards to the benefit of the Balts, but as we shall see, the Germani along the Vistula continued to thrive on this trade.

Not that Tacitus' *Germania* influenced the decision of Emperor Tiberius. It was written many years later. Yet it probably reflects the thinking that turned the tide of Roman expansionism and promoted instead the rewards of peace. Tiberius wrote, 'Nine times Augustus sent me to Germania and I accomplished more by policy than by force.'[13] It is far easier to govern by consent than to subdue a resentful populace; many peoples had discovered advantages to Roman rule. One was the cessation of local strife. Augustus himself saw the blessings of peace. When he returned to Rome victorious in 13 BC, after three years fighting in Hispania and Gaul, an altar was commissioned in his honour to Pax, the Roman goddess of peace, with his name attached – *Pax Augusta*.[14] In Roman eyes Augustus was the man who had not only ended the disruptive civil wars, but also made it possible to travel across the far-flung empire exempt even from brigandage.[15] Peace brought prosperity. Despite the fact that Augustus hounded the Germani until his death, later historians have tended to see him as the originator of the famed *Pax Romana*, the long period of relative peace in the empire that ended with the death of Marcus Aurelius in AD 180. By contrast, the end of Roman hostilities against the Germani left the tribes free to fight each other.[16]

Face to face with Romans

The economic flowering that created rich Mediterranean civilizations began later in northern Europe. The living standard of a leader among the Germani could not match that of the prosperous owner of a Roman villa. Even a chief's house was heated by a smoky central fire, which must have left a layer of dust and smuts everywhere. By contrast, Roman interiors had fine painted plaster walls and mosaic floors kept warm by underfloor heating. By settling for the Rhine as their border, the Romans established a firm frontier between the haves and the have-nots. Waves of have-nots threw themselves against the barriers, or sought less aggressive ways to gain a share of the wealth of Rome.

One method was to enter into trade or diplomatic relationships with the great southern power. 'Princely' burials can be found along the coastal plain between the Weser and Vistula and also in the west Baltic islands. They range in date from the late 1st century BC to the mid-2nd century AD. These graves are literally and figuratively set apart. They are mostly inhumations, while cremation still prevailed for most of the population. They lie in small groups away from the large cemeteries, sometimes under mounds. Above all, they are far more richly furnished than the mass of burials. Roman imports of silver, bronze and glass abound in these graves.[17] The richest single grave from the Roman Iron Age in northern Europe was found at Hoby, on the south coast of the large Danish island of Lolland. Buried there was a middle-aged man who died some time in the 1st century BC. The astonishing array of grave goods buried with him suggests diplomatic contacts with Rome.[18] [56] Tacitus remarks that silver vessels, given as presents to Germanic envoys and leading men, were as lightly esteemed as earthenware.[19] Perhaps pride dictated that this impression should be given, but in reality Roman silverware is found carefully buried in princely graves.

Another way to lay hands on Roman coinage was to serve in the Roman army. Two examples have already been mentioned: Arminius of the Cherusci (p. 105) and the man from Fallward (p. 39). They were both from Free Germania. Those Germani who had crossed the Rhine into Gaul became absorbed into the Roman empire within the provinces of Upper and Lower Germania. [see 13] Men of fighting age among them were much sought after by the Roman army as auxiliaries. Four cohorts of Batavi and two of Tungri served in Britain under Agricola, Roman governor of Britannia AD 77–85. He used them in his drive northward into Caledonia.[20]

56 *Two fine Roman beakers from the rich grave at Hoby on the Danish island of Lolland, decorated with scenes in relief from Homer's Iliad. On the left the Greek hero Philoctetes is having his foot bathed after he has been bitten by a snake. On the right is a scene in which King Priam beseeches his enemy Achilles to return his son's body.*

57 *The earliest runic alphabet is known as the Elder Futhark. Inscriptions in this script are found on artefacts (including jewelry, amulets, tools, weapons and runestones) from the 2nd to 8th centuries* AD.

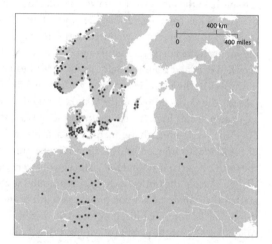

58 *The distribution of pre-6th century Elder Futhark runic inscriptions.*

As mentioned earlier (p. 36), the Batavi were from what is now Betuwe in the Netherlands. The Tungri were recruited from what is now the district of Tongres in Belgium. This presence of Germani in Britain in the Roman period could easily have introduced some Germanic DNA long before the arrival of the Anglo-Saxons. We shall return to this in Chapter 7.

Contacts with the Romans familiarized some Germani with the Latin alphabet, which was converted in around AD 150 into a runic alphabet suited to the Germanic language.[21] [57] Yet this did not instantly turn the Germani into a literate people. The Germani had little need for writing. These early inscriptions were in a language very close to Proto-Germanic. So it is interesting to see how far it spread before AD 500. [58] Germani were on the move; thus began the gradual drift into separate Germanic languages.

The parting of the ways

Linguists estimate that Proto-Germanic developed a few centuries before the birth of Christ, but no earlier than about 500 BC. Let us remind ourselves that this was the language immediately before it broke up into its daughter branches.[22]

The first branch to split away from the Proto-Germanic core was East Germanic. No language from this group is spoken today, and the clues to its existence would be slender indeed, had not the Goths left behind a Bible translated into their language. For this linguists can thank the lure of the south. In the previous chapter we saw that the Wielbark culture beside the Vistula has been regarded as the physical manifestation of the Goths (p. 100). The amber trade introduced Goths to faraway places. By this time, one amber route ran up the Vistula and Oder Rivers to the Danube. Another travelled overland from the Baltic as far as the head of the Dnieper, then downriver to the Black Sea,[23] where we find an Elder Futhark inscription. [see 58] The Goths drifted up the Vistula during the 2nd and 3rd centuries AD, or so it seems from the southern spread of Wielbark culture elements. Then the predominantly Germanic Chernyakhov culture emerged north of the Black Sea from around AD 230, while the number of settlements in the Gothic heartland around the Vistula gradually decreased. According to written sources, the Goths reached Crimea around AD 250 and from 268 they started their pirate raids upon provinces south of the Black Sea.[24] In capturing Greeks from Anatolia, they found themselves importing Christians. Among these were the parents of Wulfila (Ulfila), born c. 311, who was raised as a Goth. He became bishop of the Goths at the age of thirty and worked as a missionary there until he was forced to flee religious persecution in around 348. Settling with his flock safely inside the Roman empire, he put his mind to translating the Bible from Greek to Gothic.[25] This is one of the earliest surviving texts in any Germanic language.

Sweeping in across the steppe, the nomadic Huns displaced the Goths from their Black Sea homeland in AD 375, driving them across the Roman border.[26] Once the Goths took possession of chunks of civilization, they could have both their past and present recorded for posterity in flattering terms. Cassiodorus, a Roman in the service of Theodoric the Great, king of the Ostrogoths (r. 471–526), wrote a twelve-volume history of this people. It does not survive, but we have a summary of it written by Jordanes, a 6th-century Byzantine bureaucrat of Gothic extraction. Jordanes knew little of the early history of his people. There is a tone of uncertainty about his statement that the Goths are said to have come forth long ago from *Scandza* (Scandinavia) to mainland Europe (specifically an island in the River Vistula, in the case of the Gepids, a branch of the Goths) and from there to the coast of the Black Sea.[27]

Yet there is no reason to doubt that there was a movement of Goths from Sweden to the mouth of the Vistula. By the time Classical sources first note this people, they appear in both places, though under variant names. Ptolemy places the Gutae (*Gautae*) in southern Scandia in around AD 150.[28] Southern Sweden historically formed Gautland (Götland), the land of the Gautar in Old Norse, whose name is retained in the present region of Götaland, Sweden. Ptolemy also mentions the *Gythones* living on the east bank of the Vistula, while Tacitus renders the name as *Gotones*.[29]

There are linguistic clues that North and West Germanic developed as a single language, Proto-Northwest Germanic, after East Germanic had begun to diverge, though the period of unity may have been short.[30] [59] From 200 BC to AD 200 a warm, dry climate favoured cereal cultivation once more in Scandinavia.[31] As farmers were enticed northward, the dialect that developed into Old Norse broke away from the core. It was recorded in runes from around AD 200 onwards. By around AD 1000 Old Norse was dividing into eastern and western dialects that later evolved into the modern Scandinavian languages.[32]

West Germanic evolved from the rump of Proto-Germanic. Though a few Latin loans into Proto-Germanic seem likely, most of the earliest Latin loans in Old English can be pinned down to the Proto-West Germanic phase. They include words for 'cleric', 'coin', 'kitchen', 'miles', 'paved road' and 'wash-basin'.[33] These Germani were coming in contact with aspects of Roman life. West Germanic began to split into separate strands with the migrations

59 *The three main branches of the Germanic language family. For the place of modern languages in the tree, see 2.*

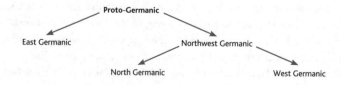

Proto-Germanic

East Germanic   Northwest Germanic

North Germanic   West Germanic

westward. The earliest split came as groups of Angles, Saxons and Jutes left for England, where Old English developed. German, Dutch and Frisian are among the other living languages on this branch. Upper German is spoken in southern Germany, Austria and large parts of Switzerland; this whole region was once Celtic-speaking.

The earliest surviving records of the name *Franci* date to around AD 300. The tribes Chamavi, Salii and Bructeri were identified as Franks.[34] They lived on the right bank of the Rhine, on the frontier with the Roman empire.[35] The Saxons initially lived further behind the frontier, but beside the ocean, well placed for raiding by sea. Virtually all of the early sources for them can be questioned in one way or another,[36] but if we take them at face value, the name *Saxones* first appears around AD 150 in Ptolemy's *Geography*. He mentions three islands off the mouth of the River *Albis* (Elbe), called the Saxon Islands, presumably the small uninhabited islands of Scharhörn, Neuwerk and Trischen. He knew of Saxons living nearby, to the north of the Elbe, on the neck of the Jutland peninsula.[37] The Saxons themselves preserved a story of setting out in ships and landing at Hadeln on the south bank of the Elbe, where they displaced Thuringians.[38] Though that comes from a late source, it could have been the memorable start of their expansion to the south of the Elbe. By the reign of Emperor Valentinian I (r. 364–75) the Saxons were launching raids on Gaul and Britain. One diatribe against them reported that they lived in inaccessible marshes on the shores of the ocean.[39] That suggests the waterlogged triangle of land between the mouths of the rivers Elbe and Weser, which preserved houses and furniture of this period so well (see p. 39). Saxon raids on Roman Britain led to the creation of a series of forts on Britain's southern and eastern coasts, under the control of the Count of the Saxon Shore.[40] [60]

The wandering of the peoples

The Roman empire held so much of Europe in its grip that the fall of its western half shook society for millions. As the Roman empire gradually crumbled in the west from AD 376, barbarians burst across its former borders. When the complex criss-crossing of their movements consolidated around AD 700, a new Europe had emerged. While some parts of it had changed relatively little from Roman times, other regions had been radically altered. The balance of power had shifted. The empires of the first

60 *Those Roman forts in Britain under the control of the Count of the Saxon Shore are illustrated here in a copy made in 1436 of a Late Roman list of officials – the* Notitia Dignitatum. *Starting from the top (l-r) is Othona (Bradwell-on-Sea), Dubris (Dover), Lemannis (Lympne), Branodunum (Brancaster), Gariannum (Burgh), Regulbium (Reculver), Rutupiae (Richborough), Anderida (Pevensey) and Portus Adurni (Portchester).*

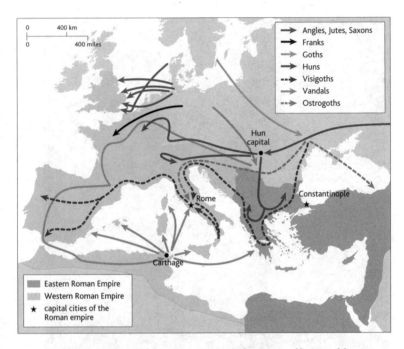

61 *Barbarian invasions as the western Roman empire began to crumble. Some of these movements were swift, others slow. The northern origins of the Goths and Vandals lay long in the past by the time they crossed the imperial border.* [61]

millennium BC all sprang from the advanced cultures of the Mediterranean. By the end of the first millennium AD, Europe was a patchwork of Christian kingdoms led by descendants of barbarians. This era of change is known as the *Völkerwanderung* (wandering of the peoples). [61]

In the 5th century the Gallo-Roman writer Sidonius Apollinaris vividly conjured up the Saxons. He tells us that 'the Saxon pirate deems it but sport to furrow the British waters with hides, cleaving the blue sea in a stitched boat'.[41] We can picture light boats made of hides stitched together and stretched over a timber framework. Sidonius Apollinaris imagined a friend of his

> ... on the look-out for the curved skiffs of the Saxons. In every one of their oarsmen you would think you were looking at an

arch-pirate ... The Saxon is the most ferocious of all foes.
He comes on you suddenly, and when you are waiting for him,
he slips away ... Shipwrecks to him are no terror, but only so
much training.[42]

Arch-pirates they may have been, but there is archaeological evidence to
suggest that by the end of the 4th century, some Saxon groups were not just
raiding but settling westwards along the coast. *Terps* (settlement mounds)
along the coast of Frisia were mainly abandoned during the 3rd century AD,
leaving the area depopulated. New arrivals in the 5th century left behind
pottery and burials connecting them with the Saxons. This has been difficult to reconcile with the fact that both the earlier and later populations
were known as Frisians to contemporaries, but it may be that the new arrivals were simply identified by the familiar name of the region. The common
thread of Saxon origin helps to explain why Frisian is the Germanic language closest to English.[43] Such sites have even been found as far west as
what is now Ponthieu in France, part of a region shortly to be conquered by
Clovis, king of the Franks.[44] [62] The Franks surged westwards into Gaul as

62 *The growth of the empire of the Franks from 481 to 814.*

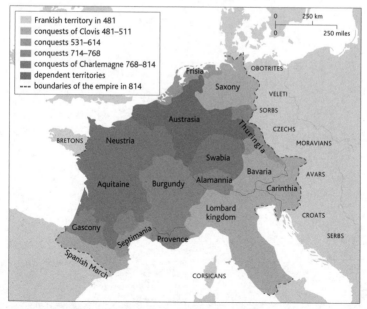

the western Roman empire fell, giving their name to modern-day France. The Franks and Saxons were rivals in the pursuit of rich, former Roman lands. The Frankish success in conquering Gaul may have been one factor in turning Saxon eyes across the Channel. Their adventures in Britain are encountered in the next chapter, but for the moment let us follow the struggles of their continental cousins.

In the 6th century, the Franks subdued the Saxons and demanded annual tribute, but had to crush Saxon rebellions in AD 555 and 556.[45] In 758 Pepin III, first king of the Franks, took the Saxon stronghold at Sythen (in Münsterland in North Rhine-Westphalia) and demanded tribute in the form of 300 horses.[46] Pepin's son and successor as king, Charlemagne (Charles the Great), captured the whole Saxon territory by AD 777. The Saxons by that time had become a federation including the Austreleudi, Westfali and Angrari.[47] The Angrari gave their name to the district of Angria, sandwiched between Westphalia and Eastphalia. These three districts, together with northern Albingia (north of the Elbe), became the Duchy of Saxony under Charlemagne. Today they are divided between the modern German states of Lower Saxony, Saxony-Anhalt, North Rhine-Westphalia and Schleswig-Holstein. The modern state in southern Germany simply called Saxony is unrelated to the ancient Saxon lands. The name arose simply from the title of its ruler.[48]

Overview

- Augustus took imperial power in 27 BC and greatly enlarged the Roman empire. From 12 BC his army commanders pushed across the Rhine into Germania. Within a few years Roman soldiers were wintering and towns were being founded in places east of the Rhine.

- In AD 7 Varus was granted command in Germania. Just two years later he led three Roman legions to their deaths in the Teutoburg Forest.

- Augustus and his successor Tiberius ordered punitive raids into Germania to avenge Rome's loss. Yet Tiberius shortly had a change of mind. The Germanic economy was too poor at the time to repay the effort of conquest, in either booty or taxes.

- The living standard of a leader among the Germani could not match that of the prosperous owner of a Roman villa. The Rhine marked a boundary between the haves and the have-nots.

- Germani could gain by diplomatic contacts with Rome, or by serving in the Roman army.

- Such contacts familiarized some Germani with the Latin alphabet, which was converted around AD 150 into a runic alphabet suited to the Germanic language.

- Proto-Germanic split into daughter branches. The first group to depart developed East Germanic, including Gothic. North and West Germanic were briefly a single language, before the dialect that developed into Old Norse broke away from the core. It was recorded in runes from around AD 200 onwards. The rump of Germanic-speakers developed West Germanic.

- The earliest split in West Germanic came as groups of Angles, Saxons and Jutes left for England, where Old English evolved.

- The Saxons lived beside the ocean, well placed for raiding by sea. By the reign of Emperor Valentinian (r. 364–75) the Saxons were launching raids on Gaul and Britain. Some settled in Frisia.

CHAPTER SEVEN

Anglo-Saxon Arrivals

> Those wild Saxons, of accursed name, hated by God and men ...
> admitted into the island, like wolves into folds ... first fixed their
> dreadful talons in the eastern part of the island.[1]

Thus raged Gildas about the strangers on his shores. Who was Gildas? Little can confidently be said about this passionate preacher. His own writing places him in the tradition of Latin Christianity surviving after Britannia left the Roman empire. His thundering denunciations of the slack morals of Celtic kings of his day reveal familiarity with what is now Wales and the southwest. A biography written in the 11th century by a Breton monk may have been based on ancient materials, which he did not entirely understand. The birthplace of Gildas is given as *Arecluta*, traditionally assumed to be Strathclyde, once known as *Alt Clut*. *Clud* is the Welsh name for the Clyde. This was puzzling, as Gildas shows no particular knowledge of that region. There is a stream that once had the same name in Cheshire, however, which bisects the village of Arclid, near Sandbach. That would be a more likely origin.[2] We are told that Gildas was educated by St Illtud (abbot of Llantwit Major, in the Vale of Glamorgan), and went on to study at 'Iren', often improbably assumed to be Ireland, but now thought to be a corruption of the Old Welsh name for Cirencester.[3] Corinium, as it was known to the Romans, was the third-largest town in Roman Britain and stands out for its maintenance of some sort of urban life for decades after the break with Rome.[4]

Of all the strange ideas generated by the desire to explain away evidence of migration, one of the most absurd is that entire communities or provinces of Romano-British took on the trappings of Anglo-Saxons out of admiration for their culture. Anglo-Saxon settlements could in this way be interpreted as Britons in disguise. Though we have only Gildas to speak for the Britons of the period, his is a powerful voice to the contrary. He blamed the immorality of the Britons for the curse of God in the form of the Saxons. The Saxons were not only loathed and feared, but also despised as pagans. They were not to be admired at all, if Gildas had any say in the matter. However, the adoption of an Anglo-Saxon lifestyle by individuals assimilated into it is more plausible. There is some evidence for this, as we shall see later in this chapter.

For the anti-migrationist school, it was tempting to cast the Anglo-Saxon advent as a parallel case to that of the earlier Roman conquest. They drew a picture of a Germanic warrior elite thinly superimposed on a mass of Romano-British. Certainly, when the emperor Claudius planned his campaign to take Britain in AD 43, he had no intention of wiping out the Celtic population there. He wanted them in harness. Claudius needed a military triumph to his name, but the more subtle arts of diplomacy paved the way. The endless rivalries between Celtic tribal leaders had opened up opportunities for Rome. When a defeated Brittonic king (Verica) sought refuge and requested allies in Rome after AD 40, it provided the perfect pretext for the Claudian invasion. Claudius was content to claim a triumph, having captured parts of southeast Britain and cemented treaties with certain other tribes. The full conquest was to take almost a century.[5] A conscious part of the programme was introducing the British Celts to the advantages of Roman life. As Tacitus cynically put it: 'And so they strayed into the enticements of vice – porticos, baths and sumptuous banquets. In their innocence they called this "civilization", when in fact it was a part of their enslavement.'[6] Governed masses of mainly Celtic descent emulated the Roman elite.

In fact, the Anglo-Saxon conquest was radically different. Far from being a planned campaign organized by a central authority, the Anglo-Saxon ingress was patchy and opportunistic. Rather than imposing their government on an existing population, they sought land to plough for themselves. Their early settlements were those of subsistence farmers. Unlike the Romans, the Anglo-Saxons brought no technological advances to Britain. Nor did they offer economic advantages. Yet there are two points of similarity. If Gildas is to be believed, the earliest arrivals came by invitation. And, like the Roman conquest, the Anglo-Saxon conquest was a drawn-out process, not a single event. It can be divided into two distinct phases, as we shall see.

As the western Roman empire broke apart, Franks and Goths snatched provinces for themselves by taking over the reins of government from the Romans. Thus they became an elite reigning over largely unchanged populations and cultures in France, Italy and Spain. The contrast with Britain is marked. France, Italy and Spain retained Christianity and developed Romance languages from Latin. In Britain a new language and religion appeared and Roman law gave way to Germanic law. Early Anglo-Saxon arrivals did not take over Britannia as a going concern. So much is evident. When the Anglo-Saxons emerged into literacy, we see Britain broken up into a patchwork of kingdoms, some created by Anglo-Saxons and others by Celtic-speakers. [see 9] With central authority weakened by the snapping of imperial bonds, the governance of Britannia seems to have devolved on to the local government units (*civitates*), which the Romans had created mainly from existing Celtic tribal territories. While some of these had continued life as Celtic kingdoms,[7] there is little sign of the Anglo-Saxons snatching the reins of local authorities. The Jutish kingdom of Cantia (Kent) retained a name based on that of a Roman *civitas*. A source composed centuries after the Anglo-Saxon advent claimed that first Thanet, and then the whole of Cantia, was granted to Jutish mercenaries in return for their protection,[8] but this has the hallmarks of myth.[9] The urban centre of local government at what is now Canterbury was left to decay. In the west, the Anglo-Saxon kingdom of the Hwicce seems similar in extent to the once-wealthy *civitas* of the Dobunni, with its capital at what is now Cirencester, but its early history is far from straightforward. In the main it seems that the Anglo-Saxons created their own polities, based initially on a people rather than a territory. Boundaries could change as a people moved, expanded or absorbed neighbouring groups.

The Romano-British

The people of Roman Britain were overwhelmingly descended from the Celtic tribes of pre-Roman times. Mixed in among them were Roman soldiers and officials stationed in Britannia, who could be drawn from anywhere in the empire. The exotic origins of certain individuals is obvious from inscriptions. Londinium (London), as the financial and administrative hub of Britannia, was probably the most cosmopolitan of British cities in the Roman era. Those whose families could afford to pay for an inscribed stone monument were mainly wealthy freedmen, military or elite figures. They include a merchant from Antioch and another born in Athens. With the comparatively new tools of isotopes and DNA, scientists can now interrogate the anonymous skeletons of ordinary denizens of Londinium.

63 *The wooden writing tablets found at Vindolanda are a remarkable survival, giving us an intimate look at life in a Roman fort in Britain. Here is a letter to Cerialis, recommending a certain 'capable fellow'.*

A teenage girl buried in what is now Lant Street, Southwark, is intriguing. She grew up in North Africa and travelled to Britain at least four years before she died at the age of fourteen. She had blue eyes and carried mtDNA HV6, common today in southeastern Europe and western Asia.[10] The people of North Africa were descended from waves of incomers from western Asia from the Palaeolithic era to the Phoenicians.[11]

The cohorts of Batavi and Tungri who served in Britain have already been mentioned (p. 108). Boggy conditions at the Roman fort of Vindolanda in Northumberland have preserved for us a rare cache of Roman writing tablets. [63] From them we learn that the garrison there from around AD 90 to 120 included the 1st Cohort of Tungri and the 9th Cohort of Batavi. The nominal strength of the 1st Cohort of Tungri was 752, including six centurions. It was led by prefect Iulius Verecundus. We know nothing of his origins, but the Batavi were generally led by their own nobles, according to Tacitus. That makes it likely that Flavius Cerialis, who commanded the 9th Cohort of Batavi, was himself of the Batavi. Officers could have their wives with them, and Cerialis did. Other ranks could not contract legal marriages, but might have families with local women in the civilian settlement adjacent to the fort at Vindolanda.[12] After the emperor Hadrian (d. AD 138) ordered a massive wall built from sea to sea north of Vindolanda, the 1st Cohort of Tungri moved to a fort midway along it called Vercovicium (now Housesteads). There they remained from the 2nd to the 4th century AD. From the early 3rd century onwards, additional Germanic units were garrisoned there. Two inscribed altars at Housesteads were raised by

64 *Gladiator figurine of bone or ivory, 1st–2nd century AD, found at Colchester, Essex, just 7 cm (2¾ inches) tall.*

Germani of a Frisian unit from Twenthe.[13] Inscriptions from locations elsewhere along Hadrian's Wall record the 1st Cohort of Batavi and 2nd Cohort of Tungri.[14]

The presence of Germanic soldiers in Britain might explain some aspects of an intriguing group of burials at Roman York. Under what is now Driffield Terrace, a cemetery was uncovered dating from the 2nd to the 4th century AD. It lay on the outskirts of the Roman town of Eboracum, across the river from the legionary fortress. It is one of many Roman cemeteries around York; what is unusual about this one is the number of bodies it contained that had been decapitated from behind at about the time of death, a pattern not found elsewhere in Roman Britain. What could this mean? Another unusual feature was that almost all were adult males, and taller than average for Roman Britain. Taken together with evidence of other injuries, including large carnivore bite marks on one individual, this looks like the last resting place of gladiators. [64]

We have genomes and isotopes from seven of these fighting men. One was clearly exotic. His closest genetic affinities lie today in the Middle East, and he spent his early life in just such an environment. The remaining six were most probably all born somewhere in Britain. Genetically their strongest matches are to modern British populations of the Celtic fringe, particularly the Welsh. Crucially, we can also compare them to a woman from pre-Roman Yorkshire (210 BC to AD 40) and an Anglo-Saxon man from Norton on Tees. [see Box p. 137] The result was clear. All of the six were more like the pre-Roman woman than the Anglo-Saxon man. It fits the expected pattern of Celtic continuity under Roman rule, while the Anglo-Saxons were new arrivals. Yet within this cohort of six were two slightly different individuals. While all six carried Y-DNA R1b haplogroups, two of these were the R1b-U106, which hints at a Germanic paternal line. These two U106 men, one a veteran and the other a youngster, were also distinct from the rest in having genetic matches in modern northeastern Europe, as well as Britain.[15] In short, they were what we might expect of a male-line descendant of a Germanic soldier based in Britain. Such ethnic mixtures could have been scattered across Britannia by the time it left the Roman empire. Presumably their loyalties lay entirely with the Romano-British when faced with waves of land-hungry Germani.

Debate has raged for more than a century over how *many* Germani it would take to overcome Britannia. All too often the battle of the numbers has been formulated as though it were a modern military question. How large an army would you need to conquer a country with a population of X million? Visions of a vast armada were conjured up, only to be exposed as implausible. This was not an invading nation with a state war budget. The approach is remote from the reality of the time and place: the Anglo-Saxons did not arrive as an army and instantly capture all of what is now England.

Heinrich Härke estimates that within the region which later became the focus of Germanic settlement the Romano-British population could have been about two million at the end of the 3rd century, declining to about one million by the middle of the 5th century, as the first Anglo-Saxon settlers appeared. It would need a significant ingress to have the dramatic impact that makes Britain's post-Roman history so different from that of France. Such mass movement is not impossible logistically. According to one computer simulation, the migration of 250,000 people from Denmark to East Anglia would require no more than thirty-eight years, using twenty boats in a continuous transport operation during a sailing season from May to August. The reality was probably a great deal less organized and could have taken a century or more.[16]

First footfalls, first settlers

The *Anglo-Saxon Chronicle* declares that the first Anglo-Saxon arrivals who responded to an invitation by Vortigern (see p. 27) were Hengest (Hengist) and Horsa in AD 449 and that they landed at Ebbsfleet (on the Isle of Thanet in east Kent).[17] These beguiling details were believed implicitly by many a Victorian author, but scorned by more recent scholars. [65] The date can be dismissed. It is taken from Bede, who must have struggled to attach dates to the imprecise account given by Gildas.[18] Neither of them was as close in place and time to the event as the author of the *Gallic Chronicle*, composed in around AD 452. He tells us that in the year AD 441–42, 'the British provinces, which up to this time had endured a variety of disasters and misfortunes, were subjected to the authority of the Saxons'.[19] He seems to be generalizing to the whole of Britannia what he presumably heard from refugees reaching Gaul. We need not imagine so complete a conquest so early. But his date accords with the archaeological evidence that the Anglo-Saxons were widely present in eastern England and the Upper Thames Valley from the 430s.[20]

Bede follows Gildas in saying that the mercenaries summoned by Vortigern landed on the eastern part of Britain, where they were granted land. There are no specifics.[21] As mentioned above (p. 112), the Romans had built a series of forts along the coast to protect Britain from Saxon raids. It was the abandonment of this line of defence that left the island open to a devastating Saxon raid in about AD 410.[22] By then Britain's garrison had been in revolt against Rome for several years. A series of local usurpers were declared emperors, the last of whom, Constantine III, led troops from Britain to Gaul in 407 in a briefly successful attempt to secure the western empire. Britain, having been thus stripped of its army, was open to attack, and all for nothing, for Constantine III was captured and executed in 411. Constantine's is the last Roman imperial coinage to reach Britain, so his death marks the end of Roman rule there.[23] We might imagine that post-Roman authorities would seek to revive the Saxon Shore defences. Several of the forts were converted to Anglo-Saxon use at a later date, such as the high-status Saxon hall at Portchester, Hampshire, and the chapel at Richborough, Kent. Yet if we seek early mercenaries, Rendlesham in Suffolk might be a better place to look. [see 9] This village, later the royal centre of East Anglia (see p. 25), is placed 10 kilometres (6 miles) from the coast. It starts with a Late Roman military presence. Unusually, it continued in use without a break, developing a Germanic character between AD 425 and 450.[24]

When Gildas wrote, the west and north of Britain were still held by Britons, while in more easterly regions they had either fled the incomers, or been slaughtered or enslaved by them, so he tells us.[25] Far from

65 *This irreverent view of the landing of Hengest and Horsa, full of amusing anachronisms, was drawn by W. W. Goodes to illustrate Bill Nye's Comic History of England (1906). Nye put his own wry twist on the story from the* Anglo-Saxon Chronicle, *rather than disputing it.*

taking on the mantle of the Romans, these newcomers seemingly had no use for Roman villas and towns in the territory in which they settled. It is rare for evidence to suggest a villa taken over in working order. The hubs of Romano-British organization were simply left to rot. Even in the Celtic west, urban life and the villa economy did not long survive the severance from empire, though it is not a story of utter abandonment. While towns there ceased to be major production centres with large populations, some do show continuing signs of life.[26]

In eastern Britain, both archaeology and place-names tell a tale of new arrivals. Farmsteads and hamlets of Germanic character appear. The incomers erected timber buildings of two types. Sunken-featured buildings we have met among the continental Germani (see p. 39). Many of these were excavated at the Anglo-Saxon settlement of West Stow in Suffolk and one was reconstructed. [66] Early Anglo-Saxon halls were generally smaller and simpler than the massive aisled longhouses of Germania. This discovery generated an argument that the early Anglo-Saxon hall owed more to Romano-British traditions. In reality, it fits the pattern of smaller, byre-less houses now recognized to exist on the continent in addition to the classic longhouse. The 'short houses' found at Wijster in the Dutch province of Drenthe provide a close parallel for halls excavated at West Stow in Suffolk. The percentage of continental Germanic buildings without byres and internal roof supports increased in the 5th and 6th centuries, the very period when early Anglo-Saxon settlements appear.[27] One can understand why new arrivals, with a limited labour force, might prefer to erect short houses, which would rapidly put a roof over their heads. Even so, the complete absence of longhouses was a puzzle until one was discovered at Eye in Suffolk in 2007. It measures approximately 19.4 metres long by 5.4 metres wide (64 × 18 feet), and is dated by pottery to the Early Saxon period.[28]

Roman fields were generally maintained by the new arrivals. It would be convenient to use already cleared land and retain existing field boundaries. One difference is that light, easily cultivated soils were often preferred, avoiding heavier soils drained by the Romans. More significantly, early Anglo-Saxon farming was less intensive. There was no need to support urban populations or standing armies.[29]

New cemeteries were laid out which bear witness to different burial rites from those of the Romano-British. Cremation was very rare in 4th-century Roman Britain, but was a common rite across northern Germany at the

66 *Reconstruction of an Anglo-Saxon village at West Stow in Suffolk. In the foreground is a sunken-featured building. Behind are short, byre-less houses, similar to a type found at Wijster in the Netherlands. All are roofed with thatch.*

time. So it is easily identified as intrusive when it appears in the first half of the 5th century in Britain. The urns within which the ashes of the dead were deposited provide further clues to origins. [67] The 'Saxon' type has parallels in the Elbe–Weser triangle of northern Germany, while the 'Anglian' type has similarities to pottery of the German-Danish border regions of Schleswig-Holstein, Mecklenburg and Fyn. Yet these styles were already

67 *Cremation urn from Spong Hill, North Elmham, Norfolk, decorated using stamps, approx. 22 cm (8½ inches) high. Galloping horses ring the pot and other designs include swastikas. Cremation was rare in Late Roman Britain, but appeared with the Anglo-Saxons.*

mixing on the continent by the late 4th century and the regional divide in Britain is not rigid. Archaeologists find no sign of surviving Romano-British in the areas settled early by the Anglo-Saxons. There is only negative evidence, in the sense that a gap in the record of Anglo-Saxon cemeteries in Yorkshire links with documentary evidence of a Brittonic kingdom of Elmet east of Leeds up until the early 7th century.[30] [see 9]

This uncompromising picture has led to much discussion of the 'Invisible Britons'. Could survivors be present in Anglo-Saxon guise? Step forward geneticists. Unfortunately, cremation effectively destroys DNA and few Anglo-Saxon inhumations are as early as the first cremations. Yet there are relatively early Anglo-Saxon inhumations which can be tested. A cemetery at Oakington, Cambridgeshire, was in use for burials in the 5th and 6th centuries. DNA was successfully extracted from four female skeletons and it has a tale to tell. To establish a base for comparison, let us first look at three samples from a Middle Anglo-Saxon cemetery at Hinxton, Cambridgeshire, which were compared with pre-Roman Iron Age samples from Hinxton and nearby Linton. The Middle Anglo-Saxon samples share relatively more rare variants with the modern Dutch than the Iron Age samples. So the evidence for population change in Britain is established. Now we come to the early Anglo-Saxon burials at Oakington. In the absence of names for the four women tested, the geneticists affixed numbers. Individuals O1 and O2 were genetically close to the Middle Anglo-Saxon samples, but O4 matched the Iron Age samples, while O3 was intermediate, suggesting mixed ancestry. So we have here evidence of intermarriage between incomers and locals at least in one area of eastern England. We should not build too much upon one small group of burials, but it is striking that the woman of presumed Romano-British ancestry died possessed of three Anglo-Saxon brooches, making hers a comparatively rich burial within this cemetery. We cannot see her as a maltreated slave.[31]

Angles, Saxons and Jutes

The earliest settlers, as we have seen, were labelled from their origins: Angles, Saxons and Jutes (p. 112). Yet geographical names such as East Saxons and West Saxons do not refer to distant origins but parts of Britain. That suggests polities or peoples formed in Britain. Two early Anglo-Saxon cemeteries, Spong Hill in Norfolk and Mucking in Essex, have been closely

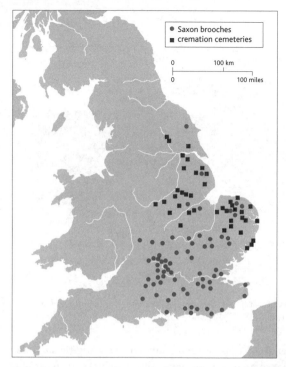

68 (above) The geography of the Anglo-Saxon settlement: the distribution of distinctively Anglian, cremation-dominant cemeteries and Saxon brooches of the second half of the 5th century.

69 A saucer brooch from Mucking in Essex. They were often worn in pairs, one on each shoulder.

studied. Comparison between them reveals differences between the Angles and Saxons. The Angles tended to practice cremation and the Saxons inhumation. Favoured brooch types differ. In Saxon areas, disc, button and saucer brooches predominate.[32] [68, 69] At Spong Hill there are close

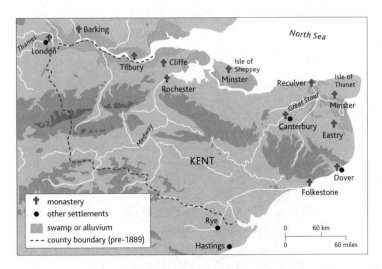

70 *The Anglo-Saxon kingdom of Kent. The Jutes appear to have settled only the territory east of the Medway (East Kent).*

parallels to material of the same period found in Schleswig-Holstein, the northernmost state of Germany, encompassing Angeln. Yet there are also occasional brooches from the presumed Saxon Elbe–Weser area. Melded together in Norfolk, the Spong Hill people developed local traditions.[33]

Another large Anglian cemetery has been almost totally excavated at West Heslerton, in the Vale of Pickering, North Yorkshire. Testing a range of the skeletons there for isotopes revealed two groups, one locally born and the other non-local. Bearing in mind that isotopes can only reveal first generation migrants and not their locally born descendants, it is still interesting that males and females are found equally in both groups and weapon burials occurred in both groups. This does not support the notion of an incoming warrior elite.[34]

Cantia (Kent) was a Jutish kingdom, according to Bede. [70] An Anglo-Saxon cemetery at Buckland, Dover, disgorged treasures in his support. Several gold bracteates (disc ornaments) worn as jewels by women buried there were probably made in Kent, but are of a type otherwise found in Norway, Denmark, northern Germany and southern Sweden.[35] [71] Others have been found elsewhere in eastern Kent. Yet Kent lay closer geographically to the North Sea coast than to Jutland. So it is not surprising to find

71 *A gold bracteate used as a pendant in a richly furnished 6th-century woman's grave in Buckland (Dover), Kent.*

Saxon influences too. Both documentary and archaeological evidence show that the Jutish kingdom was originally east Kent, while west Kent was settled by Saxons and only later absorbed into a united Kent.[36] Frankish material is scattered over much of southern Britain, but with a heavy concentration in east Kent. Indeed, the kingdom of Kent was to form so close a bond with its neighbour across the Channel, the powerful kingdom of Francia, that the impression might be created that Cantia was Frankish rather than Jutish in origin.[37] Contrary evidence comes in the form of 'pseudo-boat-burials' in Anglo-Saxon cemeteries in Kent from AD 500 onwards. In these the body is buried with parts of boats, used as grave goods. Imagine a mariner interred with the prow of his beloved boat, or lowered into the grave on a bier made of boat timbers. Since timber rots in the soil, what survives are the clench-nails which were used to fix overlapping planks together in the Scandinavian boat-building tradition. The same technique of clinker-building was used on the ocean-going vessel at Sutton Hoo in East Anglia. It was not exclusive to the Jutes. The crucial point is that the Frankish and Frisian boat-building tradition was different. Those early clench-nails tell a significant story.[38]

The second phase of conquest

The Anglo-Saxons paused in their expansion after the mid-5th century. Gildas seems to have been writing after a long period of peace. In his day the Britons still held an unbroken western swathe of the former Britannia from Cornwall to the borders of Pictland. Then in the later 6th century one group of Saxons began to push westwards and southwards, while groups of Angles spread west and north. By the time of Bede, Anglo-Saxon kingdoms covered most of England. [see 9] This second phase of conquest is characterized by endless in-fighting as expanding Anglo-Saxon kingdoms came into competition with each other. Three frontier kingdoms, Northumbria, Mercia and Wessex, gained power partly from their access to new lands to conquer. As we shall see, Britons absorbed into Wessex are not invisible, and we may suspect their continued existence in the other two kingdoms, but we have little idea of numbers.

At Yeavering in Northumberland a Celtic hillfort bears witness to the importance of the site in pre-Roman days. On lower-lying land in its lee a group of Angles created a power base that Bede knew as the royal palace of Ad Gefrin.[39] Was Yeavering an outpost in a land still largely Brittonic? The Angles certainly retained the Brittonic name, Berneich, expressed in Latin as Bernicia. An early Anglo-Saxon cemetery at Norton on Tees, just north of the ancient border between Bernicia and Deira, [see 9] has been dated to AD 540–610. It is one of only three in Bernician territory known to have more than fifteen burials. The other two are at the royal sites of Yeavering and its successor at nearby Milfield.[40] This pattern is a dramatic contrast to the massive cemetery at Spong Hill in Norfolk, where over 2,500 individuals were interred.[41]

Bede had nothing to say about early arrivals in Bernicia except that Ida, from whom the Northumbrian royal family traced their origin, began to reign in 547.[42] Bede presumably deduced this date from a regnal list similar to the one which survives in the *Historia Brittonum*, but its complications make the date problematic. Faced with such situations, historians can throw their hands in the air and declare that we will never know, or attempt to make the best possible sense of the tantalizing scraps left to us. Max Adams courageously chose the latter approach and concluded that Ida's reign actually started in 560.[43] The *Anglo-Saxon Chronicle*, which borrowed so much from Bede, simply uses Bede's date. In the early 11th century a scribe in Canterbury added a note to this entry, claiming that Ida built Bamburgh, which was first enclosed with a stockade, and thereafter with a wall. So late a source cannot be reliable on date or builder, but it tells us something of Bamburgh Castle, [72] a little over 16 kilometres (10 miles) east of Yeavering, before its reconstruction in the Norman period. The castle stands on a dolerite outcrop on the shore, a naturally defensible position.

72 A tiny Anglo-Saxon gold plaque depicting the so-called 'Bamburgh Beast', discovered at Bamburgh Castle in Northumberland.

Bede records that his people named this royal seat Bebbanburg after Queen Bebba.[44] The *Historia Brittonum* explains that Æthelfrith (d. 616), a later king of Ida's line, granted the stronghold to his wife Bebba.[45] Max Adams interprets this as part of a marriage settlement with a first wife, for Æthelfrith is also known to have married Acha, the daughter of Ælle, king of Deira.[46]

Bernicia expanded under Æthelfrith, described by Bede as 'a very brave king and most eager for glory … [who] ravaged the Britons more extensively than any other English ruler', either exterminating or conquering the natives. He defeated the Britons at Chester. Finding that monks of Bangor had come to pray there for the victory of their people, he reasoned that they were his enemies as much as the warriors. So he slaughtered them both alike.[47] It was presumably Æthelfrith who created the early 7th-century complex of buildings outside the fort at Yeavering, including a large timber hall.[48] [73] He annexed Deira on the death of Ælle to create Northumbria – the lands north of the Humber. This was to bring about his death in 616 when his brother-in-law Edwin of Deira returned from exile with the support of King Rædwald of East Anglia.[49]

In the Midlands, groups of Angles had moved up the Trent to come face to face with Britons. They were known as the Mierce – borderers. Their heartland probably lay around three significant sites: Repton in Derbyshire, where a monastery was endowed by the Mercian royal family; Lichfield in Staffordshire, where Chad established the first bishopric of the Mercians; and the royal estate at Tamworth, some 10 kilometres (6 miles) southeast of Lichfield, on the River Thame, a tributary of the Trent. Later charters

73 A digital reconstruction of the Anglian royal hall at Yeavering, Northumberland.

define all three centres as being in the territory of the Tomsæte, and it is possible that the Mercian royal line began as the leaders of these people, 'the dwellers by the river Tame'.[50] [74]

The earliest king of Mercia of whom we know more than just the name is the energetic Penda (d. 655), still a pagan at a time when other Anglo-Saxon kings were turning to Christianity. In his day almost the whole of Britain, English and Briton alike, had come under the overlordship of Edwin of Northumbria. Edwin had enlarged Deira by the conquest of the Brittonic kingdom of Elmet, taken control of Bernicia and made his presence felt in other kingdoms. Penda joined forces with Cadwallon of Gwynnedd to overturn this state of affairs. Edwin was killed in 633 and the whole of his army slain or scattered.[51] In 641 Penda killed Oswald, king of Northumbria. Penda was determined to break the overweening power of Northumbria, but died in the attempt in a third battle.[52]

Penda had expanded Mercian influence partly by creating client kingdoms around his heartland. He set his son Peada over the Middle Angles.[53] To the west were two satellite peoples. The Magonsæte lived in the district of Magana, whose name survives in the place-name Maund, Herefordshire.[54] The Wreocensæte, in what is now Shropshire, represent the heirs of the

Romano-British *civitas* of the Cornovii, with its capital at Wroxeter.[55] To the east was Lindsey, disputed between Mercia and Northumbria. It was gained by Mercia at the battle of the Trent in 679.[56] [see 74]

To the south lay the former Dobunnic polity of the Severn Valley, which became caught in a tug-of-war between Mercia and its southern rivals, the Gewisse, later to be known as the West Saxons. Anglian settlers had drifted into the northeast of Dobunnic territory in the 5th and 6th centuries, leaving their mark in pagan burials and a sprinkling of pagan place-names.

74 *The peoples of the Midlands at the time of the expansion of Mercia. The Anglo-Saxon term* sæte *meant 'dwellers, people of a district'. So* Cilternsæte = *Chiltern dwellers;* Magonsæte = *people of Magana, now Maund, Herefordshire;* Pecsæte = *Peak dwellers;* Tomsæte = *dwellers by the River Thame;* Wrocensæte *may refer to Wroxeter or the Wrekin.*

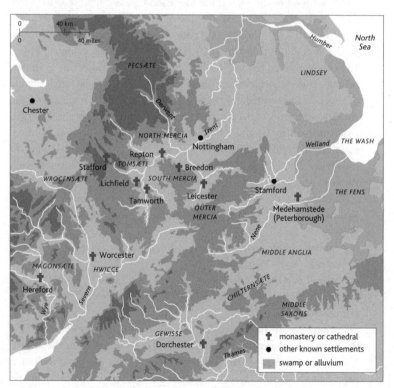

It is here that we find a rare example of continuity from Romano-British to Anglo-Saxon. At Wasperton in Warwickshire on the River Avon is a cemetery in use from the Late Roman period. Anglo-Saxon burials there start in the later 5th century. An Anglian origin is probable for those cremations in urns. Some of the early inhumations also had an East Anglian character, but others point towards the Upper Thames Valley and Wessex.[57] So we seem to have here a mixture of Angles and Saxons and probably Britons too.

The *Anglo-Saxon Chronicle* describes a battle at Dyrham in 577 in which Ceawlin (king of the Gewisse) and his son Cuthwine fought the Britons and captured three towns: Gloucester, Cirencester and Bath. This implies that the Gewisse took control of at least the southeastern part of the territory of the Dobunni. It was of strategic importance, for it formed part of a corridor west of the hilly spine of England connecting the Celtic kingdoms of the south and west to those of the north. Significantly missing from the battle list, though, is Worcester, an important Dobunnic town. So the Romano-British *civitas* may not have been taken complete in 577. The Gewisse found themselves in competition with Angles here. In 628, says the *Anglo-Saxon Chronicle*, Cynegils (king of the Gewisse) fought Penda of Mercia at Cirencester and afterwards came to terms. It is clear from the subsequent history of the area that Penda won, but he had probably forged an alliance with local leaders, for the former Dobunnic polity was not immediately amalgamated with Mercia. Instead it became the client kingdom of the Hwicce. The diocese of Worcester, created for the Hwicce, covered much the same area as that of the pre-Roman Dobunni.[58]

To the south, the Gewisse were based in the Upper Thames area, where Saxons had long been settled. A 5th-century Saxon cemetery found at Long Wittenham, South Oxfordshire, is remarkable for its rich male burials. A great hall complex, typical of royal sites, lies some 200 metres (656 feet) to the east. A few kilometres to the west is another royal hall complex at Sutton Courtenay, Oxfordshire. The two are linked by an old Roman road to Dorchester-on-Thames, where the first bishopric of the kingdom was centred.[59]

Intriguingly, the tradition preserved in Wessex names the founder of the line as Cerdic, apparently a Germanization of the Brittonic name Caraticos.[60] The Gewisse lived close to regions retained by Britons. Was peace with their neighbours at one time sealed by a marriage? If so, this did not permanently

Y-DNA I1 in England

So far Y-DNA has been obtained from only one Anglo-Saxon, a man buried at Norton on Tees, in the historic county of Durham. There were two Anglo-Saxon cemeteries there. A pre-Christian one represents early arrivals in Bernicia (see p. 132). The second, at Norton Bishopsmill, dates to 650–910 and was Christian. It is from the later cemetery that we have DNA from one man. His Y-DNA haplogroup was discovered to be I1 (M253).[61] This is one of the three haplogroups that predominate today in Scandinavia, all of which have been found in ancient DNA there. [see Box p. 90]

In 2002, when only modern DNA was available, geneticists from University College London conducted a pioneering study of Y-DNA. They took DNA from 313 males in the British towns of North Walsham, Fakenham, Bourne, Southwell, Ashbourne, Abergele and Llangefni. These places were selected as an east–west transect across central Britain from East Anglia to Wales, and as long-established market towns, rather than cities, which are more likely to be affected by recent migration. They compared the pattern of haplogroups with those in Friesland and Norway. The results showed that I1, common in Friesland and Norway, was at its highest level in East Anglia and Bourne in Lincolnshire, and decreased slightly in frequency in central England and markedly in Wales. This distribution was interpreted as reflecting Anglo-Saxon mass migrations into Britain.[62] Now we are accumulating confirmation from ancient DNA, though much more is needed.

prevent the Gewisse from expanding at the expense of the Britons. As their expansion to the north was blocked by Mercia, the Gewisse overran territory of the Britons to the southwest and south, and Jutish lands in what is now Hampshire. By the time Bede wrote, the border between the Gewisse and the South Saxons lay opposite the Isle of Wight. He remarks that the River Hamble ran through Jutish lands belonging to the Gewisse.[63] According to the *Anglo-Saxon Chronicle*, Cenwealh came to the throne of the Gewisse or West Saxons in 641 or 643. Possibly in an attempt to make peace with a fierce northern neighbour, Cenwealh married a daughter of Penda. The marriage was unsuccessful and Cenwealh repudiated her. Penda took his revenge by driving Cenwealh from his own kingdom; he had to take refuge in East Anglia until 648. It was under Cenwealh that the Old Minster at Winchester was built for Wine when he became bishop of Winchester in 660. This marked a shift southward of the heart of the kingdom, away from the dangerous Mercian border.[64] After the death of Cenwealh in 672, sub-kings took upon themselves the government of Wessex, dividing it up and ruling for about ten years, until Cædwalla took over Wessex in 685.[65]

This kingdom was to become central to the creation of the English nation. Yet it appears less solidly Anglo-Saxon than, for example, the kingdom of the East Angles, established earlier. The name Cædwalla is an anglicized version of the Brittonic name Cadwallon. After Cædwalla abdicated in 688, in order to make a pilgrimage to Rome, Ine assumed the throne.[66] His laws for Wessex are revealing. They made separate provision for Ine's English and Brittonic subjects, the latter called *Wilisc*, translated as 'Welsh', though not in the modern sense of 'the people of Wales' (see also p. 151).

The Anglo-Saxons had a compensation culture. For example, *wergeld* (man-payment) was the legal value set on a person's life. If you killed a man you would have to pay that compensation to his family. The *wergeld* provides the clearest proof that the Anglo-Saxons did not regard all men as equal. One man could literally be worth more than another. At the bottom of the ladder were slaves. Above them we have the *ceorl*, whose *wergeld* was 200 shillings. The word has descended into Modern English as 'churl', but simply meant a man or husband in Old English, and denoted a rural head of household in the laws. They could be upwardly mobile. An 11th-century text spells out that ownership of five hides, a bell and a castle-gate, together with a seat and special office in the king's hall, entitled a *ceorl* to the status of *thegn*.[67] (A hide was an unit of land measurement which depended more on its value than its extent.) A king's *thegn*, also called a *gesith* (compan-ion), was indeed among the king's close companions. His *wergeld* was 1,200 shillings. In the laws made by Ine, the *wergeld* of a 'Welsh' taxpayer was 120 shillings, a slave only 60 shillings, while the *wergeld* of a 'Welsh' horseman in the king's service as a messenger was 200 shillings, and for a 'Welshman' who held five hides of land the *wergeld* was 600 shillings.[68] So in Wessex a free Briton was protected by law and could be a substantial land-owner, but there is no indication that he could rank equally with the English nobility.

Whatever interaction there was between Britons and Anglo-Saxons, it left little linguistic trace. The Brittonic impact on Old English was minimal. If millions of Celtic-speakers had shifted to the language of a handful of Anglo-Saxon lords, Old English should show signs of a Brittonic 'accent', but it does not. Even the number of words borrowed from Celtic is small.[69] The overwhelming majority of English place-names outside Cornwall are Anglo-Saxon in origin, indicating that the incomers generally created their own settlements. Yet the few names with a Brittonic element are not evenly spread across the country. There is a marked difference between the early-settled east and the later-settled west, with far more Brittonic survivals in the latter.[70] So the signals point to the taking of territory complete with natives *in situ* more often in the second phase of expansion.

Overview

- The Romano-British population was overwhelmingly Celtic, but included individuals from many parts of the Roman empire, including some Germani within the Roman army. This may explain the Germanic Y-DNA U106 carried by two gladiators in Roman York.

- The Anglo-Saxon ingress was dissimilar to the Roman conquest of Britain in almost every way. The exceptions are that both began by invitation, and both were protracted affairs, rather than a single event.

- Ancient DNA from individuals before and after the Anglo-Saxon advent indicates that the Anglo-Saxons were indeed incomers.

- There was no reason for the Romano-British population on the whole to imitate the Germanic way of life, but individual Britons could adopt it by marriage or other assimilation.

- Bede's geography of the Angles, Saxons and Jutes in Britain finds confirmation in archaeological evidence. This should be seen as a broad picture, within which Germanic influences might cross boundaries or change over time.

- A second wave of expansion into Brittonic territory coincided with the rise of Anglo-Saxon kingdoms and power struggles between them. The expansionist kingdoms of Northumbria, Mercia and Wessex were born from the borders with Britons and show signs of the absorption of Britons.

CHAPTER EIGHT

Embracing Christianity

Now we must laud the heaven-kingdom's Keeper ...[1]

S o begins *Cædmon's Hymn*, the earliest religious verse written in English. But how and why did the Anglo-Saxons become Christian? They had brought with them from their continental homelands a Germanic pantheon which reflected a warrior ethos. The predominant trio of deities, Woden, Tiw and Thunor (Thor), all appear in English place-names.[2] All expressed aspects of war (see pp. 42–45). Yet this religion, so well tailored to the heroic values of *Beowulf*, was exchanged for a single all-powerful deity, who laid Ten Commandments upon His adherents. While the first four of these protected the religion itself, the other six promoted a stable society in which people could live peaceably together. Christianity took this further, enjoining us to love our neighbours as ourselves. In hindsight, we may see this as a message suited to a people moving from the annexation of a new homeland to the creation of kingdoms under the rule of law. Was there some notion at the time that peace promised greater prosperity than war? If so, such mundane considerations do not surface in the account of the conversion of the English that Bede conscientiously produced. Instead the stress at one key point falls on rewards in the afterlife, just as hinted in the opening of *Cædmon's Hymn*.

Keeping the faith

Christianity had first arrived in Britain in Roman times. [75] As we know from St Patrick and Gildas, the faith continued among Britons after Britannia left the empire. Writing in the 5th century, Patrick suggests that religious apathy was so common as to bring down the wrath of God upon the Britons. Yet he was raised in a Christian environment. He was the son of a deacon and grandson of a priest.[3] It was a Romano-British Christianity that he took to Ireland, and that was to return to Britain with Irish monks. Though Gildas in the 6th century found much to complain about in his sinful countrymen, he never accused them of a return to paganism. In western Britain there are scattered clues to the continuation of Latin Christianity in the 5th to 7th centuries, such as Christian commemorative inscriptions and place-names incorporating *ecles*, from the Latin *ecclesia* (church). A number of Brittonic monasteries are known from the literature by around 650, but evidence on the ground has proved elusive, except for the signs of large sub-circular enclosures around some Welsh and Cornish churches.[4]

So a recent discovery is a breakthrough. In May 2016 a team from the South West Heritage Trust excavated the cemetery attached to Beckery Chapel near Glastonbury in Somerset. The chapel stood on a prominence which once would have been an island within the wetlands. This was the type of remote site attractive to those seeking seclusion. In a previous excavation some fifty to sixty skeletons were found. Most of them were adult males, which strongly suggested a monastic site. Now radiocarbon dating has revealed that the remains are from the 5th or early 6th century. That was before the conquest of Somerset by the West Saxons.[5] The medieval monks of Glastonbury Abbey are commonly thought to have invented tales of a pre-Saxon antiquity for their monastery as a fund-raising tactic, but perhaps they were confounding their own history with that of this earlier monastic house nearby. Glastonbury Abbey itself appears to be of Saxon foundation. The site was occupied in Roman times, but there is nothing to indicate that this was by a religious community.[6]

Bede blamed the Britons for making no attempt to preach the faith to pagan Angles and Saxons.[7] Yet it is possible that some Anglo-Saxons chose to receive the faith as they intermarried and intermingled with Britons. The Hwicce are a case in point. Bede, whose aim was to provide a detailed account of the conversion of the Anglo-Saxons, fails to tell us how the Hwicce became Christian. He simply tells us that they were.[8] So Britons were probably responsible.[9]

75 *Roman gold finger-ring found at Brentwood in Essex. Its octagonal bezel carries the Christian chi-rho monogram (reversed), a bird and a vine or tree.*

Roman vs Irish

When Bede came to tell the story of the conversion of the Anglo-Saxons to Christianity, he gave most of the credit to the mission of St Augustine, but was scrupulously fair to the work of the Irish from Iona, despite his bias in favour of Rome.

It was Pope Gregory the Great (d. 604) who decided that the Anglo-Saxons should be brought into the Church. He chose a man he doubtless knew well to head the mission. Augustine was prior of the monastery founded by Gregory on his own family property on the Cælian Hill in Rome. In 596 Augustine set out with a group of monks, but they had only gone a little way when they became 'paralysed with terror'. One can only imagine that they had encountered someone familiar with the worst the Anglo-Saxons could do. 'They began to contemplate returning home rather than going to a barbarous, fierce and unbelieving nation whose language they did not even understand'; but buoyed up by exhortations from Pope Gregory, the mission doggedly pressed onward, acquiring interpreters from the Franks.[10]

Augustine and his companions landed on Thanet, just off the coast of Kent, where they waited until they were sure of their welcome. Æthelberht (d. 616), king of Kent, had married the Frankish princess Bertha, whose parents had insisted that Bertha be allowed to practise her Christian faith. So Æthelberht was not unfamiliar with Christianity, but met the delega-tion from Rome with reserve. He could promise them no conversions, but granted them a dwelling in Canterbury and the right to preach. On the east side of the city was the Church of St Martin, which Bede thought had sur-vived from Roman times. [76] This church certainly incorporates Roman material. It had been used as a chapel by Queen Bertha and became the first church of the mission. In due course Æthelberht was baptized, along with others of his people.[11]

The Anglo-Saxons emerge into a brighter light as they adopted Christianity, which brought literacy with it. The convenience of records was readily perceived by kings as much as by churchmen. The earliest-known Anglo-Saxon law code is that of Æthelberht of Kent. It was partly designed to integrate the fledgling English Church and its property within the existing Germanic legal system. As Christianity spread, kings would grant land for the foundation of monasteries and cathedrals. The Church zealously preserved the charters which recorded such grants, as proof of their rights.

76 *The Church of St Martin, Canterbury, was in origin Roman. It was built outside the walls of the Roman city in a cemetery, and may therefore have been a mausoleum or cemetery church. It was the first church used by Augustine, missionary to the English.*

After his success in Kent, Augustine returned to Gaul to be consecrated archbishop of the English. He informed Pope Gregory that the harvest was great and the workers few, so the Pope sent him more colleagues, including Mellitus and Paulinus, of whom we shall hear more, with instructions on the organization of the English Church and 'very many manuscripts'. [Pl. xix] Presumably guided by knowledge of the Roman administration, Pope Gregory envisaged London as the seat of a southern archbishop and York as the seat of a second archbishop, both with the power to consecrate twelve bishops to be under their authority.[12] The political realities encountered by Augustine dictated that Canterbury should be his seat, rather than London. Canterbury Cathedral remains the mother church of the Anglican Church. The present cathedral, though, is the result of multiple rebuildings, increasing its size, and now bears no resemblance to Augustine's building. Excavation in the nave in 1993 revealed remains of the first Anglo-Saxon cathedral, which was built on top of soils which had accreted when the Roman town was abandoned. Stone and bricks from decayed Roman buildings were re-used in its foundations.[13]

This was the first of a number of cases where former Roman towns were considered suitable places for cathedrals and monasteries, as Christianity began to spread across Anglo-Saxon England. However, Augustine chose a site outside the city wall at Canterbury for a monastery, which he envisaged as a burial place for himself and later archbishops of Canterbury and the kings of Kent.[14] Thus he respected the Roman rule that burials should be outside the town walls, and also separated the pastoral and contemplative arms of the Church. The monks had their own establishment in which they could concentrate on prayer, while the cathedral would be served by ordained clergy, who would also aid the bishop in administrative tasks. This was entirely logical, yet too ambitious, it seems, for most of Anglo-Saxon England. There is no evidence for centuries afterwards of such strict segregation of bishops and their staff from monks.[15] Nor were later Anglo-Saxon burial grounds separated from population centres.

The first church of St Augustine's Abbey had a rectangular nave and apsidal chancel. The earliest Christian churches were modelled on the Roman civic basilica, or administrative hall and law court. This was an aisled hall on an east–west axis, with an entrance at the east end and usually a semi-circular apse opposite. Most of the early churches in Rome followed that pattern, and so had their altars at the west end. Yet Christians preferred to face east to pray, towards the rising sun, symbol of Christ as the light, so gradually the orientation was switched around.[16]

Mellitus was the first member of the mission consecrated to work outside Kent. In 604 Augustine sent him to preach in the land of the East Saxons. At that time it was ruled by Æthelberht's nephew Sæberht, the son of his sister. According to Bede, Æthelberht was the overlord of all the southern kingdoms. He certainly seems to have had influence enough to support the mission to the East Saxons. Mellitus having had some success in Essex, Æthelberht built a church for him, dedicated to St Paul, in London.[17] London was in the territory of the Middle Saxons, [see 9] who left their name in the county of Middlesex. [see 104] By this time they were evidently controlled by the East Saxons, who later lost Middlesex and London to Mercia.[18]

The English Church, so dependent upon the goodwill of Æthelberht, suffered a severe setback on his death in 616. His son Eadbald had refused to adopt the faith. Objects related to the cult of Woden buried in two graves in a cemetery at Finglesham, Kent, may date as late as this.[19] Likewise, the death of Sæberht left his three robustly pagan sons in charge of the East Saxons. Bishop Mellitus was expelled from the kingdom.[20]

This climate of religious swing and sway provides the background to a remarkable discovery. At Prittlewell in Essex lies an Anglo-Saxon cemetery dating to the 6th and 7th centuries. In 2003 a team from the Museum of London Archaeology Service was asked to investigate a previously unknown part of the site. What they found made headlines. There was an undisturbed burial chamber, 4 metres (13 feet) square, which contained an array of riches second only to the ship burial in Mound 1 at Sutton Hoo. [77] As at Sutton Hoo, the skeleton had dissolved in the soil, all but a few fragments of teeth, but such a high-status burial with weapons indicates a male,

77 *This reconstruction drawing of the Prittlewell burial chamber by Faith Vardy displays the wealth of goods provided for the 'Prittlewell Prince'.*

and indeed most probably a king. He was dubbed the 'Prittlewell Prince'. The grave goods include the paraphernalia of a warrior: a gold-mounted iron sword and remnants of a shield and two spears. More numerous were items that would be used for feasting and entertainment in the lord's hall, such as drinking horns, cooking and serving vessels, an iron folding stool of Italian type, the remnants of a lyre, dice and gaming pieces. The deceased wore a gold belt buckle similar in type to that at Sutton Hoo, [see Pl. ix] but bare of decoration. Two Merovingian coins date the burial to the late 6th or 7th century, while the grave goods are all characteristic of the early 7th century.[21]

Thus far the burial appears entirely pagan and it resides within a pagan cemetery. Yet certain features tell a different tale. The body was laid in the east–west alignment typical of Christian burials. A Byzantine silver spoon with an inscription in Roman letters and a cross incised in it could have been baptismal. Uniquely in England, two gold foil crosses had been placed on the head, perhaps on the eyes, of the corpse. [78] Such crosses are otherwise found only in Lombardic Italy and Almannia (southwest Germany and northern Switzerland) around AD 600. So it is likely that this was the burial of the Christian Sæberht by his pagan sons. Two different influences were brought to bear on the burial. It had all the magnificence that a pagan royal family would expect, yet someone had injected a Christian element with a probable Italian origin.[22] Bishop Mellitus, sent from Rome by Pope Gregory, would be the obvious person.

The setback to the Roman mission was only temporary. Eadbald of Kent had a change of heart and accepted the new faith. So when Edwin, king of Northumbria (d. 633), sought the hand in marriage of Eadbald's sister Æthelburh, he was informed that it was unacceptable for a Christian

78 *These two gold foil crosses were placed on the head of the 'Prittlewell Prince'. His body had dissolved in the acid soil, but the position of the crosses suggests that they had been placed over his eyes.*

maiden to marry a heathen. Edwin could not promise to adopt a religion of which he knew nothing, but he did promise to put no obstacles in the way of Christian worship by Æthelburh and all who came with her. So Paulinus was consecrated bishop in July 625 to accompany the princess. Edwin was in no haste to change his religion, learning about Christianity gradually from Bishop Paulinus, and debating its merits with his counsellors. From Bede's perhaps apocryphal description of the decisive council session comes the famous metaphor for the evanescence of human life as a sparrow flying swiftly through a royal hall from one door to the other, briefly sharing the warmth of the fire-lit interior. What followed that flight? The argument went that if the new doctrine brought certainty on the hereafter, it was right to accept it. Thus Edwin and his people came to Christianity in 627.[23]

Edwin was baptized at York in the church of St Peter the Apostle, which he had hastily built of wood as he prepared for baptism. Soon afterwards he began building a more magnificent cathedral of stone for Paulinus, encasing the timber chapel. Before the walls were fully up, Edwin was slain in battle. But after a year of chaos, he was succeeded by Oswald (see below), who completed the construction.[24] The cathedral at York did indeed become the seat of an archbishop in 735, as planned by Pope Gregory. It is commonly known as York Minster.

The Anglo-Saxon word *mynster* is a borrowing from the Latin *monasterium*, which we translate as 'monastery', but as far as we can understand the meaning for Anglo-Saxons of this time, it denoted any kind of religious establishment with a church. Some might be enclosed and contemplative communities living to a monastic rule, such as Monkwearmouth and Jarrow, to which Bede belonged, but probably many were not.[25] Bede himself was critical of laymen who obtained charters of land under the pretext of building monasteries, but really as a means of freeing their land of military obligations to the king. They ruled over such supposed monasteries as laymen and had no real notion of monastic life.[26]

Oswald of Northumbria was a son of Æthelfrith, the first king to unite Bernicia and Deira (p. 133). When Æthelfrith was killed, Oswald and his brother Oswiu had fled into exile among their northern neighbours. There they encountered Christianity. The Irish enclave in Argyll had welcomed St Columba from Ireland in 565 to found a monastery on the small Hebridean island of Iona.[27] So when Oswald came out of exile to take the throne of Northumbria, he requested the 'Irish elders' to send him a bishop.

When Aidan arrived from Iona he was granted Lindisfarne, off the coast of Northumbria, which becomes an island at high tide. Thus Northumbria developed a type of Christianity slightly different from the Roman variety. Bede famously waxed wroth at their way of calculating the date of Easter.[28] According to Bede, Oswald was the overlord of much of Britain.[29] It seems that he used his influence to promote Christianity, for he stood sponsor at the baptism of Cynegils, the first king of the West Saxons to become Christian. The two kings established a bishopric at Dorchester-on-Thames.[30]

Frankish influences were still at work to promote the Roman tradition. Rædwald's successor in East Anglia was persuaded to accept Christianity by Edwin of Northumbria, but was killed by a heathen not long afterwards. So it was not until Sigeberht became king of the East Angles in around 630 that the new faith made much headway in that kingdom. Sigeberht had been in exile in Gaul, where he became a devout Christian and a man of learning. He was eager to share the faith with his subjects and was ably assisted by Bishop Felix from Burgundy. Together they founded a school. Sigeberht also founded a monastery, to which he retired.[31]

Marriage diplomacy brought Christianity to the Middle Angles. Their chief, Peada, son of the militantly pagan Penda, sought the hand in marriage of Alhflaed, daughter of Oswiu, the brother and successor of Oswald of Northumbria. Oswiu stipulated that Peada and his nation should accept baptism. The East Saxons, too, were persuaded by Oswiu to accept the faith. Overcoming Penda himself took an army. Oswiu triumphed over Penda in 655 and ruled Mercia himself until 658, converting the kingdom.[32]

The resultant patchwork of Irish and Roman influences on Anglo-Saxon Christianity created odd situations. Oswiu of Northumbria followed the Irish calendar, while his wife had a chaplain from Kent who followed the Roman calendar. So the king could be keeping Easter Sunday while his queen was still in Lent. Ultimately a meeting was called to decide on one uniform system. It was held in the monastery at Whitby headed by Abbess Hild, who was on the side of the Irish. Vehement in the Roman cause was Wilfrid (d. 709), at that time abbot of Ripon and shortly to become bishop of Northumbria. The Synod of Whitby in 664 was a turning point for Christianity in England. Oswiu ruled that his kingdom would calculate Easter according to the customs of Rome.[33] Thus the English Church was knitted together into a single organization led by Canterbury and ultimately the Pope.

The final pieces of the jigsaw of the conversion fell into place when Æthelwalh of the South Saxons was baptized in Mercia, under the patronage of King Wulfhere of Mercia (d. 674 or 675). The outspoken and controversial Bishop Wilfrid had been ejected from his see and chose to come to the still-pagan kingdom of the South Saxons (Sussex) to aid in its conversion. But Wulfhere had overreached himself by granting Æthelwalh the Isle of Wight and land in Hampshire that belonged to the West Saxons. Cædwalla had other ideas. He was a young and vigorous prince of the Gewisse, in exile from his own land, but clearly protective of it. He arrived among the South Saxons with an army and slew their king. Once he became king of Wessex in 685, he incorporated the Isle of Wight into his kingdom, wiping out the pagan natives, and resettling the island with his own people. He had won over Wilfrid beforehand by promising him a large estate on Wight.[34] England was fully Christian, at least nominally.

Changing burial customs

Cremation declined in popularity even before the conversion of the Angles. So by around AD 600, the standard practice of all Anglo-Saxons was inhumation with possessions, but in the next two decades the deposition of grave goods also declined rapidly, except in high-status burials under barrows. This was the transitional period from pagan to Christian.[35] In England bed burial appears unique to the 7th century. It appeared earlier on the continent. [see 16] There is a link in England to high-status women. At Street House near Saltburn, Yorkshire, an Anglo-Saxon cemetery was discovered in 2004, dating to the second half of the 7th century. Many of the higher-status objects found there have a Kentish origin or inspiration. The central burial on the site was that of a woman dubbed the 'Saxon Princess', buried in her bed. She wore a pendant unparalleled in Anglo-Saxon England, with cloisonné garnets surrounding a central gem incised to create a scallop shape.[36] [Pl. xii]

Early Christian cemeteries among the Anglo-Saxons can be recognized by a combination of features. East–west orientation alone is insufficient, as this occurred in some English regions during the pagan period, though it became standard practice for Christians. Other clues are Christian artefacts such as crosses, and otherwise few objects beyond the knife carried at the belt for domestic use. It seems that the austere burial mode long favoured by Christian monks and clergy was gradually adopted by English Christians, as the responsibility for burial shifted from kindred to Church.[37] The views of the English Church on burial were not spelled out at the time, but it seems likely that they were much the same as those decreed for the continental Saxons by Charlemagne in the 780s, which forbade cremation and ruled that the bodies of Christian Saxons should be taken to the Church's cemeteries and not to pagan burial mounds.[38]

Slavery

Christianity had no immediate effect on the institution of slavery, though the Church encouraged the freeing of slaves. When Wilfrid arrived in Sussex, he was granted 87 hides of land in Selsey, where he established a monastery. The land came complete with stock, fields and the people who worked them. [79] Among these were 250 male and female slaves, whom Wilfred baptized and rewarded with freedom.[39] Misleading comparisons have been made to the slave plantations of the American South.[40] These belong in a different economy. Plantations grew cash crops for export or

79 *The great majority of Anglo-Saxons worked on the land. This depiction of farm workers and their tools was used to illustrate a passage from Exodus in a Late Saxon manuscript.*

sale to distant markets; by contrast, early Anglo-Saxon estates aimed to be largely self-sufficient. Anglo-Saxon slaves on the land seem to have lived like other peasants, each with a simple dwelling and a small plot of land on which crops could be grown or a few animals kept.[41] This is akin to the role of slaves in Germania, remarked on by Tacitus (p. 42).

Slavery was deeply embedded in Anglo-Saxon society. The Normans took over an England where about 10 per cent of the population were slaves. The men mainly worked as agricultural labourers. The women had the tedious task of grinding corn, or were serving maids, wet-nurses, dairy maids, weavers and seamstresses. War was probably the biggest source of slaves.[42] Bondage could also be a punishment for theft or other crimes. The laws of Ine (king of Wessex 688–726) laid down that if a thief's wife and children were privy to a theft, the entire household could be enslaved.[43] Some of these captives were traded out of the country and ended up in slave markets such as the one in Marseilles in the south of France.[44] Yet this was against the laws of Ine. If anyone sold one of his own countrymen overseas he was obliged to pay for him with his own *wergeld* (see p. 138) and make full atonement with God for his crime.[45] It seems that the Church frowned on sales which could result in Christians coming under a heathen master.

Christian soldiers

Embracing the gospel of the Prince of Peace did not bring an end to warfare in England either. Even if we did not have the *Anglo-Saxon Chronicle* to list bloody battles, we could read the same message in the staggering Staffordshire Hoard. Discovered in July 2009 close to the village of Hammerwich, near Lichfield, in the heart of Mercia, it is the largest collection of Anglo-Saxon gold and silver metalwork ever found. Among its thousands of items, nearly all from war gear, are remarkable Christian objects. One metal strip carries a biblical inscription which matches the martial mood of the hoard: 'Rise up, O Lord, and let Thy enemies be dispersed and those who hate Thee be driven from Thy Face' (Numbers 10:35). It might have been attached originally to a wooden cross which could be carried into battle against pagans. Moses had brought the Ten Commandments to his people, including 'Thou shall not kill', but by the time that Christianity reached the Anglo-Saxons, the concept of the just war had been developed by St Augustine of Hippo.[46]

80 *The York Helmet (750–75) is one of the finest objects of the Anglo-Saxon period. It was discovered in Coppergate in the city. The decoration of the nose-guard is a beautiful example of Anglo-Saxon craftsmanship in Style II, with two interlaced animals.*

We do not know who buried this great hoard or exactly when. It can only be dated by stylistic comparison with objects with a known date elsewhere. A pectoral cross from the hoard can be compared with one taken to his grave by St Cuthbert, who died in 687. [PL. xvi] Sword fittings from the hoard are similar to those found at Sutton Hoo. Although there are a few pieces decorated in Anglo-Saxon Style I (for an example of this style see Frontispiece), most of the decoration used in the hoard is in Anglo-Saxon Style II, based on interlaced animals. Experts are converging on a date of 650–70 for the deposition of the hoard. That could place it in the last years of the pagan Penda of Mercia, or in the reign of one of his Christian sons, Peada (d. 656), or Wulfhere (d. 674 or 675). Could it be Penda's battle booty? He was certainly the scourge of Christian kings and could have captured Christian items. The hoard may represent the spoils of a single battle, or the accumulation from a longer period of warfare.[47]

A wonderful helmet found by chance in York shows an Anglo-Saxon warrior placing himself under heavenly protection. [80] On the crest is an inscription in Latin which translates as 'In the name of our Lord Jesus Christ, the Holy Spirit and God; and to all we say amen Oshere.' Only a nobleman would own so magnificent an object. Perhaps Oshere was a member of the Northumbrian royal family.

Building to last

Together with influences from Rome came a gradual revival in England of building in stone, at least for key Christian buildings. The Germanic tradition of timber construction continued unabated for the overwhelming majority of buildings. Even Anglo-Saxon palaces were built in timber. Early churches could be timber-built, too.[48] Since timber was not ideally suited to creating a semi-circular apse, timber churches would have a square-ended chancel. The preference for a square end continued in many places into the era of stone-building, for example at the twin monasteries of Monkwearmouth and Jarrow.[49]

Bede gives us a useful account of how his own monastery was built. Its founder was a Northumbrian noble, Biscop Baducing, who took the Christian name of Benedict. At the age of twenty-five he abandoned worldly ambition to embrace a spiritual life, making the first of five journeys to Rome.[50] Eventually returning to Northumbria in 674, Benedict Biscop founded the

81 *The Latin dedication stone of St Paul's Church, Jarrow, the oldest surviving in England. It was laid on 23 April 685.*

monastery of Monkwearmouth at the mouth of the River Wear, as its name suggests. He crossed into Gaul to obtain masons 'to build him a church in the Roman style, which he had always admired'. When the work was near completion, he sent messengers to Gaul to fetch glass-makers, at this time unknown in Britain, that they might glaze the windows of his church, the cloisters and refectory. They not only did so, but taught some local people their handicraft. A few years later Benedict Biscop founded Jarrow as a second part of the same monastery, though some miles away.[51] [81; Pl. xxiii] A 12th-century source credits St Wilfrid with glazing the windows at York Minster, to keep out the birds and rain, but let in the light.[52] If so, that would pre-date the work on Monkwearmouth, yet Wilfrid, too, may have resorted to importing glaziers, so Bede's claim that glaziers were unavailable locally is not necessarily invalid. At Glastonbury Abbey a craft-working complex of five glass furnaces has been radiocarbon dated to around AD 700, which makes it the earliest solid evidence for glass-working in Anglo-Saxon England.[53]

Aldhelm (d. 709 or 710), abbot of Malmesbury and bishop of Sherborne, wrote a laudatory poem in Latin on a newly built church. It was rectangular, lofty and glowed with gentle light when the sun shone through the glazed windows.[54] One can imagine the impact. This would be a grander interior than any other that Anglo-Saxons knew in their daily lives. Voices magnified by the acoustics would seem to float to heaven. Externally, a lofty stone church would tower over the single-storey cottages huddled around it. [Pl. xxii] The church as the largest and most enduring structure of a settlement evoked the power of faith and its immortality, a rock amid the shifting sands of humanity.

The fine Anglo-Saxon church at Brixworth, Northamptonshire, has been considerably altered over the centuries, but its original plan can be reconstructed. [82; Pl. xxi] It looks back to the early churches of Kent [see 76] in its basilican inspiration. It has the semi-circular apse so favoured by the early Church, but surrounding it, and apparently original, is a ring crypt, which became popular in the 9th century. Excavation in 1982 revealed that the church was built into a ditch containing 8th-century material, which gives the earliest possible date, and experts now consider that it was probably built late in the reign of the powerful King Offa of Mercia (r. 757–96). The scale of this church and European parallels suggest a patron of Offa's standing.[55]

82 *The interior of the Anglo-Saxon church of All Saints, Brixworth, Northamptonshire, looking east to the altar. Its semi-circular arches are built of re-used Roman bricks. Those in the side walls originally divided the nave from the later-removed aisles, in a plan inspired by the typical Roman basilica.*

83 *The Ruthwell Cross was carved in the early 700s, when Ruthwell, now in Scotland, lay within the Anglian kingdom of Northumbria.*

84 *(below) Detail of the Ruthwell Cross, showing Mary Magdalene washing the feet of Christ, as explained by the Latin inscription around the border.*

Where constructing a church was impractical, or the church was too small to contain the whole congregation, people might gather instead beside a stone cross. The famed Ruthwell Cross features large figurative reliefs on its broad faces, surrounded by explanatory inscriptions in Latin. [83, 84] On the narrower sides, runic inscriptions surround the bird and vine tracery, symbolizing Christ as the 'True Vine' (John 15: 1–7). It is a masterpiece of its period. A standing cross might be erected in a churchyard as a grave marker, as we are told was the case for a cross at Worcester. Here Bishop Oswald (d. 992) would preach to the multitudes who could not be accommodated in his cathedral. Carved stone crosses were still being produced in some numbers in the first quarter of the 11th century, but by the time of Edward the Confessor (r. 1042–66) such crosses were seen as antiquated. The cross at Worcester was demolished and its stone re-used in the enlargement of the cathedral. Many Anglo-Saxon sculptures have been discovered re-used as building material.[56]

Some of the finest and best-preserved Anglo-Saxon sculptures are in the priory church of St Mary and St Hardulph, Breedon-on-the-Hill, Leicestershire, in the heart of Mercia, dating from the 8th and 10th centuries. [85; Pl. xxiv] They are believed to have been removed from a long-since-vanished Anglo-Saxon church and incorporated into a new complex of religious buildings in the 13th century. Breedon was founded as a colony from the monastery of Medeshamstede (Peterborough).[57] [see 74]

85 A section of the decorative vine scroll frieze behind the high altar at Breedon-on-the-Hill in Leicestershire, which contains some of the finest and best-preserved Anglo-Saxon sculptures.

Learning

Christianity brought literacy, learning and Latin, the language of the Church. The monasteries developed scriptoria, where books were laboriously copied by hand and often illuminated with decorated initial letters [86, 87; Plate xviii] or full-page depictions related to the text. [Pl. xvii] They would be beautifully bound in decorated leather. The unique pocket gospel found in the tomb of St Cuthbert when his remains were translated to Durham in 1104 retains its original red goatskin binding, with an appealing combination of interlace and plant scroll decoration.[58] [88]

Scribes could use a stylus to scratch letters on a wax tablet for everyday purposes, but books were written on vellum, which was animal skin which had been soaked, stretched and scraped clean. One of the most valuable books held by York Minster is the York Gospels. [Pl. xvii] It is thought to have been written around the turn of the first millennium in the scriptorium of St Augustine's monastery, Canterbury, and then brought to York by Archbishop Wulfstan in around 1020. Now DNA analysis has established that it was written on expensive parchment made of calf skin.[59] It was a few surviving bristles that revealed that the same is true of the famous Lindisfarne Gospels, one of the most magnificent manuscripts of the time in all of Europe. [86, 87, 89]

86, 87 (opposite) *The Lindisfarne Gospels, created at Lindisfarne Abbey c. 700, are seen as the pinnacle of Anglo-Saxon art. The initial letter M of Marcus in St Mark's Gospel is beautifully illuminated (above). Under the original Latin script is the translation into Old English added in the 10th century. The opening words of the Gospel of St Luke become a delight to the eye with a profusion of decoration (below). The initial letter dominates the page and becomes part of the frame for the rest of the text.*

88 (left) *St Cuthbert's Gospel of St John was written in the joint monastery of Monkwearmouth and Jarrow and placed in the tomb of St Cuthbert, bishop of Lindisfarne, in the early 8th century. It is the earliest intact European book.*

89 *Each Gospel in the Lindisfarne Gospels is preceded by a 'carpet' page – a vibrant weaving together of geometric and interlaced elements. All have a complex cross at the heart of the design, while at the margins the natural world breaks out of the frame into bird or animal heads. This one introduces the Gospel of St Mark.*

xvii Luke the Evangelist depicted in the York Gospels, thought to have been created in Canterbury *c.* 1000 and taken to York by Archbishop Wulfstan.

BEATVS VIR QVINON ABIIT IN CON SILIOIMPIORVM

i A richly decorated initial letter B from the Ramsey Psalter, probably made for
Oswald, founder of Ramsey Abbey in 969, as part of the Benedictine reform. The he
a fox joins the two curves of the letter and spews out foliage which curls within th
er, while knotwork embellishes the head and base of the vertical stroke.

xix Scenes from the Passion depicted in the St Augustine Gospels made in Italy in the 6th century and possibly among the books sent to England with the group including Mellitus and Paulinus. It was in the library of St Augustine's, Canterbury, until the dissolution of the monasteries.

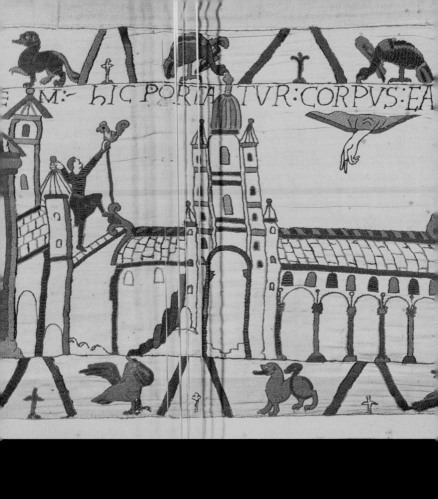

M:- hIC PORTATUR:CORPVS·EA

xx This scene from the Bayeux Tapestry depicts the solemn funeral of Edward the Confessor on 6 January 1066. He was buried in the church of Westminster Abbey, the rebuilding of which on a magnificent scale he had ordered. It had been consecrated just a few days earlier. On the left we see a workman putting the finishing touch to it: adding a weather vane.

xxi Early Anglo-Saxon churches could re-use Roman materials from dilapidated buildings. At All Saints, Brixworth, Northamptonshire, thin Roman bricks are arranged in a double row to strengthen the arch above the door.

xxii A stone tower to house bells was not a feature of the earliest English churches, but began to appear in the Late Saxon period. No two early towers were alike. The magnificent 11th-century tower of St Mary, Sompting, West Sussex, has an oak-shingle helm roof inspired by Rhenish architecture.

xxiii Anglo-Saxon coloured glass discovered in excavations has been placed in this tiny original window, just 18 cm (7 inches) in diameter, in St Paul's church, Jarrow.

xxiv Reproduction of the carved angel at Breedon-on-the-Hill, Leicestershire, one of the finest surviving Saxon figure sculptures. One hand holds a cross-headed staff, while the other is raised, with the third finger and thumb touching in a Byzantine-style blessing.

The Lindisfarne Gospels were made by Eadfrith, bishop of Lindisfarne from 698 to 721. They were written in Latin, but around 970, the monk Aldred added an Anglo-Saxon translation beneath the original Latin [see 86]. This is the oldest surviving version of the gospels in any form of English.[60] It is estimated that approximately 130 calf skins would have been needed for this book.

The monasteries had their own schools and some became centres of learning. Bede tells us of the large quantity of books that Benedict Biscop brought from Rome for his double monastery of Monkwearmouth and Jarrow.[61] And Bede advised his former pupil, Archbishop Ecgbert of York (d. 766), not to neglect the duty of teaching.[62] He did not. Under Ecgbert and his successor Ælberht, a keen collector of books, the school at York became a noted hub of intellectual activity. Indeed, York seems to have been the first place in Europe to create a cathedral school of this character.[63] Its most famous student was Alcuin of York (d. 804), whose reputation for learning led to an invitation, when he was approaching fifty, to join the court of Charlemagne. There he was regarded as the greatest scholar of his day, and taught Charlemagne rhetoric, dialectics and astronomy.[64]

What books were available? Apart from the Bible itself, Alcuin was much influenced by the works of Bede, whom he took as a model of scholarship. Both men were masters of lucid Latin prose and poetry.[65] Bede himself urged Ecgbert to read the works of Gregory the Great,[66] which had a strong impact on the English Church. In a long poem in praise of York, Alcuin provided a partial list of the books there. They included the works of the Church Fathers, such as Augustine of Hippo and Jerome. The late Latin poetry of the Christian Church was well represented, but also Virgil. *The Consolation of Philosophy*, written in AD 524–25 by Anicius Manlius Severinus Boethius, a Roman senator, was present at York. While not specifically Christian, it was so compatible with Christianity that it was among the works translated into English by Alfred (see p. 25). Much of the literature of the ancient Greeks and Romans was shunned in Bede's day as pagan, unless it came through the filter of a Christian author, such as Isidore of Seville. Yet the library at York possessed work by Aristotle, and Alcuin was familiar with Pliny. So great was Alcuin's regard for the knowledge of the ancient Greeks that in a letter to Charlemagne in 799 he dared to hope that Athens was being reborn in Francia.[67]

Monastic reform

Long after Bede had complained of abuses of the monastic system, Dunstan, as archbishop of Canterbury 960–88, attempted the reform of the English Church. He had the support of Æthelwold, bishop of Winchester, who compiled the *Regularis concordia*, which stipulated monastic observance for reformed English Benedictine houses. Another supporter was Oswald, whom Dunstan consecrated bishop of Worcester in 961 and promoted to the see of York in 972. The most powerful friend to Dunstan was Edgar, king of England 959–75. Dunstan enforced monastic celibacy and the rule of St Benedict where he could. In his day this committed reformer was seen as a man of exceptional sanctity; after his death he was rapidly raised to the ranks of the saints.[68]

Overview

- Christianity survived among Britons from the Roman period, but Christian Britons played a minor part in the conversion of the Anglo-Saxons.

- St Augustine was sent by Pope Gregory from Rome with a mission to convert the Anglo-Saxons.

- St Columba was invited to settle on Iona among the Irish of Argyll. Oswald of Northumbria was baptized by this Irish Church and invited members of it to Northumbria. He influenced the conversion of other kings.

- The process of Anglo-Saxon conversion depended heavily on the baptism of kings, who would then encourage conversion among their subjects.

- The patchwork of conflicting influences from Rome and Ireland was removed by the Synod of Whitby in 664, in which Oswald declared in favour of Rome.

- As conversion spread across the country, burial customs gradually changed to an east–west alignment without grave goods.

- The institution of slavery was largely unaffected by the conversion, though the Church encouraged manumission and frowned on the sale of English people abroad.

- Warriors could put themselves under the protection of the Christian God by wearing items with a Christian dedication or having a processional cross carried into battle.

- Christianity brought with it a revival of building in stone for important churches and monasteries. Stone carving developed within such buildings and on standing crosses.

- Some monasteries and cathedrals became seats of learning.

- Dunstan, archbishop of Canterbury, reformed the monasteries.

CHAPTER NINE

Forging a Nation

Zadok the Priest, and Nathan the Prophet anointed Solomon
King. And all the people rejoiced, and said: God save the King!
Long live the King!

The concept of kings

The words above, based on the Bible passage 1 Kings 1:38–40, have been
used in every English, and later British, coronation since that of King Edgar
at Bath Abbey in 973, the first coronation of a king of England. The coronation service devised for Edgar by Archbishop Dunstan embodies the
concept of a king as chosen by God. Such a notion first appeared in England
when the mighty Offa of Mercia had his son Ecgfrith anointed as co-ruler in
787.[1] In this, it seems that he was following in the footsteps of monarchs
of the Franks and their heirs who sought papal anointing from the 750s.[2]

How were Anglo-Saxon kings chosen in the world of mortals? By the
time that literacy shines a light on the process, it appears that the king's
council, known as the *witan* (literally 'wise men'), had a key role. [90] This
was an elite gathering. It would include members of the royal house, archbishops and bishops, prominent abbots and laymen with administrative
or military roles. They needed to approve a new king, and could depose
one who proved unsatisfactory.[3] Two themes appear: pedigree and feats of
arms. At the very beginning of *Beowulf* we have the story of Scyld (p. 13), who
had arrived alone and destitute, but became a great king by his prowess in
arms.[4] He did not owe his throne to noble birth, though we see that pedigree becomes important elsewhere in the poem. Likewise, Tacitus tells
us that the Germani chose their leaders for their valour. Yet the Germanic
word *kuning* (*cyning* in Old English) seems to carry with it a connotation of
kindred (p. 101). There is no doubt that Anglo-Saxon kings were expected to
lead their armies: many of them died on the battlefield. So an adult warrior
was required. Thus kingdoms could pass from brother to brother, or cousin
to cousin, when more practical, rather than father to son. That does not

90 *An Anglo-Saxon king with his* witan *(council) used to illustrate a story from Genesis in an 11th-century manuscript.*

mean that a man of another kindred could not seize a throne by force. It happened. Nonetheless, pedigrees for Anglo-Saxon kings were carefully constructed and recorded in the *Anglo-Saxon Chronicle* and elsewhere. The pedigree of Penda of Mercia claims descent, real or imagined, from Offa, king of Angeln, and from him to Woden.[5]

Almost all of the surviving Anglo-Saxon royal genealogies claim descent from Woden, which may seem strange, since they were recorded in the Christian era. But Snorri Sturluson (see p. 47) was not the first to realize that a clash with Christianity could be removed by treating Odin/Woden as an historical figure. A Latin version of the *Anglo-Saxon Chronicle* was written in around 975 by Æthelweard, a noble of Wessex. He commented on the genealogy of the kings of Kent, which starts with Woden, 'who also was king of a multitude of barbarians. For the unbelievers of the North are oppressed by such delusion that they worship him as a god even to this day, namely the Danes, the Northmen and the Suevi.'[6] Woden embodied the attributes of a great leader and the inclusion of Woden in an Anglo-Saxon family tree was restricted to royalty.[7]

Bede believed that seven kings were also overlords over all the kingdoms south of the Humber.[8] The *Anglo-Saxon Chronicle* added Ecgberht of Wessex as the eighth in 829, on his conquest of Mercia and 'all that was south of the Humber', quoting Bede for the previous seven. In all but one of the surviving manuscripts, the chronicler used the term *Brytenwalda* ('wide ruler') to describe this overlordship. The other version gives *Bretwalda*. As we see from the fact that Ecgberht gained this hegemony by conquest, it was not an hereditary position. Bede's list begins with Ælle of the South Saxons, who supposedly arrived on the southern shore near Selsey in 477, with his three sons in three ships, and fought the Britons there to gain a land for his people.[9] This reads like an attempt in a literate age to make sense of a poetic oral history preserved among the South Saxons, which may have exaggerated the power of an early leader of their people. Bede would have been on stronger ground with rulers closer to his own time. To the extent that we can place any faith in his list, it includes kings of different kingdoms, reinforcing the evidence that hegemony shifted from kingdom to kingdom as military power waxed and waned. We need not imagine a permanent office with fixed duties and powers, but a situation in which a particularly strong ruler could command tribute from other kingdoms would make sense of the Tribal Hidage.

Mighty men and the landscape

The mysterious document known as the Tribal Hidage may have been a 7th-century tribute list in origin, assessing how much tribute was expected by an over-king. Mercia was clearly already large at that time, for its core was assessed at 30,000 hides, the same as East Anglia. Only Wessex was larger, assessed at 100,000 hides. (Northumbria is missing from the list.)[10] A few of the minor peoples named appear on the map here illustrating the expansion of Mercia. [see 74] The names of some endured. The Pecsæte and Wrocensæte are mentioned in charters of 963.[11] The Magonsæte, apparently the equivalent of the Westerna in the Tribal Hidage, are recorded in a charter of 958,[12] and as late as 1016 in the *Anglo-Saxon Chronicle*. By these late dates they were not independent polities. The last ruler of the Magonsæte had ceased to rule by 740 and his place seems to have been taken by an ealdorman.[13] Similarly, a charter of Offa in 778 refers to his under-king Aldred, *dux* of his people, the Hwicce.[14] The title 'ealdorman' seems to be the Old English equivalent of the Latin *dux* (duke). With the appearance of these magnates, the *thegns* were no longer the top rank of the nobility. As major kingdoms were divided into shires, each shire was led by an ealdorman. This process was under way in Wessex by the time of Ine (r. 688–726), for a penalty included in his laws is that an erring ealdorman shall forfeit his shire.[15] Thus independent peoples or kingdoms were absorbed by neighbouring kingdoms. So by around AD 800 there were three great powers: Northumbria, Mercia and Wessex, the greatest of which was Mercia.

A king and his court were supported by renders in kind, known as the *feorm*. The supplies would be delivered to royal sites, which the king and his entourage would visit in a circuit. The laws of Ine lay down what was to be delivered from every 10 hides.[16] The king, therefore, had a vested interest in the productivity of land within his kingdom. So did the recipients of royal land grants, which could include the right to receive the *feorm*.[17] Most of the earliest are grants to the Church, but kings could and did reward their chief retainers with lands.

Britain, warmed by the North Atlantic Current, has a climate milder than one might expect from its latitude, and generally escapes the harsh winters of a continental climate. The lands of lowland Britain had a potential that was to be more fully realized under the rise of kingdoms and land-rich churchmen, who had the power and incentive to organize and innovate. It would take a powerful landlord to impose the kind of upheaval that created, from a landscape of scattered farms and hamlets, the English village, surrounded by its open fields. This more efficient land-use could yield a greater surplus, attractive to kings, magnates and abbots, who needed to support their households, building projects and nascent towns. Indeed, the intensification of agriculture was a prerequisite of early state formation. Not only in England, but in the Germanic-speaking world as a whole, greater planning of settlements appears from the 8th century onwards.[18]

In 1901 historian Peter Ditchfield published a plan of what he saw as the typical layout of an English medieval village and its lands. [91] The arable land was divided into two open fields, each divided into strips that were allocated to individual tenant farmers living in the village. (Three-field systems are also known.) Villagers would be able to graze their cows or sheep in the common pasture. Ditchfield saw each villager having in addition a separate 'close' or enclosed field near the village. That is one way of expressing a pattern in which each villager had a plot of land, which in early layouts could surround the house, so that village houses were more spaced out.[19] Ditchfield portrays the close relationship of manor house and church.

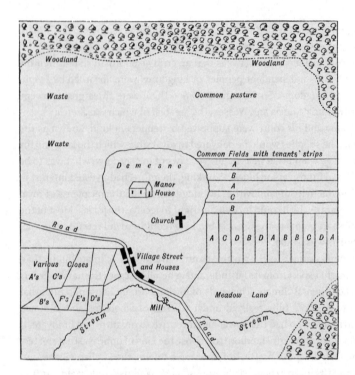

91 A diagram of a typical layout of a medieval English manor, with manor house, church and village, surrounded by open fields divided into strips, and pasture, meadows and woodland used in common, drawn by Peter Ditchfield in 1901. The practice of enclosing land previously in open fields began in the later Middle Ages and continued for centuries, almost wiping out this farming system in England.

Many a parish church owes its origin to a manorial lord's desire for a chapel for his own household and tenants, conveniently close to his own house.[20] The demesne land that surrounded the manor house was the farm for the direct support of the manorial lord's household.

Noting that most English place-names are derived from Old English, Ditchfield assumed that the pattern of nucleated village and land held in common by the villagers was established by the earliest Anglo-Saxon arrivals.[21] In this he was following the scholar Frederick William Maitland, who wrote in 1897, 'we are compelled to say that our true villages, the nucleated villages with large open fields, are not Celtic, are not Roman, but are very purely and typically German'.[22] Howard Gray in 1915 recognized that the classic open field systems were not ubiquitous throughout England, but were found in the central areas in a rough triangle from mid-Dorset to Sussex to Durham. He, too, felt that what he called the 'Midland System' had been imported fully formed from the Anglo-Saxon homelands.[23]

In a radical rethinking of the topic, Joan Thirsk proposed in 1964 that the fully functioning open field system only appeared after the Norman conquest.[24] This idea proved highly influential and generated lively debate over the following decades. Evidence against so late a date came from both documents and archaeology. In fact, Gray had already pointed out the many Anglo-Saxon land grants referring to x acres in one field and y acres in another field, indicating open field systems.[25] The laws of Ine provide for redress where some have fenced their portion of a common meadow or other partible land and others have not, and cattle get in and eat their common crops or grass.[26] Iron Acton in Gloucestershire was divided into two manors before 1066. The division runs through the village beside the church, indicating that the village was laid out before the Norman conquest.[27] Most convincingly, archaeologists had found beneath early Norman monuments evidence for the ridge and furrow ploughing that characterized open field agriculture.

Since the 1970s enough Anglo-Saxon settlements have been excavated for patterns to emerge. It is now clear that the Midland System was not imported fully formed in the 5th century. Early Anglo-Saxon houses tend to be dispersed and groupings of them lack signs of planning. They range from single farmsteads to conglomerations such as West Heslerton in Yorkshire, and Mucking in Essex, where at times perhaps 100 individuals lived. Most early settlements, though, would accommodate between thirty and fifty people. Although certain individuals were buried with greater wealth than others, there is little sign of social ranking in house size. Then in the Middle Anglo-Saxon period (c. 650–c. 850) rectilinear settlements appeared, with greater evidence of planning, foreshadowing the medieval village. At the same time there was an increased emphasis on arable farming. Bread wheat predominated, but a wider range of crops appeared. Heavier soils were being brought into cultivation. Corn dryers and watermills appeared, pointing to an increase in the scale of agricultural operations.[28]

An intensive study of the parish of Shapwick in Somerset was begun in 1989 by archaeologists Mick Aston and Chris Gerrard to examine the chronology of the village, which has a ladder pattern, with the church half-way up the ladder. One crucial reason for selecting Shapwick was that a survey of the parish in 1515 included furlong names (within the two open fields) of Anglo-Saxon habitative form, for example Sladwick, suggesting settlements earlier than the village with its open fields. The furlong-name 'Oldechurch' indicated that an early church had lain outside the village. It was probably founded during the first half of the 8th century, when the estate was granted to Glastonbury Abbey. Presumably the village did not exist at the time. Field-walking and test-pitting revealed a lack of early Anglo-Saxon material in the village. By contrast, 10th- and 11th-century pottery was found throughout the village plan. So the evidence favours a date for the laying out of the village after the 8th century and by the 10th. Shapwick fits a pattern of planned villages on the pre-conquest estates of Glastonbury Abbey. Might the reorganization of the abbey estates be the work of the energetic St Dunstan (909–988), when he was abbot of Glastonbury? He established the rule of St Benedict at Glastonbury in around 946.[29]

Key innovations boosted the increase in yields that would make such reorganization worthwhile. First, the mouldboard plough enabled farmers to cultivate heavier, more fertile soils. [92] A simple type of plough, the ard, had been in use since prehistory. It is best suited to loamy or sandy soils. So the early Anglo-Saxon preference for lighter soils suggests the use of the ard initially. The addition of a mouldboard turns the topsoil over, bringing

92 *Ploughing with oxen, with the sower following behind, from January in* The Anglo-Saxon Calendar *(1025–50). A team of oxen pulling a mouldboard plough could bring heavier but more fertile soils into cultivation.*

93 *Silver penny of King Offa of Mercia, depicting the king.*

nutrients to the surface. A wheel or wheels could be added to support the heavier frame. Such a plough, together with a team of oxen to draw it, was a major investment, but could be shared between several farmers in the open field system. Secondly, crop rotation, for example planting with winter wheat followed by spring barley, kept fields in permanent cultivation, with the aid of intensive manuring and short fallow periods every third year or so, when the field could be used for grazing.[30]

The rise of mighty men triggered other changes in the landscape. The formidable Offa, king of Mercia from 757 to 796, [93] took direct control of the Hwicce and Middle Angles. His predecessor, Æthelbald, had a claim over London and the lands of the Middle Saxons (Middlesex) which passed to Offa, but Offa himself took Sussex and Kent by conquest, and expanded Mercian authority over the East Angles.[31] By the end of his reign he controlled a huge swathe of England. Offa's life and deeds are poorly documented, but in recent decades archaeological evidence has helped to flesh out his achievements. He was determined to guard his borders. He built the massive Offa's Dyke for protection against the Welsh. [94] That staggering feat illustrates the workforce at his command. During decades in which archaeologists were uneasy with the concept of war and defence, there was a reluctance to see such great earthworks as defensive. It was argued that they simply marked boundaries. Certainly a gigantic bank and ditch will become a practical boundary, but such huge effort speaks of a greater need. The border was not impermeable. Rather, it controlled the passage of people, funnelling them towards specific places such as Chepstow, whose name, from Old English *cēap* (meaning 'purchase', 'sale', 'bargain', 'market') reveals that it was a trading centre.[32]

Elsewhere, Offa controlled a far more important market. The walled Roman city of Londinium had long been deserted, apart from the building there of St Paul's, but an Anglo-Saxon trading town called Lundenwic had been established to the west. Excavations have discovered a settlement dated from the 7th to the early 9th century along the north side of what is

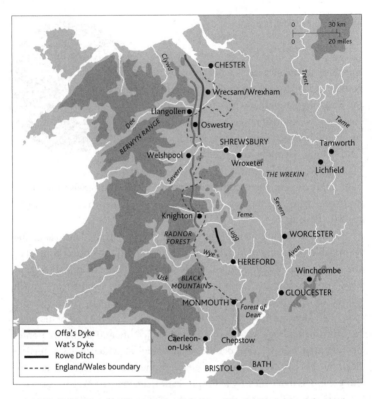

94 *The relationship between the present border between Wales and England and the Mercian frontier earthworks known as Offa's Dyke.*

now the Strand, between Trafalgar Square and Covent Garden. To the south of the Strand are traces of an embankment shored up with timber.[33] One of the sources of income from Lundenwic, harbour fees, is revealed by charters. For example, in 733 Æthelbald of Mercia granted to Mildrith, abbess of Minster-in-Thanet, remission of the toll due on a ship in the harbour of London.[34] Bede described London as an emporium for many nations, who came to it by land and sea.[35] The name Aldwych (old *wic*) in London preserves its memory.

In Old English *wic* could mean anything from a single dwelling to a village, but Lundenwic is not the only case where it referred to a port. At Eoforwic (York) a trading centre dating to the same period as Lundenwic grew up outside the Roman walls of Eboracum. Remains of it have been found at Fishergate, on the bank of the River Foss as it joins the River Ouse. Seagoing vessels could reach York via the Ouse. They brought items from the continent, such as Rhenish glass, as well as goods from closer to home. By the end of the 8th century, when Alcuin of York wrote his poem in praise of his home city, he used the term *emporium*, as Bede had of London. He even mentions a colony of Frisian traders there.[36]

Other examples of port markets developing at around the same time are Gipeswic (Ipswich) and Hamwic (Southampton). It has been assumed that both were founded by kings. Yet there is no particular evidence of this at Ipswich. Indeed, it is argued that the impetus could have come from foreign traders.[37] At Hamwic a rich Anglo-Saxon cemetery was probably in use by Jutes earlier than the annexation of the area by the West Saxons.[38] [95] Yet, if Hamwic was not actually founded by a West Saxon king, it soon came under royal control. It was partnered in what is now Southampton with the royal estate of Hamtun.[39]

Fordwich, now a tiny town on the River Stour in Kent, was once the main port for Canterbury. It began life as part of the royal estate of nearby Sturry and so here we can presume the direct involvement of the kings of Kent in its development.[40] It is first mentioned in AD 675.[41] Then in 763 or 764 the king of Kent granted to Sigeburga, abbess of St Peter's Minster, Thanet, the remission of toll due on two ships at Fordwich and on a third at Fordwich and Sarre.[42] The Isle of Thanet had its own trading site at Sarre. A large Anglo-Saxon burial ground in use there in the 6th and 7th centuries

95 *A gold pendant with inlaid garnets found in an exceptionally rich Anglo-Saxon cemetery at Southampton, which dates back to the late 7th century.*

96 *An example of the gold* thrysma *or shilling issued by Eadbald of Kent in 620–25, with his head on one side and his name on the other.*

yielded fascinating grave goods. One male was interred with a set of balances, which we can imagine in use on a market stall. There were imported luxury goods, too.[43]

A market economy thrives on coinage. The law code of Æthelberht, issued around AD 600, calculated compensation in shillings.[44] The earliest Anglo-Saxon coins, presumably the shillings, were produced around that time, but sustained production began in the 630s. These were small, gold coins, modelled on Merovingian types. [96] The gold coins were superseded by the silver penny in around 675. The new, thin, Carolingian-style penny introduced by Offa in around 760 began the custom of coins carrying the names of both the ruler and the moneyer issuing them.[45] [see 93] Concentrations of Middle Anglo-Saxon coins found at specific spots in the rural countryside may mark the locations of smaller markets and fairs.[46]

Town creation by Alfred the Great (r. 871–99) has never been forgotten, whereas that by Offa fell into obscurity and needed archaeologists to uncover. He created proto-towns at Hereford, Worcester and other riverine sites. The common features of these settlements were a fortified enclosure and a bridge or ford.[47] It is significant that the first mention in England of the public duty of defending fortresses and maintaining bridges comes in Mercian charters. It occurs first in 749, along with the older duty of military service at need. So it seems that Offa's predecessor had seen the value of defended crossings even before the Viking incursions began. Offa spread it into Kent in 792, specifically to guard against 'seaborne pagans with migrating fleets'.[48] Viking ships were on the prowl.

The Mercian hegemony collapsed in the 820s after the death of Coenwulf I, king of Mercia 796–821. The West Saxons under Ecgberht (d. 839) rose to the fore. They took control of the southeastern provinces after a battle in 825 in which they defeated Mercia. East Anglia regained its independence in the same year. Indeed Ecgberht was recognized as overlord of England after defeats of Mercia and Northumbria in 829.[49]

Alfred and the Viking menace

In 793 the monastery founded by St Aidan on the tiny island of Lindisfarne was sacked by 'the heathen'.[50] Alcuin of York was aghast. His reaction echoes that of Gildas, who was convinced that the backsliding kings of the Britons had brought down the wrath of God in the form of the Saxons. Now pagans were attacking Christians once more. Alcuin chastised Æthelred, king of Northumbria, and his court for wallowing in luxury while the poor starved. He had a point. Loyalty can wear thin in those circumstances. But for the devout Alcuin, Christianity itself should be a shield: 'There is no better defence of a country than the equity and piety of princes and the prayers of the servants of God.'[51]

The word Viking spread terror far and wide. Peaceful monks and farmers learned to fear the sail on the horizon that presaged a lightning attack by massive, axe-wielding pirates of the north. Though there was much more to the Viking Age than piracy, it will be forever defined by wanderlust and warriors. *Viking* in Old Norse meant sea-warriors, as far as we can tell.[52] Young Scandinavian men went a-viking in the invitingly warm summers around AD 800, in search of plunder and adventure. The paganism of the Vikings set them apart from the rest of the Germanic-speaking world, by then absorbed into Christendom.[53]

In 865, says the *Anglo-Saxon Chronicle*, 'a great raiding army came to the land of the English and took winter quarters in East Anglia'. Æthelweard's Latin translation names their leader as Ívarr. Ívarr and his brothers Óláfr, Ásl and Halfdan campaigned fiercely on both sides of the Irish Sea. Their impact was so great that when Ívarr died in 873, the *Annals of Ulster* described him as king of all the Northmen in Ireland and Britain. Where had they come from? The dynasty of Ívarr introduced a new Viking modus operandi to the British Isles. Instead of the hit-and-run raid, they exacted tribute. Furthermore, the attacks were orchestrated by a leadership of royal descent. Since Norway had no royalty when Ívarr and his family appeared, this points to the Danes. Ívarr and his brothers were probably the sons of Godfrid, son of Harald Klak, briefly king of Denmark 812–14 (as I argue elsewhere). Late attempts to weave Óláfr and Ívarr into the royal line of Norway or the saga of Ragnarr Loðbrók, legendary king of Denmark, are unconvincing.[54]

King Edmund of East Anglia accommodated Ívarr's army in 865 and provided them with horses, no doubt to encourage them to move on. So they did, initially. The army took York the following year. The Northumbrians were in disarray at the time, in the grip of a power struggle fomented by the devil, says the pious churchman Asser (d. *c.* 909). They had expelled their 'rightful' king, Osberht, and put in his place Ælle, who was not of the royal line. Faced with the Vikings, the two kings finally joined forces and assembled an army to descend upon York. They were cut to pieces within its walls. Virtually the entire Northumbrian force was annihilated there, including the two kings. The remnant who escaped made peace with the Vikings.[55] This was the turn of the tide, when Scandinavian raiding gave way to settlement in England. The Anglo-Saxon Eoforwic became the bustling Viking town of Jorvik, the life of which has been marvellously uncovered by excavation. Waterlogged soils beneath Coppergate preserved the remains of buildings as well as cloth, leather shoes and other items that usually disintegrate in the soil.

In 867, however, Ívarr's army was still on the move. They established their winter quarters at Nottingham in Mercia. Burgred, king of Mercia, called upon his brother-in-law Æthelred, king of the West Saxons, for help

97 *The family tree of Alfred the Great.*

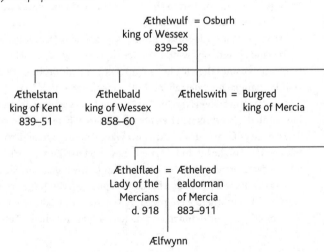

Æthelwulf = Osburh
king of Wessex
839–58

Æthelstan
king of Kent
839–51

Æthelbald
king of Wessex
858–60

Æthelswith = Burgred
king of Mercia

Æthelflæd = Æthelred
Lady of the | ealdorman
Mercians | of Mercia
d. 918 | 883–911

Ælfwynn

98 *The ring of Queen Æthelswith of Mercia, wife of King Burgred and daughter of Æthelwulf of Wessex. On the bezel is the Agnus Dei (Lamb of God). It is inscribed with her name on the inside.*

in overcoming the menace. [98] Æthelred was the youngest but one of four brothers who became kings of Wessex in turn after the death of their father Æthelwulf. Æthelwulf had successfully fought off a large Viking raiding army in Surrey in 851. His son Æthelberht had barely taken the throne of Wessex when Vikings ravaged his capital, Winchester. As they were returning to their ships with immense booty, the ealdormen of Hampshire and Berkshire fell upon them with their men and cut them down, putting the remnant to flight. But Æthelred and his brother Alfred were powerless in 867 against the great army of Ívarr. The Danes had ensconced themselves at Nottingham within defences which could not be breached.[56] A rampart and massive ditch have been discovered by archaeologists, but it is unclear whether they were thrown up swiftly by the Danes or were simply taken over by them.[57] Either way, the value of defences must have made an impression on the young Alfred, who went on to make good use of them.

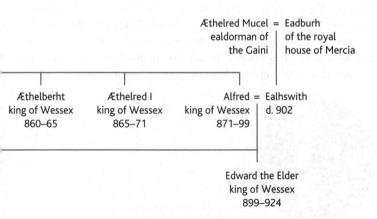

		Æthelred Mucel	=	Eadburh
		ealdorman of		of the royal
		the Gaini		house of Mercia

Æthelberht	Æthelred I	Alfred = Ealhswith
king of Wessex	king of Wessex	king of Wessex	d. 902
860–65	865–71	871–99

Edward the Elder
king of Wessex
899–924

In the following year Alfred gained a link to the royal family of Mercia by his marriage to Ealhswith, daughter of Æthelred Mucel, ealdorman within Mercia, and his wife Eadburh, a member of the Mercian royal family.[58] Thus Alfred's children would have some claim to Mercia in times to come, as we shall see.

The Viking army returned to York, but subjugated East Anglia in 870, killing King Edmund, later venerated as a saint. Next they threatened Wessex again in 871, supported by reinforcements from overseas. After fighting several battles against them, Æthelred died. Alfred, the youngest brother, was left to take up the crown of Wessex and the fight for its survival. [99] Within a month he found himself and his men hopelessly outnumbered fighting the whole Viking army at Wilton. It seems that in the end he paid them to go away. Naturally they returned. If ruthless men find that they can gain money by menaces, why stop? The men of Kent had purchased peace in 865. The Mercians appear to have done the same in 872, but it availed them nothing. Burgred of Mercia was forced out of his kingdom in 874 and joined the Anglo-Saxon community in Rome. The Vikings reduced Mercia to a satellite kingdom with a puppet king.

The Danes rampaged around Wessex until Alfred was famously forced to flee to the marshes of Somerset with a small band of his supporters. There at Athelney he made his first fortress, from which he could sally forth to attack the foe. He was probably already familiar with the site, whose name at the time was *Æthelinga eigge*, meaning 'island of the princes'. Since this is an Old English name, it must date after the West Saxon conquest of Somerset. St Æthelwine, a brother of Cenwealh, king of the West Saxons from 642 to 672, chose to become a hermit on the island. Yet Athelney was a high-status site before then, as revealed by a Roman bronze mask and late 6th-century pottery imported from the eastern Mediterranean. It already

99 A silver penny of Alfred the Great, showing his head and name.

had both man-made and natural defences. Asser, who wrote a *Life of Alfred*, describes Athelney as surrounded by an impassible morass of marsh and water on every side. The only access was by punts and a causeway connecting Alfred's fort at Athelney with one he built nearby at Lyng. It was the perfect guerrilla base for the beleaguered king. From this bolt-hole, Alfred succeeded in rallying the men of Wessex and defeated the Viking army at Edington in Wiltshire in 878. This proved to be a pivotal point in the history of England. Guthrum, leader of the Danes, even accepted baptism at the hands of Alfred. The Danish army retreated to settle in East Anglia.[59] Meanwhile, Halfdan had become the first Scandinavian king of York, but died fighting in Ireland in 877.[60]

In 886 Alfred occupied Lundenburh, the old walled Roman city of London. Soon afterwards a treaty was drawn up between Alfred and Guthrum, dividing England into an English south and west and a Danish north and east, the Danelaw, where Scandinavian settlement is recorded in many place-names ending in -by or -thorpe.[61] Cornwall, long a Brittonic enclave, had lost its last king in 875, and now increasingly came under the control of Wessex.[62]

Alfred the Great built defensive *burhs* (fortified places) around Wessex in his successful fight back against the Danes. His hand also spread over Mercia, but at one remove. A certain Æthelred sought the backing of Wessex to free Mercia from Danish shackles. Alfred's price was dominance. Mercia and Wessex were to be welded into one kingdom. Alfred was described in charters of the late 880s and early 890s either as 'king of the Angles and Saxons' or by composite forms such as *Angulsaxonum rex*, which we could translate as 'king of the Anglo-Saxons'.[63] Æthelred married Alfred's daughter Æthelflæd, and they ruled Mercia as the Lord and Lady of the Mercians. Æthelred and Æthelflæd too created *burhs*. [100]

Alfred may have regarded London as part of Mercia, for in 886 he entrusted the walled city to Ealdorman Æthelred.[64] Although some *burhs* were no more than forts, others were laid out as towns. A charter of Worcester demonstrates their twin purposes. Æthelred and Æthelflæd stated that, having ordered the borough at Worcester to be built for the protection of the people, they now granted to the church of St Peter half their rights in the market and borough, including the tax levied for repair of the borough wall.[65] A successful market town would generate revenue and pay for its own defence. Some sites, such as Bath and Winchester,

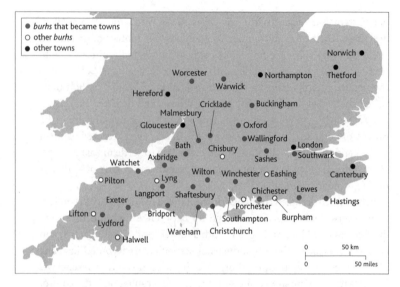

100 *The fortified sites created by Alfred, Æthelred and Æthelflaed, as listed in the early 10th-century 'Burghal Hidage'. This is by no means the total tally of Anglo-Saxon towns.*

were selected because they already had Roman city walls, which could be repaired or rebuilt on Roman foundations. Elsewhere Alfred generally built in earth and timber for rapid security, but stone walls could follow.[66] A document composed in the early 10th century has been given the name the 'Burghal Hidage'. It survives in seven medieval and early modern versions which together list thirty-three places. The list is primarily that of Alfred's fortresses, but includes several in Mercia.[67] [100]

With the expansion of market towns beyond the early emporia came a new class of people, the burgesses, and greater encouragement to specialize in a particular craft, the products of which could be sold in the market. Under Alfred's son Edward the Elder, mints were confined to 'ports', which were market towns, both coastal and inland. Edward ordered that all buying and selling should be done in a port, with a portreeve as witness,[68] partly to hinder the sale of stolen property. (The portreeve was the royal official in charge of a market town.) Anglo-Saxon society was becoming more urban and more complex, with a greater variety of niches into which an individual might hope to fit.

101 Æthelflæd 'the wise' from a 13th-century genealogical chronicle in Anglo-Norman French.

The unification of England

Edward the Elder took the throne of Wessex on the death of his father in 899 and continued the battle against the Danes, working with his sister and brother-in-law in Mercia. After the death of Æthelred in 911, Edward took London and Oxford into his own hands, but left his sister Æthelflæd in charge of Mercia. She continued to fortify places, creating strongholds at Tamworth and Stafford in 913. She also pushed into the Danelaw, taking Derby in 917 and Leicester in 918, the year in which she died. She enjoyed considerable posthumous acclaim. She was described by a Norman historian as 'so powerful that in praise and exaltation of her wonderful gifts, some call her not only lady, or queen, but even king'. A later chronicle calls her the wisest of secular women. [101] The Mercians accepted her daughter Ælfwynn as her successor, but Edward frustrated this plan six months later by taking Ælfwynn into Wessex, and seizing control of Mercia himself. Edward then led his armies deeper into the Danelaw. He conquered East Anglia and took the submission of the Northumbrians, Scots and Strathclyde Britons in 923, the year before his death. In theory he had united England.[69]

In reality Sigtryggr, grandson of Ívarr, appeared on the scene. Known to the English as Sihtric, he had left his kingdom of Dublin to claim the crown of York. One of his first acts on English soil was an attack on Davenport in Cheshire. He showed no sign of bowing the knee to Edward, and minted his own coins, including some in Lincoln, which suggests that he controlled not only Northumbria, but some land south of the Humber. Edward's son Æthelstan took a diplomatic approach to Sigtryggr. They met at Tamworth in 925 and Æthelstan gave his sister to Sigtryggr. It was a short marriage, for Sigtryggr died the following year and another descendant of Ívarr came from Dublin to claim the throne. He had a wasted journey. Æthelstan drove him out and took Northumbria under his own rule in 927.[70] [102] England was now united.

Yet it was not the end of Scandinavian ambitions in England. In the reign of Æthelred the Unready (r. 978–1016) the Vikings returned, more organized, more disciplined, more formidable than before. The *Anglo-Saxon Chronicle* was once again a record of battles. One became famous because of a poem about it. Most versions of the *Chronicle* give it a terse line under the year 991: 'Ealdorman Byrhtnoth was killed at Maldon' (in Essex). But one version is more forthcoming. It tells us that Olaf (Tryggvason, later king of Norway) came with ninety-three ships and raided around Folkstone, Sandwich,

102 *Æthelstan portrayed on his tomb in Malmesbury Abbey, Wiltshire.*

Ipswich and finally Maldon, where he and his men killed the ealdorman and slaughtered the English army. In the early 11th-century poem *The Battle of Maldon*, the poet turns defeat into a victory for the English ethos. The Vikings landing on Northey Island in the Blackwater estuary expected to be bought off. Byrhtnoth defied them: 'Do you hear, sea-wanderer, what this nation says? They will give you spears as tribute.' There was only one approach to the mainland, via a narrow causeway which was easily held by a small group of his warriors. To break the stalemate, Byrhtnoth allowed the Vikings to cross the causeway. His staunch followers were willing to defend their ancestral home and gain glory thereby. Struck down, Byrhtnoth commended his soul to God. His men fought on out of loyalty to him.[71] It has the heroic values of *Beowulf* with one significant difference. The ancestral land was no longer overseas. It was England.

It has been argued that the Anglo-Saxons saw royal success or failure as a measure of the relationship between king and subject. So Alfred saved Wessex by his ability to raise the army of the West Saxons, while Æthelred lost his kingdom through his failure to keep the loyalty of his men.[72] Certainly Æthelred was condemned by posterity. In the 13th century a pun was made on the literal meaning of his name 'noble counsel' and 'un-ræd', meaning 'no counsel' or 'ill-advised counsel'. The epithet stuck, and he became Æthelred the Unready to history.[73]

By 994 the intruders were led in person by King Sweyn Forkbeard of Denmark, who succeeded in his long campaign of conquest in 1013, but had little time to enjoy victory. He died on 2 February 1014. So England in 1016 had its first crowned Scandinavian monarch: Sweyn's son Cnut (d. 1035), king of Denmark, England and Norway. This union of crowns was not to last. Cnut had consolidated his position in England by marrying Emma of Normandy, the widow of Æthelred. He intended his triple crown to descend undivided to Harthacnut, his son by Emma. Instead, his son Harold by an earlier wife seized the throne of England and murdered one of Emma's sons by Æthelred. On the death of Harold at the age of twenty-five, Harthacnut did replace him as king of England, as well as Denmark, but died drinking at a wedding feast in 1042. So the throne went to the remaining son of Æthelred by Emma, the pious half-Norman Edward the Confessor, who had spent much of his earlier life in Normandy. He was childless, so on his death in 1066 a tussle began between three claimants to the throne. [Pl. xx]

103 *This scene from the Bayeux Tapestry depicts the coronation of Harold, son of the powerful English earl Godwin, on 6 January 1066. The new king sits enthroned with nobles to the left and Archbishop Stigand to the right. Beyond Stigand the people hail their king.*

Harold Godwinson, earl of Wessex, was the Anglo-Saxon choice. [103] According to the *Anglo-Saxon Chronicle*, Edward named Godwinson as his successor on his deathbed. However, William of Normandy, a cousin of Edward the Confessor, claimed that Edward had promised the throne to him. Meanwhile Harald Hardrada, king of Norway, was invited to seize the throne by Tostig Godwinson, brother of Harold. This act of sibling rivalry meant that Harold Godwinson was famously forced to fight two rivals in succession, disposing of Harald Hardrada at Stamford Bridge, Yorkshire, on 25 September 1066, and then marching his army south to meet William at Senlac Hill, near Hastings in East Sussex, where he himself was killed on 14 October 1066.

Some Anglo-Saxons fled their homeland, moving to Denmark, Norway or even travelling the length of the Mediterranean, where some joined the Varangian Guard of the Byzantine emperor.[74] Yet England survived as a nation. Indeed its system of administration was taken over more or less intact by William I, whose great survey of his captured nation in 1086, Domesday, left us a wealth of information about the late Anglo-Saxon organization of England. Built into it are constant references to the state of affairs in the time of Edward the Confessor. The units of government from manor to hundred to shire simply continued from Saxon times.[75] [104]

1 Snothinghamscire
2 Roteland
3 Wirecestrescire
4 Northantonescire
5 Huntedunscire
6 Grentebrigescire
7 Oxenefordscire
8 Bochingehamscire
9 Bedefordscire
10 Hetefordscire
11 Midelsexe

—— Northern limit of the Domesday survey

SCOTLAND

Northymbraland

North Treding

Eurvyscire

East Treding

West Treding

North Sea

Irish Sea

Inter Ripam et Mersham

Cestrescire

Derbyscire

Lincolnescire

1

Stadfordscire

Ledecestre

2

Nordfulc

Sciropescire

WALES

Herefordscire

3

Warwicscire

4

5

6

Sudfulc

9

Glowecestrescire

7

8

10

Exsessa

11

Wiltescire

Berrochescire

Sudrie

Chenth

Sumdrsete

Hantescire

Devenescire

Dorsete

Sudsexe

Cornvalge

English Channel

0   50 km

0   50 miles

104 *The shires of England as designated in the Domesday survey of 1086. The names gradually changed their spelling, but their boundaries remained much the same until reorganization in 1974. East Anglia was divided into Norfolk (North Folk) and Suffolk (South Folk). The name of Surrey derived from the Old English for South Region. Several shires were named after their chief town, such as Wiltshire (Wilton) and Hampshire (Hamton, now Southampton).*

William of Normandy had gained the throne by conquest. One of the first acts of his son Henry I (r. 1100–35) as king was to marry a descendant of Alfred the Great. It was a shrewd concession to the Anglo-Saxon feeling for royal pedigree. His wife Matilda (d. 1118) was the daughter of Malcolm III of Scotland and St Margaret, grand-niece of Edward the Confessor by his brother Edmund Ironside.[76]

Overview

- Anglo-Saxon kings generally rose to the throne by a combination of royal pedigree and fitness to fight.

- By around 800 there were three great powers in England: Northumbria, Mercia and Wessex. Gradually these were divided into shires, each headed by an ealdorman, creating the system of administration revealed in 1086 by the Domesday survey.

- Great kings and land-rich churchmen had the power to change the landscape. From the 8th century onwards a pattern of scattered farms and hamlets changed into planned villages surrounded by open fields in much of England. Key innovations boosted the increase in yields, creating a greater surplus to feed non-farmers.

- The earliest Anglo-Saxon trading towns were emporia such as Lundenwic and Hamwic. Coinage to support trading activities was struck from the mid-600s.

- Offa of Mercia (d. 796) created Offa's Dyke, a great defence work to protect Mercia from Welsh incursion. He also created proto-towns in Mercia, such as Hereford and Worcester.

- Vikings from Scandinavia began by raiding England and ended by settling in parts of it. A treaty between Alfred the Great and Guthrum of the Danes divided England.

- Alfred the Great in Wessex and his daughter and son-in-law in Mercia created fortified market towns that could pay for their own upkeep. English society became more urban and complex.

- England was united under one crown by Alfred's grandson Æthelstan in 927. The Anglo-Saxons had come to see themselves as native English, defending their land against invaders.

- In the reign of Æthelred the Unready the Vikings returned. From 1013 England had a series of Scandinavian monarchs, followed by Edward the Confessor, king of England 1042–66, the last descendant of Alfred in the male line to rule England.

CHAPTER TEN

The Rise of English

> We seem, as it were, to have conquered half the world
> in a fit of absence of mind.[1]

Incomings and outgoings

The year 1066 was of course far from the end of the story of the English language or the English people. More than nine and a half centuries have passed since the battle of Hastings. In that time English people have travelled around the world, and people from across the world have entered England. Both processes have helped to shape the language and culture of the English. It would be surprising if we could see no change at all in the English genepool after Anglo-Saxon times. [see Box p. 193]

The army that William the Conqueror brought to Britain included Bretons, Flemings and French, as well as his own Norman barons and their men. The Normans themselves were a mixture. The Franks had imposed their control on the Gallo-Roman people of Gaul. They gave their name to France, but did not settle in sufficient numbers to change the Romance language to a Germanic one. Nor did the Vikings who came after them. During the reign of Charles the Simple (r. 898–922), a band of Vikings under Rollo settled in the Lower Seine area. In 911 the Franks managed to prevent Rollo seizing Paris and Chartres and took the opportunity to make a treaty ceding territory around the Seine to Rollo, in return for Rollo's acknowledgment of Charles as his feudal lord. In 924 Rollo received a further grant of Maine and the Bessin. By 933 the Duchy of Normandy had enlarged to include the Cotentin peninsula. So the Duchy by then covered roughly the area of modern Normandy.[2]

To gain acceptance into the kingdom of the Franks, Rollo agreed to convert to Christianity. In 911 he contracted a marriage with the daughter of Charles the Simple. His successors William Longsword and Richard I also made political unions.[3] Meanwhile, no doubt, a good deal of mixing went on among their followers and local women. If the children of Vikings were raised by French-speaking mothers, it is not surprising that Old Norse vanished in Normandy over just the few generations between Rollo and William the Conqueror. The Normans who arrived in England in 1066 spoke Norman French and were culturally homogeneous, whether or not they had a Viking among their ancestors.

William the Conqueror replaced most of the Anglo-Saxon aristocracy with his own supporters. This has led to a popular supposition that the modern English aristocracy must be full of Norman Y-DNA haplogroups. In fact, few baronial male lines have lasted from Norman times down to the present day. Nearly a third failed to produce male heirs just in the century after the Norman conquest. Barons were expected to fight for the king, and might turn out for war with every able man of their family. Lineages could be lost on the battlefield. Risings against a monarch tended to start among the barons, too. So some over-mighty subjects were condemned to death as traitors. Among the earls, Norman male lines had shrunk to de Vere, Percy and Talbot by 1600, though new earldoms had been created for some old Norman families.

Subsequent centuries saw more Norman male lineages disappear from the ranks of the aristocracy. The present Percy family, Earls of Northumberland, has twice descended through female lines, adopting the Percy surname.[4] The last de Vere Earl of Oxford died without issue in 1625. Many male lines of manorial lords also ended in daughters. This does not mean that there are no Norman male lines surviving at all in England. Cadets of the landed classes could enter the professions or trade, severing the link between a Norman surname and landed estates.

England was ruled jointly with parts of France for centuries. After the civil wars that followed the death of Henry I with no legitimate male heir, the throne was taken in 1154 by Henry II, the first Angevin king of England. He was the son of the Count of Anjou and Matilda, daughter of Henry I. Henry II ruled an empire greater than that of any English king before him: England, Wales, Ireland, Normandy, Anjou, Brittany and Aquitaine. Aquitaine was acquired when Duchess Eleanor of Aquitaine married Henry in 1152. Henry II's son John (r. 1199–1216) and grandson Henry III (r. 1216–72) were powerless to prevent the loss of Normandy, Anjou and Poitou to the king of France. Yet Aquitaine remained English until the end of the Hundred Years' War in 1453. Wine from Bordeaux was one of many foreign goods traded into England.[5]

Trade brought people, too. Towns in the rich lowlands of England gradually turned into cities, which attracted people from afar. In London, York, Bristol, Southampton and Norwich, there were high concentrations of foreigners by the mid-15th century, including merchants from the great trading towns of Flanders and northern Italy. Out in the countryside unskilled labourers from Scotland, Ireland, France and the Low Countries were seasonal workers on the land. In 1440 the English Parliament imposed a new tax on resident foreigners, generating valuable records of immigrants. The survey of 1440 recorded around 20,000 named persons of foreign birth. To pluck some examples out of the database, there was an Irish woman spinning wool in Leicestershire and a Scottish chaplain working in the rural parish of Sledmere in the East Riding of Yorkshire. Benedict Nicoll is one of the few people specifically identified in the tax records as coming from Sweden. He was a student at the University of Cambridge. Alexander Plaustrell, or Palestrelli, was a prominent Italian merchant in London, while Henry Phelypp, a Flemish sculptor, was working on the rebuilding of the parish church at Long Melford in Suffolk.[6]

In the 16th and 17th centuries, England opened its heart to a flood of refugees. The persecution of Protestants, called Huguenots, in Catholic France drove many into exile. An estimated 50,000 fled to England. Given that the population of England was only about five and a half million at the end of the 17th century, they had a considerable impact. The great majority were accustomed to urban life. Many were skilled craftsmen, especially weavers, but also silversmiths, watchmakers and others. Some were professional people – clergy, doctors, merchants, soldiers and teachers. London was the greatest magnet for these incomers, but they were also attracted to other English cities and towns, such as Norwich and Canterbury. They were so well assimilated into Protestant England that many an English person has a Huguenot somewhere in their family tree. The descendants of Huguenots made their mark in many walks of life. The great actor and theatre manager David Garrick (1717–1779) was the grandson of a Huguenot refugee.[7] It seems that England was far from insular, even before it turned its sights on more distant shores.

England lagged behind the Portuguese, Spanish and Dutch in the Age of Exploration, but once they began, English explorers became the trailblazers of what was to become a vast global empire. [105] The foundation of the East India Company in 1600 was a key turning point. With it, the English

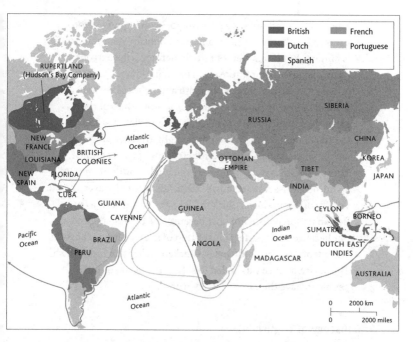

105 *European colonial expansions followed a period of exploration which vastly enlarged the European map of the world and understanding of its assets.*

broke the Spanish and Portuguese monopoly of the East Indian spice trade. The company was gradually drawn into political and military intervention in India to protect its trading interests, that 'absent-minded' acquisition of empire. In the 18th century Britain led the Industrial Revolution, which boosted the country to superpower status. Meanwhile, explorers were claiming territories such as Australia for the British Crown, though Britain lost much of its North American territory in the American Revolution. Britain famously ended up with an empire upon which the sun never set. In the post-war period Britain divested itself of empire in a relatively painless way, encouraging former colonies to join a more equitable organization now known as the Commonwealth of Nations. Many Commonwealth citizens have come to Britain to study and to work, as have citizens of the European Union, of which Britain is still a member as I write. The result is a multi-cultural Britain. Robin Cook, when Foreign Secretary in 2001, said:

The idea that Britain was a pure Anglo-Saxon society before the arrival of communities from the Caribbean, Asia and Africa is fantasy. But if this view of British identity is false to our past, it is false to our future too. The global era has produced population movements of a breadth and richness without parallel in history. Today's London is a perfect hub of the globe. It is home to over 30 ethnic communities of at least 10,000 residents each. In this city tonight, over 300 languages will be spoken by families over their evening meal at home. This pluralism is not a burden we must reluctantly accept. It is an immense asset that contributes to the cultural and economic vitality of our nation ... Chicken Tikka Massala is now a true British national dish, not only because it is the most popular, but because it is a perfect illustration of the way Britain absorbs and adapts external influences. Chicken Tikka is an Indian dish. The Massala sauce was added to satisfy the desire of British people to have their meat served in gravy.[8]

The history of English

The result of so much adventuring into and out of an island on the fringe of Europe is a remarkably rich language. Norman England had an elite speaking Anglo-Norman French, but Old English remained the language of the people. Old English arose from a blending and changing in Britain of the Germanic dialects of the incoming Angles, Saxons and Jutes. Regional dialects persisted in disunited England. We have most evidence of the West Saxon dialect, since the vast bulk of surviving texts are in West Saxon, or had been recopied by West Saxon scribes in a superficially West Saxon form, reflecting the dominance of Wessex from Alfred's time onwards. The Northumbrian, Mercian and East Anglian dialects share a number of features and are grouped together as Anglian. The Kentish and Essex dialects have left traces in charters, but are less well known.[9]

Although Modern English is fundamentally a Germanic language, it has a huge number of words derived from Latin and French. Some of these were acquired in the Anglo-Saxon period. Augustine and his colleagues had brought Latin to Britain with them, and hundreds of Latin words were adopted into Old English. Then the Viking settlers brought Norse speech,

Norman and later additions to English DNA

A recent study using the People of the British Isles (PoBI) database (p. 29) showed that the population of southern and eastern England cannot be modelled as a simple mixture of Celts and Anglo-Saxons. The English on average have slightly less steppe ancestry (ANE) than the Scots, Welsh and the ancient Anglo-Saxon samples. Within Europe, steppe ancestry decreases from north to south, so the authors of the study suggested that this subtle difference was the result of the centuries in which what is now England lay within the Roman empire.[10] Yet the Anglo-Saxons displaced many of the most Romanized people, who were pushed west and north into the regions that remained Celtic-speaking. It would seem more logical to suspect that immigrants from the Normans onwards added a pinch of southern spice to the English genetic mix.

which added fundamental vocabulary. About a thousand such words eventually became part of standard English. They include words which use the Norse *sk-* sound, such as 'skirt', 'sky' and 'skin'. A handful of French words also entered Old English from contacts with Francia. Even so, only 3 per cent of the words in Old English were non-Germanic loanwords, compared to 70 per cent in Modern English.[11]

The language was enriched in the Norman period by the absorption of far more vocabulary derived from French and Latin, and a sprinkling of words from other languages, such as 'marmalade' (from Portuguese), 'sable' (from Russian) and many words from Arabic, especially to do with the sciences, such as 'algebra' and 'alkali'. There was also a more fundamental change. The effort to communicate between peoples of different origin may lie behind the simplification of Old English, including the loss of grammatical gender and cases, as it developed into Middle English (1100–1500).[12] This period of simplification would later make Modern English a relatively easy language to learn. Also its mixture of Romance and Germanic vocabulary gives it a certain familiarity to speakers of a range of European languages.

Middle English was the language in which the poet Geoffrey Chaucer (c. 1343–1400) wrote *The Canterbury Tales* [106] and the anchoress Julian of Norwich (1342–c. 1416) wrote the comforting *Revelations of Divine Love*, the first book in the English language known to have been written by a woman. By this time English kings could speak English. It had become one of the

106 *Chaucer depicted as a pilgrim in the Ellesmere Manuscript, an early 15th-century copy of his* Canterbury Tales.

languages of the royal court. When William Caxton introduced the printing press to England in 1476, *The Canterbury Tales* was among his earliest publications. As he translated a number of other works into English, he made a tentative start to a process of standardizing the English language by adopting the dialect of London. Yet his own spelling was highly inconsistent, and a true standard English was centuries in the future.

In the Tudor period there was a renaissance of Classical learning, together with new developments in science, medicine and the arts. It coincided with the European exploration of Africa and the Americas. There were no words in English to accurately convey the new concepts, innovations and discoveries, so yet more words were borrowed from Latin, together with others from Greek, French, Italian, Spanish and Portuguese.[13] Queen Elizabeth I was a product of the new humanist education and was well versed in French, Greek and Latin. In her day Early Modern English (1500–1800) was developing. This was the language of Shakespeare, [107] which pioneers took to the early British colonies in North America. The expansion of the lexicon continued long after Shakespeare, as English-speakers invented

107 *This is the only portrait of playwright and poet William Shakespeare that has a good claim to have been painted from life.*

new technology and encountered a whole world full of objects, places and living things new to them. The word 'bungalow', for example, comes from Hindi *banglā* 'belonging to Bengal', referring to a type of cottage built for early European settlers in Bengal. As Terry Pratchett put it:

> These islands of ours have the richest language in the world,
> mostly because we stole useful words from everybody else,
> besides frantically inventing new ones for ourselves.[14]

The empire has long gone, but its linguistic legacy lives on. English became the lingua franca in India and in former British colonies in Africa – the language of convenience in polyglot lands. Most importantly, it was the language of those thirteen American colonies that Britain lost. Though the United States expanded to take in Spanish-speaking territory, and drew migrants from a multitude of nations, English remained its primary language. So as the US overtook Britain in the 20th century to become the superpower it is today, its influence more than any other turned English into a global lingua franca. Currently nearly two billion people around the globe understand it. It is the language of aviation, science, computing, international trade and diplomacy.

Rediscovering the Anglo-Saxons

By the mid-12th century, those Normans interested in the history of this island could choose between fact and fancy. It has to be admitted that fancy took the popular vote. Two authors worked in vivid contrast. William of Malmesbury (d. c. 1142) was a scholarly monk at Malmesbury Abbey in Wiltshire, of mixed Norman and English family. He settled into the position of abbey librarian and prolific historian. Queen Matilda, the half-English, half-Scottish wife of Henry I, triggered his work on English history. She asked for a written account of the connection between the English royal family and the abbey's founder, St Aldhelm. Thus began the *Gesta regum Anglorum* (Deeds of the Kings of the English), a history of England from the death of Bede in 735 until his own day, completed in around 1125–26. William greatly admired Bede's work and took him as an exemplar, pursuing both truth and clarity. William's history was widely influential, but soon found itself in competition with a book of another ilk entirely.[15]

The History of the Kings of Britain was completed about 1138 by Geoffrey of Monmouth. He was probably of Breton stock. William the Conqueror had granted Monmouth Castle to a Breton and it descended in his family until after Geoffrey's time. So Geoffrey's parents may have been part of the entourage of the Breton lords of Monmouth.[16] The Bretons and Welsh spoke similar Celtic languages; no wonder Geoffrey of Monmouth wallowed in nostalgia for a golden Celtic past. In default of any true history, Geoffrey succumbed to a prevailing thirst among European nations for a Trojan ancestry and traced a royal line from one Brutus of Troy, whom he imagined to be the founder of Britain, through a host of supposed pre-Roman sovereigns to three genuine 7th-century kings of Gwynedd. Geoffrey devoted most space to a detailed and loving treatment of Arthur, that shadowy symbol of resistance by the Britons to the Anglo-Saxons. Subsequently the character of Arthur was embellished in poetry and prose and placed in a context of medieval chivalry. The Trojan and Arthurian vision of the British past remained predominant throughout the Middle Ages. The world of the Anglo-Saxons was almost lost to sight.

The second edition of *Holinshed's Chronicles* (1587), famed as the inspiration for over a third of Shakespeare's plays, still clung to pseudo-history to fill the gap in knowledge before records, with supposed characters Albion and Brutus conjured up from the names of Britain in Classical sources. Yet the coverage of the Anglo-Saxon advent draws on Bede's *Ecclesiastical History*, first printed in Strasbourg at around the same time that Caxton set up a printing press in England. An English translation by the Catholic exile Thomas Stapleton was published in 1565[17] The religious upheavals of the Reformation spurred advocates of varied viewpoints to delve into ecclesiastical history in hope of support for their cause. On the Protestant side was Matthew Parker, archbishop of Canterbury 1559–75. The dissolution of the monasteries from 1536 to 1540 had released manuscripts into the hands of scholars such as Parker, who amassed such treasures as the St Augustine Gospels [Pl. xix] and one version of the *Anglo-Saxon Chronicle*. He left his collection to his former college at Cambridge, thus making it available to later scholars. Many charters had been recorded by monastic scribes. They became a staple source for antiquarians writing the national and county histories that began to appear from the 16th century. Some authors took all apparently Anglo-Saxon charters at face value. The recognition that some were later forgeries fed a mini-industry of commentary and critique in more recent times.[18]

While Anglo-Saxon chronicles, laws and charters were being plundered by a new generation of historians, Anglo-Saxon literature lay dormant. The English language had changed so markedly in the Middle Ages that Old English became impenetrable to ordinary English-speakers. Anglo-Saxon poetry largely vanished from the national consciousness. The poetic anthology in the *Exeter Book*, [4] now listed in UNESCO's Memory of the World register, was scarcely known until its first publication with translation in 1842.[19] It was the start of a revival of scholarly interest in the Anglo-Saxons and their literary heritage. Frederick James Furnivall, one of the co-creators of the *New* (later *Oxford*) *English Dictionary*, felt the lack of accurate early texts from which the dictionary could quote when tracing the origins of a word. In 1864 he founded the Early English Text Society, which brought out volume after volume of works in Old English and Middle English, approximately 250 during his lifetime.[20]

By the latter part of the 19th century, national pride in the achievements of Britain was coupled with pleasure in Anglo-Saxon heritage. The Victorian public embraced two contrasting images of Alfred the Great. In one we see the king at his lowest ebb, hiding from the Danes: in a story for which there is no contemporary evidence, the king is pictured taking shelter with

108 *A Victorian portrayal of the apocryphal story of Alfred allowing a cottager's cakes to burn in his abstraction, as he pondered the fate of England.*

109 *Sculptor Hamo Thornycroft's bronze statue of Alfred the Great, erected in 1899 at Winchester, depicts him as a Christian warrior, with the cross of his sword hilt held aloft as a symbol of his faith.*

a humble cottager, who scolds him for carelessly allowing her cakes to burn.[21] [108] The counterpoint was a vision of the king as a noble defender of a Christian realm. [109] The latter takes strength from the former. Alfred had won against the odds.

The race pseudo-science that emerged in 19th-century Germany and the United States has already been touched upon (see p. 97). The form it took in Britain was the ugly assertion of the racial superiority of the

Anglo-Saxons over the Irish,[22] and indeed over the rest of humankind, in supposed justification of the brutalities of colonialism. Two world wars in which Germanic-speakers fought each other did nothing to bolster a sense of Germanic solidarity. Moreover, the evils of racism were dramatically exposed by the deeds of the Nazis. Indeed the backlash against the 'Germanist school' in the post-war years inclined some historians against treating the Anglo-Saxon advent as a folk migration.[23] Thus they harmonized with the stream of anti-migrationism in post-war archaeology.

There was a more critical approach to sources, an improvement on the more credulous of earlier views, but it could be taken too far. The claim that Asser's *Life of Alfred* was a fake has a long history, but it was most prominently proclaimed in 1964 by eminent historian V. H. Galbraith. Thus one of the most useful sources for a vital era in England's history could have been a needless sacrifice on the altar of scholarly scepticism. Fortunately, the work of Asser was rescued from ignominy by less profligate historians.[24]

At the more popular level, John Ronald Reuel Tolkien's hugely popular fantasy novel *The Hobbit* (1937), followed by *The Lord of the Rings* in three volumes (1954–55) drew on Old English literature, among other influences. [110] Tolkien described *Beowulf* as one of the most valued sources for *The Hobbit*.[25] He took the term 'Middle-earth' from *Beowulf*. Yet Tolkien was no blindly uncritical admirer of the heroic ethos. He subjected the poem *The Battle of Maldon* (p. 183) to piercing moral analysis. While self-sacrificing bravery may be admired, the pride which led Byrhtnoth to imperil his own men by allowing the enemy too much room to manoeuvre was a fault. Indeed the poet actually says so, a point not often noticed. Beowulf too, in insisting on unarmed combat with Grendel, puts himself in unnecessary peril for his own greater glory.[26] Nor was Tolkien in the remotest accord with Nazi philosophy. In 1938 he was perturbed to be asked by a German publisher if he was Aryan. His satirical response made it clear that he rejected the misappropriation of the term Aryan, and did not subscribe to 'the wholly pernicious and unscientific race-doctrine'.[27]

110 *An 8th–10th century Anglo-Saxon gold ring with a untranslatable runic inscription, perhaps of magical intent. The idea of a magical ring appears in Tolkien's* The Lord of the Rings, *drawing on folk tales.*

Tolkien had been interested in Old English and Middle English from his schooldays and gained a degree in English language and literature from Oxford before serving in the First World War. After the war he began his academic career at the University of Leeds, and in 1925 he returned to Oxford as Professor of Anglo-Saxon. There he made a translation of *Beowulf*, which was finished in 1926 but remained unpublished in his lifetime. It was finally edited by his son and published in 2014. His British Academy lecture of 1936, 'Beowulf: The monsters and the critics' (quoted in Chapter 1, p. 17), marked a turning point in *Beowulf* research. Yet his fame sprang from his fiction. *The Lord of the Rings* generated a genre of heroic fantasy which remains highly successful today.[28]

Terry Pratchett left us a description of the Tolkien effect. After reading the whole three volumes of *The Lord of the Rings* at a gulp in his early teens:

> Enthralled I was. To the library I went back and spake thusly:
> 'Have you got any more books like these? Maybe with maps in?
> And runes?'[29]

Grown to manhood, Pratchett threw Nordic myth into the bubbling cauldron of his imagination, along with an extraordinary range of other ingredients, to produce his best-selling series of Discworld books. A recurrent character is the redoubtable witch Granny Weatherwax, whose mind can hitch a lift in the those of birds and animals (and even, on one occasion, a swarm of bees) to gather information near and far, leaving her own body temporarily in a near-death coma. Readers of the *Ynglinga Saga* will recognize this gift as an attribute of Odin (see p. 44). Unlike Tolkien and most of his imitators, Pratchett could never treat his imagined world entirely seriously. The Discworld series began as affectionate satire of the genre of heroic fantasy and never lost its comic genius, even when delving into the darker reaches of the human condition. He puts into the mouth of one of his characters what could be his own ironic comment on *The Battle of Maldon*:

> Putting up a statue to someone who tried to stop a war is
> not very, um, statuesque. Of course if you had butchered five
> hundred of your own men out of arrogant carelessness, we'd be
> melting the bronze already.[30]

Film-makers, too, have mined this rich lode. *The Lord of the Rings* was converted into three highly successful films directed by Peter Jackson, released from 2001 to 2003. The *Beowulf* story itself has been adapted for cinema and television a number of times. A film released in 2007 brought it to the notice of Anglophone audiences worldwide. [see 7]

The Anglo-Saxons have been directly fictionalized by Bernard Cornwell in his series of Saxon stories (2004–15), which formed the basis for a BBC television series, *The Last Kingdom*. Cornwell chose a tense time in England's history, when the fate of the nation hung in the balance between Anglo-Saxon and Viking. His fictional hero is the son of a Northumbrian ealdorman based at Bamburgh Castle, who finds himself at ten years old orphaned and dispossessed by the Danes, yet adopted by one. To regain his inheritance he must join Alfred the Great. This convoluted plot enables Cornwell to explore the outlook of both pagan and Christian, as well as giving his readers the vivid battle scenes that they expect of him. In an interview with Emerson College, Cornwell explained:

> Years ago, when I was at university, I discovered Anglo-
> Saxon poetry and became hooked on that strange and often
> melancholy world. For some reason the history of the Anglo-
> Saxons isn't much taught in Britain (where I grew up) and it
> struck me as weird that the English really had no idea where
> their country came from. Americans know, they even have
> a starting date, but the English just seemed to assume that
> England had always been there, so the idea of writing a series
> about the creation of England was in my head for a long time.[31]

Bernard Cornwell's recollections of his schooldays may seem unfair to teachers making an honest effort to instil the National Curriculum today into English schoolchildren aged seven to eleven. It includes 'Britain's settlement by Anglo-Saxons' and 'the Viking and Anglo-Saxon struggle for the Kingdom of England', but this comes in an ambitious scheme to cover the history of Britain from the Stone Age to 1066. And who can say that this is the wrong approach? The story of people on this island did not start with the Anglo-Saxons. The point Cornwell is making, though, is that Americans can champion 1776 for the Declaration of Independence, whereas few English people could give a date for the birth of their country *as a nation state*. Indeed English historians themselves might disagree on exactly which point marks that birth. The political unification of England was a complex and drawn-out process. Some might argue that England was born not in a blaze of battle, but in the beavering of bureaucrats. It is Domesday Book that most clearly reveals a state, centrally organized and taxed. It may be the earliest such nation state in Europe.[32] Since its development was organic, rather than to a plan by a revolutionary steering committee, England has no written constitution. It lacks an elevating motto to rival the '*Liberté, égalité, fraternité*' of the French Republic. What it has instead is a whole lot more history.

A more tangible contact with the past was made by Terry Herbert with his metal detector in an otherwise unremarkable field in Staffordshire in July 2009 (see p. 151). He picked up one piece of glittering metal after another. The field seemed full of gold and silver. [Pls xv, xvi] In the previous autumn, the farmer's plough had swept a long-buried treasure to the surface. It proved to be a staggeringly huge hoard. Archaeologists were contacted, but found no clue to its context. It was not part of a cemetery or shrine or any other Anglo-Saxon feature. It simply seems to have been buried with the intention of returning for it. The place where it lay is the end of a hillock overlooking Watling Street, the Roman road from Dover to Wroxeter, so a traveller might have chosen to hide the treasure in fear of theft, or fear of being detected in theft.[33] Crowds queued for hours to see the first exhibition of pieces from the Staffordshire Hoard at the Birmingham Museum and Art Gallery, and it continues to re-ignite popular interest in the Anglo-Saxons.

Buried treasure has a perennial fascination for the public, but could they get as excited by a lump of slag? One television programme aimed to find out. *Time Team* was another brainchild of archaeologist Mick Aston, noted above (p. 169) for his work on the English village. He wanted to bring into our living rooms the *process* of discovery in archaeology.[34] This was a brand-new concept for television and hugely ambitious, for scripted programmes, with all the content known in advance, are far easier to make. There was an immediacy about *Time Team* that captured the excitement of digging up the past. The first programme of the first series, aired on 16 January 1994, focused on Athelney in Somerset, a site at the heart of Alfred the Great's fight against the Danes (see p. 178). Perhaps it was felt that so well-known a background story would hook the public's interest. Yet the real hook proved to be the format. Viewers became entranced as they watched the team bicker amiably over objects that had last seen the light of day hundreds or thousands of years before. Yet the first programme on Athelney was unlike any other in the twenty series of *Time Team*. As Athelney is a scheduled monument the team was not allowed to dig. This proved to be a shining triumph for geophysical survey, as we watched the layout of the long-demolished Athelney Abbey emerge amazingly clearly on a printout.[35]

The other star of the show was a lump of slag discovered by field-walking. Together they proved that there is more to archaeology than digging. An expert on ancient technology, Gerry McDonnell, was so excited on hearing of the lump of slag that he jumped into his car in Bradford, Yorkshire, to travel the 250 miles to Athelney to lay his hands on it. Could Alfred the Great have had a forge in his camp to make weapons to equip his army? Did their quality aid the turn of the tide in English history? It was a tantalizing thought. In 2002, for their 100th episode, *Time Team* returned to Athelney, this time with permission to dig. It was this excavation that uncovered a defensive ditch at Athelney that pre-dated Alfred's works.

This site was one of many selected by *Time Team* that brought to life the Anglo-Saxon period in English history. Mick Aston aimed to cover all periods in *Time Team*, but he had a personal interest in the development of monasteries, towns and villages that brought the programme back to the Anglo-Saxons time and again. *Time Team* was the antithesis of a chronicle of kings and battles. It gave us glimpses into the daily lives of ordinary people of the time, as indeed archaeology in general does so well. As the public face of British archaeology, *Time Team* naturally reflected the anti-migrationism prevailing then. Times change, but the thrill of discovery never goes out of fashion.

Geneticists, too, have been fuelling interest in the Anglo-Saxons, first by ferreting around in modern DNA for clues to their genetic input, and more recently by tapping directly into the DNA of Anglo-Saxons. This exciting development is yet in its infancy. The unfolding story from ancient DNA still has much to tell us, but has already given us glimpses of its potential. It can make 'Invisible Britons' visible. It can consolidate or refute deductions based on other evidence. Already we know from an anonymous woman at Oakington that not *all* Britons absorbed into early Anglo-Saxon groups were doomed to slavery (p. 128), whatever might be inferred from the rumblings of Gildas. Did more Britons survive *in situ* in the second

111 *The Anglo-Saxons left a lasting mark on the English countryside in those few churches which have not been completely rebuilt since their day. The jubilant display of ornament on the Late Saxon tower of All Saints, Earls Barton, Northamptonshire, shows the increasing confidence and competence of English stone masons.*

phase of Anglo-Saxon conquest than the first? Such questions can now be addressed by DNA.

Above all, ancient DNA can link us directly with our ancestors. One recent study estimated that, on average, the present population of eastern England derives 38 per cent of its ancestry from Anglo-Saxon immigrants.[36] The English reader may wonder what that means for him or her. The modern population of eastern England is richly varied. Individuals within it range from having zero Anglo-Saxon ancestry to so high a level that ancestry DNA tests tend to score them as German. The natural indignation of a man with a solid East Anglian pedigree going back many generations, who finds a DNA test incapable of even identifying him as English, feeds back useful information to the geneticists responsible. Curiosity about our ancestors seems likely to generate a new wave of interest in the practical but poetry-loving people who gave a name to England. Today the Anglo-Saxons seem in no danger of being forgotten.

Overview

- In 1066 England was conquered by the Normans, who replaced the English aristocracy. In the medieval period there was immigration into England from continental Europe, as well as from Scotland, Wales and Ireland.

- The DNA of the modern English cannot be modelled as a simple mixture of Anglo-Saxon and Celtic. Migration from 1066 onwards has left its mark.

- Old English, the language of the Anglo-Saxons, developed into Middle English (1100–1500), followed by Early Modern English (1500–1800) and Modern English.

- Though Modern English is a Germanic language, 70 per cent of its vocabulary is non-Germanic, borrowed from many other languages, notably Latin and French. This polyglot vocabulary makes English the richest language in the world.

- English today is a global lingua franca, partly as the legacy of the British empire, but mainly due to the superpower status of the United States of America.

- In the Middle Ages a pseudo-history of Britain was far more popular than the genuine article.

- Interest in the Anglo-Saxons began to revive in the Tudor period and greatly increased in the Victorian period.

- The surge of national pride in the 19th century encouraged racism and an inflated concept of the Anglo-Saxon achievement, which produced a backlash after the Second World War.

- Tolkien was a scholar of Anglo-Saxon who changed the scholarly view of *Beowulf*, but left a greater legacy in his popular fiction, now brought to the cinema screen.

- Archaeology can reveal those details of everyday life in Anglo-Saxon times that documentary sources omit.

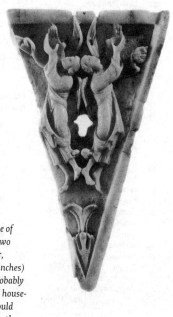

112 *Carved relief plaque of walrus ivory depicting two angels, from Winchester, 10th century, 7.6 cm (3 inches) high. The plaque was probably mounted at one end of a house-shaped shrine and so would originally have been seen the other way up.*

Notes

Prologue

1. Freeborn 1992, 24.

Chapter 1: How the Anglo-Saxons Saw Themselves (pp. 13–32)

1. *Beowulf*, trans. Hall, XLIII, lines 33–45.
2. The name was so interpreted in a 12th-century history of the Danes: Sven Aggesen, vol. 1, 96–97.
3. *Beowulf*, trans. Swanton, lines 78 and 780.
4. Thietmar of Merseburg, I.17.
5. Christensen 2015, summarized in English in *Medieval News*, May 2016, no. 5; Niles 2007.
6. *Beowulf*, trans. Swanton, Introduction; *Beowulf*, trans. Tolkien, commentary.
7. *Anglo-Saxon Poetry*, Maxims II, 21.
8. *Saga of the Volsungs*, 13.
9. See Williams 2015 for a more complex and nuanced interpretation.
10. Tolkien 1937.
11. Gregory of Tours, III, 3, translated in Murray 2008, 290.
12. *Beowulf*, trans. Swanton, lines 175–78.
13. Neidorf 2013, Beowulf; *Beowulf*, trans. Swanton, Introduction, 2–3.
14. *Beowulf*, trans. Swanton, Introduction, 15–18; *Beowulf*, trans. Tolkien, commentary.
15. Chase 1981.
16. Neidorf 2014; *Beowulf*, trans. Swanton, Introduction, 3.
17. Davis 2006.
18. Bede, *The Ecclesiastical History of the English People (EH)*, IV.24.
19. Neidorf 2013, *Widsith*.
20. *Anglo-Saxon Poetry*, 337.
21. Dales 2013, 236.
22. Bede, *EH*, IV.24.
23. Wood 1991.
24. Brookes 2007; Ljungkvist 2008.
25. Bill 2008.
26. Williams 2011; Adams 2010.
27. Williams 2011, 30–31.
28. Williams 2011.
29. Bede, *EH*, II.15, III.18.
30. Carver 2000, 36–37; Williams 2011.
31. Drauschke 2007, 67; Birmingham Museums Trust 2014, 49.
32. Drauschke 2007.
33. Harrington and Welch 2014, 94, 173–80.
34. Bede, *EH*, II.15.
35. Bede, *EH*, III.18.
36. Wood 1991.
37. Carver 2000, 32.
38. Bruce-Mitford 2005, especially 27–29.
39. Bede, *EH*, III.22.
40. Scull, Minter and Plouviez 2016.
41. Keynes and Lapidge 1983, III: Extracts from the writings of King Alfred.
42. Alfred the Great, *Boethius*, trans. Sedgefield, II, xix.
43. *Beowulf*, trans. Tolkien, lines 365–67.
44. *Anglo-Saxon Poetry*, Deor 362–65 and Waldere 510–11.
45. Webster 2012.
46. Keynes and Lapidge 1983, I: Asser, *Life of King Alfred*, 1; Anlezark 2002.
47. Keynes and Lapidge 1983, I: Asser, *Life of King Alfred*, 22.
48. *ASC*, Introduction by Swanton.

49. Gildas, II, 18–23.
50. Bede, *EH*, I.15.
51. John 1996, 4–5; Higham 1992.
52. Rix 2014, 87–90.
53. Bede, *EH*, V.9.
54. e.g. Pohl 1997, 14.
55. *ODNB*: Boniface [St Boniface], entry by I. N. Wood.
56. Boniface, 194–95.
57. See Rix 2014 for a more detailed discussion.
58. Clark 1966.
59. Härke 2007.
60. Weale et al. 2002; Capelli 2003.
61. Leslie 2015.
62. Kershaw and Røyrvik 2016.
63. Geary and Veeramah 2016.
64. Schiffels et al. 2016; Martiniano et al. 2016.
65. Jobling et al. 2014, chapter 2.
66. Jobling et al. 2014, Appendix.

Chapter 2: The Germani (pp. 33–49)

1. Tacitus, *Germania*, 2. The original gives Ingaevones. The translator's substitution of Ingvaeones is omitted here.
2. Ptolemy, 2.10.
3. Pliny, IV. 30, VIII.16. There are spelling variations in the original Latin.
4. Rix 2014, 8–12.
5. Caesar, I.1.
6. Tacitus, *Germania*, 28.
7. Tacitus, *Germania*, 4.
8. Jobling et al. 2014, 328–29.
9. Smith 1986, 24–25.
10. Hall 2002, 26–29.
11. Smith 1986, 26–28.
12. Tacitus, *Germania*, 43.
13. Posidonius, vol. 1, fr. 73.

14. Tacitus, *Germania*, 2.
15. Ptolemy, II.10.
16. Tacitus, *Germania*, 29.
17. Tacitus, *Annals*, II.6.
18. Toorians 2006.
19. D. H. Green 1998, 59.
20. Caesar, IV.1–15.
21. Tacitus, *Annals*, II.44.
22. Tacitus, *Germania*, 38–39.
23. Tacitus, *Germania*, 40.
24. Todd 2004, 112.
25. Tacitus, *Germania*, 40.
26. *Beowulf*, trans. Swanton, lines 902, 1072, 1088, 1141f; Neidorf 2015.
27. *Widsith*, ed. Malone, 108, 215–16 (line 27 in plural form *Ytum*).
28. Florence of Worcester, 206.
29. Caesar, VI.21–22.
30. Tacitus, *Germania*, 5, 7, 14–15; for the Celts, see Manco 2015, *Blood of the Celts*, 12.
31. Todd 2004, 76–79.
32. Tacitus, *Germania*, 16.
33. Hamerow 2002, 5, 77–79 and figs 2.1, 2.8, 3.21.
34. Hamerow 2002, 5–15, 22–23 and fig. 2.1; Behre 2004; Christensen 2015.
35. Ramqvist 1992.
36. Hamerow 2002, 31–34.
37. Tacitus, *Germania*, 22; Fischer 2005.
38. Hamerow 2002, 40–43; Looijenga 2003, 48, 64; Fischer 2004, 277.
39. *Beowulf*, trans. Swanton, lines 168, 2196.
40. M. Green 1991, 46–48.
41. Theune-Großkopf 2008.
42. Tacitus, *Germania*, 2, 16, 18–19, 23–24.
43. Murray 2008, 136: Salvian of Marseilles, *On the Governance of God*.
44. Tacitus, *Germania*, 7, 11, 25–26; Caesar, VI.4.22.
45. Caesar, VI.21.
46. M. Green 1991.
47. *Prose Edda*, Gylfaginning, XI; *Poetic Edda*, The Seeress's Prophecy, 5.

48. Tacitus, *Germania*, 9.
49. Tacitus, *Germania*, 11.
50. D. H. Green 1998, 246–53.
51. D. H. Green 1998, 16 and chapter 13; Ringe 2006, location 1700–5; Mallory and Adams 2006, 409, 431; Todd 2004, 103.
52. Wicker 2015, 27.
53. *Prose Edda*, Gylfaginning, XXXIV.
54. *Prose Edda*, Prologue III, Gylfaginning, III, IX, XX.
55. *Heimskringla*, vol. 1, *Ynglinga Saga*, II–IX; *Prose Edda*, Gylfaginning, XXXVIII.
56. Lindow 2002.
57. *Prose Edda*, Prologue IV.
58. *Heimskringla*, vol. 1, *Ynglinga Saga*, V.
59. Wicker 2015.
60. D. H. Green 1998, 124.
61. Mallory and Adams 2006, 410; *Prose Edda*, Prologue III, Gylfaginning XXI.
62. D. H. Green 1998, 248.
63. *Prose Edda*, Prologue III, Beguiling of Gylfi, IX, XX; *Heimskringla*, vol. 1, *Ynglinga Saga*, III.
64. D. H. Green 1998, 252.
65. *Poetic Edda*, Loki's Quarrel, 29.
66. Strabo, VII.2.3.
67. Caesar, I.50.
68. Tacitus, *Germania*, 8; Tacitus, *Histories*, IV. 61, 65, V.22 and 24.
69. Schröder 1999.
70. *Poetic Edda*, The Seeress's Prophecy.
71. Flavius Josephus, I.6.
72. Isidore, IX.ii.27, 89.
73. ASC, under year 855; Anlezark 2002.
74. Rose 2014, 278–81; Rix 2014, chapter 1.
75. *Prose Edda*, Prologue III–V.
76. *Heimskringla*, vol. 1, *Ynglinga Saga*, I–V.
77. Lazaridis et al. 2014; Raghavan et al. 2014; Haak et al. 2015; Jones et al. 2015; Allentoft et al. 2015.

Chapter 3: The Long and Winding Road (pp. 50–72)

1. *Anglo-Saxon Poetry*, 342: The Fortunes of Men, 27.
2. Mallory and Adams 2006, 4–6.
3. Mallory 1989; Anthony 2007; Pereltsvaig and Lewis 2015.
4. Haak et al. 2015.
5. Larichev, Khol'ushkin and Laricheva 1990; Kuzmin and Keates 2016.
6. Lbova and Volkov 2015.
7. Pitulko et al. 2016.
8. Kuzmin and Keates 2016; Pitulko et al. 2012; Pitulko et al. 2004.
9. Moreno-Mayar et al. 2018.
10. Kivisild 2017.
11. Raghavan et al. 2014: https://yfull.com/ supplied the Y-DNA haplogroup of Afontova Gora 2 as Q-F746.
12. Gladkih, Kornietz and Soffer 1984; Iakovleva and Djindjian 2005.
13. Fu et al. 2016 and additional information on SNPs from Sergey Malyshev pers. comm.; Mathieson et al. 2018, sample Iboussieres 31–32.
14. Mathieson et al. 2018.
15. Wu 2012.
16. Jordan 2010; McKenzie 2010; Vasilieva 2011; Gibbs and Jordan 2013.
17. Haak et al. 2015; Mathieson et al. 2015.
18. Jones et al. 2017; Mittnik et al. 2018; pers. comm. on Y-DNA from Sergey Malyshev.
19. Lazaridis et al. 2014; Haak et al. 2015; Günther et al. 2018.
20. Lazaridis et al. 2014; Haak et al. 2015.
21. Calculated by https://yfull.com/.
22. Mallory and Adams 2006, 101–3.
23. Mallory and Adams 2006.

24. Pereltsvaig and Lewis 2015, 192–202.
25. Anthony and Ringe 2015.
26. Anthony 2007, 147–59, 174–82.
27. Jones et al. 2017; Y-DNA haplogroup from Anatas Kumbarov.
28. Jones et al. 2017; Y-DNA haplogroup from Anatas Kumbarov.
29. Roberts, Thornton and Pigott 2009.
30. Anthony 2007, 182–86; Olsen 2006.
31. Mathieson et al. 2015; Lazaridis et al. 2016.
32. Mallory and Adams 1997, 540–41.
33. Mathieson et al. 2018, sample I6561.
34. Anthony 2007, 239–45, 274–75.
35. Morgunova and Turetskij 2016.
36. Parpola 2008; Greenfield 2010.
37. Anthony 2007, 328–39.
38. Harrison and Heyd 2007, chapter 9; Kristiansen 2005.
39. Harrison and Heyd 2007, chapter 9; Kristiansen 2005.
40. Kremenetski, Chichagova and Shishlina 1999; Kremenetski 2003.
41. Anthony and Ringe 2015.
42. Mallory 2013.
43. Ringe 2006, 3.4.5 (ii).
44. Krahe 1963.
45. Włodarczak 2009.
46. Harrison and Heyd 2007, 201; Kristiansen et al. 2017.
47. Furholt 2014; Bradley et al. 2016, 122.
48. Müller et al. 2009.
49. Price 2015, 166–67.
50. Manco 2015, *Ancestral Journeys*, 100.
51. Bradley et al. 2016, 121.
52. Mathieson et al. 2018.
53. Woidich 2014; Mallory and Adams 1997, 226–27.
54. Lõugas, Kriiska and

Maldre 2007; Cramp et al. 2014.
55. Kristiansen 1989.
56. Włodarczak 2014.
57. Bramanti et al. 2009; Malmstrom et al. 2009.
58. Haak et al. 2015.
59. Mathieson et al. 2018.
60. Mittnik et al. 2018, samples Gyvakarai1 and Plinkaigalis 242; Jones et al. 2017; Mathieson et al. 2018, sample I4629.
61. Jones et al. 2015.
62. Jones et al. 2017.
63. Allentoft et al. 2015.
64. Allentoft et al. 2015; Mathieson et al. 2015, sample RISE61; Additional information on SNPs from Vladimir Tagankin.
65. Mittnik et al. 2018.
66. Manco 2015, *Blood of the Celts.*
67. Vandkilde 2005; Sarauw 2006; Melheim 2012; Melheim and Prescott 2016.
68. Mathieson et al. 2015, sample RISE98. For a description of his burial in grave 49 see Fornander 2011, 44–47 and Olausson 2015.
69. Ringe 2006, chapter 3.
70. Andersen 1996, 49–50.
71. Ringe, Warnow and Taylor 2002, 110–11; Ringe 2006, 3.4.5 (ii).
72. Manco 2015, *Blood of the Celts,* 94–96.
73. Anthony 2008.
74. Kroonen 2012; Iverson and Kroonen 2017.
75. Włodarczak 2014; Anthony 2007, fig. 14.1.
76. Furholt 2014.
77. Larsson 2009.
78. Aikio 2012.
79. Iverson and Kroonen 2017.
80. Ringe and Taylor 2014, 2.
81. Kallio 2015.
82. Kallio 2012; Parpola 2012, 132; Aikio 2006.

Chapter 4: Travel, Trade and Bronze (pp. 73–92)

1. Hesiod, *Works and Days,* lines 140–55.
2. Lucretius, V.
3. Murray 2007, 206–8.
4. Roberts, Thornton and Pigott 2009, 1012–17; Thornton 2009; Pernicka and Anthony 2010; Yener et al. 2015; Boscher 2016.
5. Norquist et al. 2012.
6. Prescott 2006; Vandkilde 2011.
7. Price 2015, 178; Kristiansen and Larsson 2005, 113–15, 136–38, 140.
8. Pokutta 2014.
9. Pare 2000; Kristiansen and Larsson 2005, 118, 186; Vandkilde 2011.
10. Ling et al. 2014; Ling and Stos-Gale 2015.
11. Kristiansen 2017.
12. Ling et al. 2014.
13. Field 1998.
14. McKinley, Schuster and Millard 2013.
15. Woodward and Hunter et al. 2015, chapter 7 and figs 7.4.4 and 12.10.
16. Maran 2013.
17. Murillo-Barroso and Montero-Ruiz 2012.
18. Kristiansen and Larsson 2005, 125–27; Czebreszuk 2008; Czebreszuk 2013; Cwaliński 2014.
19. Mukherjee et al. 2008.
20. Varberg et al. 2015; 2016.
21. Cline 2014, especially p. 173.
22. Czebreszuk 2008.
23. Ling 2012.
24. Kristiansen and Larsson 2005, 207–8 and fig. 92; Mörner and Lind 2015.
25. McGrail 2004, 36, 113–17, 2011.
26. Anthony 2007, chapter 15; Kristiansen and Larsson 2005, 174–223; Johannsen 2010.
27. Goldhahn 2009.
28. Barjamovic 2011, chapter 1.

29. Kristiansen 2017.
30. Frei et al. 2015.
31. Frei et al. 2017.
32. *Rigveda*, Hymn XXXV.
33. Johannsen 2010; Kaul 2014.
34. Kaul 2014; Kaul 1998.
35. M. Green 1991, 41–43, 76–77; Kristiansen and Larsson 2005, fig. 129.
36. Kristiansen and Larsson 2005, 298–302.
37. Mallory and Adams 1997, 226–27.
38. Bagnasco et al. 2017.
39. Haak et al. 2008.
40. Suggested by Michał Milewski, pers. comm.
41. Olausson 2015.
42. Moffat and Wilson 2011, 181–83.
43. YFull calculation. https://yfull.com/.
44. Szécsényi-Nagy et al. 2015.
45. Batini et al. 2015.
46. YFull calculation. https://yfull.com/.
47. Allentoft et al. 2015 and pers. comm. from Allentoft.

Chapter 5: The Iron Cradle of Germanic (pp. 93–103)

1. Pliny, 37.11.
2. Pliny, 37.11.
3. Roberts 2007: entry for Pytheas.
4. Barber et al. 2004.
5. Hannon et al. 2008.
6. Kristiansen 1998, 233; Kaliff 2001.
7. Makhortyk 2008.
8. Dzięgielewski 2010.
9. Brandt and Rauchfuß 2014, Vorwort.
10. Martens 2014.
11. Piotrowska 1998.
12. Pereltsvaig and Lewis 2015, 21–22.
13. Schrader 1883, trans. 1890, part I, chapter 4; part IV, chapter 15.
14. Pereltsvaig and Lewis 2015, 23–24; Müller 1888, 116–21.

15. Rives 2012, 51.
16. Arnold 1990 and 1992.
17. Piotrowska 1998.
18. Wozniak, Grygiel, Machajewski and Michalowski 2013; Michalowski 2014.
19. Martens 2010; Todd 2004, chapter 4; Poznan Archaeological Museum exhibition text.
20. Bochnak 2006 and 2011.
21. Tacitus, *Germania*, 43.
22. Sims-Williams 2006, 86, 191.
23. Bochnak 2006; Andrzejowski 2010.
24. Bochnak and Harasim 2012; Teska 2014.
25. Kaliff 2001.
26. Babik 2001.
27. D. H. Green 1998, chapters 7 and 8; Ringe 2006, 4.6.
28. D. H. Green 1998, 162–63; Ringe and Taylor 2014, 308.
29. Caesar, VI.24.

Chapter 6: The Haves and the Have-Nots (pp. 104–17)

1. Tacitus, *Annals*, I.3.6.
2. Cassius Dio, XLV–LVI, especially LVI.18; Goldsworthy 2014.
3. http://www.roemerforum-lahnau.de, last accessed 30 April 2018; *Science* 27 August 2009: Bronze horse head hints at Roman ambitions in Germany.
4. Goldsworthy 2014, 447.
5. Cassius Dio, LVI, 18–24.
6. Goldsworthy 2014, 446–57.
7. Tacitus, *Annals*, II.26.
8. Murdoch 2006.
9. Tucker 2011, 75–76.
10. Goldsworthy 2014, 453.
11. Heather 2009, 5.
12. Tacitus, *Germania*, 5.45.
13. Tacitus, *Annals*, II.26 (3).
14. Augustus, 12.
15. Velleius Paterculus, II.90.1.
16. Tacitus, *Annals*, II.44.2.
17. Todd 2004, 33–34.

18. Price 2015, 282–83.
19. Tacitus, *Germania*, 5.
20. Tacitus, *Agricola*, 36.
21. Spurkland 2010; Robertson 2012.
22. Ringe 2006, section 4.1.
23. Jovaisa 2001.
24. Heather and Matthews 1991, chapter 3; Kokowski 2013.
25. Heather and Matthews 1991, chapter 5.
26. Heather 2009, 439.
27. Jordanes, chapters 4 and 17. Jordanes gives no date for the move to mainland Europe, but his claim (chapter 60) that the race of the Ostrogoths in AD 540 was overcome in almost its 2,030th year produced the commonly quoted calculation of 1490 BC, which has no historical value.
28. Ptolemy, 2.10.
29. Ptolemy, 3.5; Tacitus, *Germania*, 44.
30. Ringe and Taylor 2014, chapter 2.
31. Perdikaris 2004.
32. Mallory and Adams 1997, 22.
33. Ringe and Taylor 2014, section 4.3.4.
34. Murray 2008, chapter 1.
35. Heather 2009, chapter 6.
36. Springer 2003; Flierman 2017.
37. Ptolemy, II.10.
38. Widukind of Corvey, 6.
39. Murray 2008, 25: Orosius, *Histories against the Pagans*, VII.32.
40. *Notitia Dignitatum. in Partibus Occidentis*, XXVIII.
41. Murray 2008, 182: Sidonius Apollinaris, *Panegyrics*.
42. Murray 2008, 216: Sidonius Apollinaris, Letter to Namatius.
43. Nieuwhof 2013; Bazelmans 2009; Schrijver 2014, 129; Hines and Ijssennagger 2017.

44. Soulat 2009.
45. Murray 2008, 105: *Chronicle of Marius of Avenches*, and 307-8: *Histories of Gregory of Tours*.
46. *Carolingian Chronicles*, 42.
47. *Carolingian Chronicles*, 51, 53.
48. Springer 2003.

Chapter 7: Anglo-Saxon Arrivals (pp. 118–39)

1. Gildas, II.23.
2. Breeze 2008.
3. Breeze 2013.
4. Russo 1998, 72–74.
5. Manco 2015, *Blood of the Celts*, 154–55; De la Bédoyère 2013, chapter 2.
6. Tacitus, *Agricola*, 21.
7. Manco 2015, *Blood of the Celts*, 165–67, 177–80.
8. *Historia Brittonum*, 31, 37.
9. Yorke 1990, 26.
10. Redfern et al. 2016; Eaton et al. 2015.
11. Henn et al. 2012; Schuenemann et al. 2017.
12. Bowman and Thomas 1994, 22–30.
13. *RIB* 1593 and 1594.
14. *ILS* (vol. 1), 2549 and 2554.
15. Martiniano et al. 2016.
16. Härke 2011.
17. *ASC*, under the year 449.
18. Bede, *EH*, I.15; Gildas, II.23.
19. Murray 2008: *Gallic Chronicle of 452*, 84.
20. Higham and Ryan 2013, 76.
21. Bede, *EH*, I.15; Gildas, II.23.
22. Murray 2008: *Gallic Chronicle of 452*, 80.
23. *ODNB*: Constantine III [Flavius Claudius Constantinus], entry by R. S. O. Tomlin.
24. Scull, Minter and Plouviez 2016.
25. Gildas, II.25.
26. Higham and Ryan 2013, 42–47 and chapter 2; Hamerow 2012, 11–14.
27. Hamerow 2012, chapter 2.

28. Caruth and Goffin 2012.
29. Hamerow 2012, 144–47.
30. Higham and Ryan 2013, chapter 2.
31. Schiffels et al. 2016.
32. Higham and Ryan 2013, chapter 2.
33. Hills and Lucy 2013.
34. Montgomery et al. 2005.
35. Bakka 1981.
36. Yorke 1990, 13; Harrington and Welch 2014, 6.
37. Harrington and Welch 2014, 6, 173–80.
38. Brookes 2007.
39. Hope-Taylor 1977.
40. Sherlock and Welch 1992.
41. Hills and Lucy 2013.
42. Bede, *EH*, II.14, V.24.
43. Adams 2013, Appendix A.
44. Bede, *EH*, III.6, III.16.
45. *Historia Brittonum*.
46. Adams 2013, Appendix A.
47. Bede, *EH*, I.34, II.2.
48. Hamerow 2012, 102–4.
49. Bede, *EH*, II.12.
50. Yorke 1990, 102.
51. Bede, *EH*, II.5, II. 20.
52. *ASC*.
53. Bede, *EH*, III.21.
54. Finberg 1961, 217.
55. Yorke 1990, 104; Charles-Edwards 2013, 16, 387–96.
56. *ASC*; Bede, *EH*, IV.21.
57. Carver, Hills and Scheschkewitz 2009.
58. Manco 1998.
59. Hamerow 2012, 102–3; Hamerow, Ferguson and Naylor 2013.
60. Lapidge et al. 1999, 93, 203–4: Yorke 1990, chapter 7.
61. Martiniano et al. 2016.
62. Weale et al. 2002. This study was carried out in the early days of construction of the Y-DNA phylogeny, so I1 is not identified as such, but as haplogroup 2.
63. Bede, *EH*, IV.16.
64. Yorke 1990, 136; Yorke 1982.
65. Bede, *EH*, IV.12, 14, 16; *ASC* 685, 686.

66. *ASC*.
67. *EHD* I, 2nd edition (1979), no. 51 (p. 476).
68. *Laws*, 36–61.
69. Tristram 2007.
70. Higham and Ryan 2013, illustration 2.24.

Chapter 8: Embracing Christianity (pp. 140–63)

1. *Anglo-Saxon Poetry*, 4: Cædmon's Hymn.
2. Gelling 1973.
3. Patrick, *Confessio*, 1.
4. Blair 2005, 14–27.
5. South West Heritage Trust news: 5 December 2016.
6. Gilchrist and Green 2015.
7. Bede, *EH*, I.22.
8. Bede, *EH*, IV.13.
9. Sims-Williams 1990, 79–83.
10. Bede, *EH*, I.23–25.
11. Bede, *EH*, I.25–26.
12. Bede, *EH*, I.27–29.
13. Canterbury's Archaeology 1992/1993, The 17th Annual Report of Canterbury Archaeological Trust Ltd.
14. Bede, *EH*, I.33.
15. Blair 2005, 68.
16. Gough 1973, 56–57.
17. Bede, *EH*, II.3, 5.
18. Yorke 1990, 46–47.
19. Chadwick Hawkes 1982.
20. Bede, *EH*, II.5.
21. Webster 2011.
22. Hirst et al. 2004.
23. Bede, *EH*, II.6, II.9–14.
24. Bede, *EH*, II.14.
25. Blair 2005, 3.
26. Bede, Letter to Egbert.
27. Bede, *EH*, III.4.
28. Bede, *EH*, III.3–5.
29. Bede, *EH*, II.5.
30. Bede, *EH*, III.7.
31. Bede, *EH*, II.15, III.18–19.
32. Bede, *EH*, III.21–24.
33. Bede, *EH*, III.25.
34. Bede, *EH*, IV.12–13, 15–16; *ASC* 685, 686.
35. Higham and Ryan 2013, 127–30; Blair 2005, 240.

36. Sherlock and Simmons 2008.
37. Higham and Ryan 2013, 127–30; Blair 2005, 240.
38. Sims-Williams 1990, 76.
39. Bede, *EH*, IV.13.
40. Fischer 1989, 243.
41. Pelteret 1985.
42. Pelteret 1985.
43. *Laws*, 39.
44. Pelteret 1985.
45. *Laws*, 41.
46. Augustine of Hippo, *City of God*, I.21.
47. Leahy and Bland 2014; Birmingham Museums Trust 2014; Higham and Ryan 2013, 173–78.
48. Blair 2005, 83, 206–8, 213.
49. Smith, Hutton and Cook 1979, 13–14.
50. Bede, *EH*, V.19.
51. Bede, *Lives of the Holy Abbots*; Benedict Biscop entry, in Lapidge et al. 1999, 60–61.
52. *Vita Sancti Wilfridi auctore Edmero*.
53. Gilchrist and Green 2015.
54. *Aldhelm: The Poetic Works*, 47–49.
55. Parsons and Sutherland 2013.
56. Hare 2014.
57. Blair 2005, 83; Stenton 1970.
58. Breay and Meehan 2015.
59. Teasdale et al. 2017.
60. *ODNB*: Eadfrith, entry by A. Thacker; Backhouse 1981.
61. Bede, *Lives of the Holy Abbots*.
62. Bede, Letter to Egbert.
63. Dales 2013, 31–32.
64. Einhard, *Life of Charlemagne*, 25.
65. Dales 2013, chapter 1.
66. Bede, Letter to Egbert.
67. Blair 1970, 259, 270, note 2, chapter 26; Dales 2013, 25, 32–33.
68. *ODNB*: Dunstan, entry by M. Lapidge; Blair 2005, 350–54.

Chapter 9: Forging a Nation (pp. 164–87)

1. ASC 785 for 787.
2. Higham and Ryan 2013, 188–90.
3. Lapidge et al. 1999, 124–26.
4. *Beowulf*, lines 5–11.
5. ASC, A 626.
6. *Old English Chronicles*, 5.
7. John 1996, 55.
8. Bede, *EH*, II.5.
9. ASC 477.
10. Henson 2006, Appendix 3; Lapidge et al. 1999, 455–56; Higham and Ryan 2013, 139–40.
11. Sawyer 1968, no. 723; Electronic Sawyer 712a.
12. Sawyer 1968, no. 677.
13. Yorke 1990, 113.
14. Sawyer 1968, no. 113.
15. *Laws*, 49, cap. 36.
16. *Laws*, 59, cap. 70.
17. Lapidge et al. 1999, 181–82.
18. Hamerow 2002, 87, 139–41.
19. Hamerow 2012, 73–76.
20. Blair 2005, 381–82, 387–93.
21. Ditchfield 1901, chapter 7.
22. Maitland 1897, 222.
23. Gray 1915.
24. Thirsk 1964.
25. Gray 1915, 450–509.
26. *Laws*, 49, cap. 42.
27. Manco 1995.
28. Hamerow 2012, chapters 2 and 5.
29. Gerrard with Aston 2007, 74–101, 974–81.
30. Hamerow 2002, 139–43; Hamerow 2012, 90, 147–51.
31. Yorke 1990, 113–14.
32. Ray and Bapty 2016.
33. Blackmore 2002.
34. Sawyer 1968, no. 86.
35. Bede, *EH*, II.3.
36. Spall and Toop 2008.
37. Scull 2002.
38. Stoodley 2002.
39. Sawyer 1968, no. 288; Electronic Sawyer for full text.
40. Russo 1998, 146.
41. Sawyer 1968, no. 7.
42. Sawyer 1968, no. 29.
43. Russo 1998, 146–47.

44. *Laws*, 5–17.
45. Lapidge et al. 1999, 113–15.
46. Ulmschneider 2002.
47. Haslam 1987, 86.
48. Brooks 1971; Sawyer 1968, no. 134 and Electronic Sawyer for full text.
49. ASC E 823 (for 825), 827 (for 829).
50. ASC.
51. Browne 1908, 128–32.
52. Brink 2008.
53. Ferguson 2009, 377.
54. Manco 2015, *Ancestral Journeys*, 250–51.
55. ASC; Keynes and Lapidge (trans.) 1983, Asser 27.
56. ASC; Keynes and Lapidge (trans.) 1983, Asser 5, 18, 30.
57. Lomax 2013, Kindle location 660.
58. Keynes and Lapidge (trans.) 1983, Asser 29 and note 58; *ODNB*: Ealhswith, entry by Marios Costambeys.
59. ASC; Keynes and Lapidge (trans.) 1983, Asser 31–53, 92 and notes; William of Malmesbury, II, 92; Haslam 2014, 52–56.
60. ASC 876 for 875; Downham 2007, 238.
61. Keynes and Lapidge (trans.) 1983, 171–72 or Laws, 98–101 for the text of the treaty; Higham and Ryan 2013, 284–89.
62. Charles-Edwards 2013, 431.
63. Keynes and Lapidge (trans.) 1983, 227, note 1.
64. ASC.
65. Sawyer 1968, no. 223; Electronic Sawyer for full text.
66. Biddle and Hill 1971.
67. Hill and Rumble 1996.
68. *Laws*, 114–17.
69. ASC; Lapidge et al. 1999, 162–63; *ODNB*: Æthelflæd, entry by Marios Costambeys; Henry of Huntingdon, 168.
70. Downham 2007, 97–100.

71. *Anglo-Saxon Poetry*, 518–28.
72. Sheppard 2004.
73. Lapidge et al. 1999, 15.
74. Godfrey 1979.
75. Campbell 2000, chapter 1.
76. *ODNB*: Henry I, entry by C. Warren Hollister.

Chapter 10: The Rise of English (pp.188–207)

1. Seeley 1883, 10.
2. Neveux 2008, chapter 4; Ferguson 2009, chapter 9.
3. Neveux 2008, 89.
4. Hey 2000, 33–36, 51–52.
5. Aurell 2007, introduction and 196.
6. Ormrod 2013.
7. Gwynn 1985.
8. *Guardian*, 19 April 2001.
9. Ringe and Taylor 2014, 7–9.
10. Galinsky et al. 2016.
11. Crystal 2003, 24–27.
12. Crystal 2003, 32–48.
13. Crystal 2003, 60–66.
14. Pratchett 2014, 291.
15. *ODNB*: Malmesbury, William of, entry by R. M. Thomson.
16. Crick 2004.
17. *ODNB*: Bede, entry by J. Campbell.
18. Sawyer 1968: bibliography.
19. *Codex Exoniensis*.
20. *ODNB*: Furnivall, Frederick James, entry by William S. Peterson.
21. Martínez Pizarro 1996.
22. Curtis 1971; De Nie 2004.
23. e.g. John 1996, chapter 1.
24. Keynes and Lapidge 1983, 50–51; Campbell 2000, 129–30.
25. Tolkien 1981, letter no. 25.
26. Tolkien 1953.
27. Tolkien 1981, letter nos 29 and 30.
28. *ODNB*: Tolkien, John Ronald Reuel, entry by T. A. Shippey; *Beowulf* trans. Tolkien.
29. Pratchett 2014, 156–63.
30. Pratchett 1997, 405.
31. *Entertainment Monthly*, 31 January 2014.
32. Campbell 2000, xxi and chapter 1.
33. Leahy and Bland 2014, 6–8; Birmingham Museums Trust 2014.
34. Aston 2000, 28.
35. Croft, Gaffney and Gater 1993.
36. Schiffels et al. 2016.

Bibliography

Abbreviations

ASC: *The Anglo-Saxon Chronicle*, trans. and ed. Michael Swanton. London: Dent 1996.

BAR: British Archaeological Reports.

EH: Bede, *The Ecclesiastical History of the English People*, trans. B. Colgrave, ed. J. McClure and R. Collins. Oxford and New York: Oxford University Press. 1994.

EHD: *English Historical Documents*. London: Routledge.

ILS: *Inscriptiones Latinae Selectae*, ed. H. Dessau. Berlin: Weidmann. 1892–1916.

ODNB: *Oxford Dictionary of National Biography*. 2004; online ed., May 2008.

RIB: *The Roman Inscriptions of Britain*, ed. R. G. Collingwood and R. P. Wright. Oxford: Clarendon Press. 1965.

Primary Sources

Aldhelm: *The Poetic Works*, trans. M. Lapidge, J. L. Rosier, N. Wright. Cambridge: D. S. Brewer. 1985.

Alfred the Great, *Boethius. King Alfred's Anglo-Saxon Version of Boethius, de Consolatione Philosophiae*, ed. and trans. W. Sedgefield. Oxford: Clarendon Press. 1899.

Ammianus Marcellinus, *Roman History*. London: Bohn. 1862.

The Anglo-Saxon Chronicle, trans. and ed. Michael Swanton. London: Dent. 1996.

Anglo-Saxon Poetry, ed. and trans. S. A. J. Bradley. London: J. M. Dent. 1982.

Augustine of Hippo, *City of God*, trans. M. Dods, 2 vols. Edinburgh: T. & T. Clark. 1871.

Augustus, *Res gestae divi Augusti/ The Deeds of the Divine Augustus*, trans. F. W. Shipley. Loeb Classical Library. Cambridge, MA: Harvard University Press. 1924.

Bede, *The Ecclesiastical History of the English People*, trans. B. Colgrave, ed. J. McClure and R. Collins. Oxford and New York: Oxford University Press. 1994.

Bede, Letter to Egbert, included in *The Ecclesiastical History of the English People*, ed. J. McClure and R. Collins. Oxford and New York: Oxford University Press. 1994.

Bede, *The Lives of the Holy Abbots of Weremouth and Jarrow*, in *Ecclesiastical History of the English Nation*, trans. J. A. Giles, Everyman's Library 479, 349–66. London: J. M. Dent; New York: E. P. Dutton. 1910.

Beowulf: An Anglo-Saxon Poem Translated from the Heyn-Socin Text, trans. J. L. Hall. Boston, New York and Chicago: D.C. Heath and Co. 1892.

Beowulf: Text and Facing Translation, ed. and trans. M. Swanton (2nd ed.). Manchester: Manchester University Press. 1997.

Beowulf: A Translation and Commentary, together with Sellic Spell, by J. R. R. Tolkien, ed. C. Tolkien. London: Harper Collins. 2014.

Boniface = *The English Correspondence of Saint Boniface*, ed. and trans. E. Kylie. London: Chatto and Windus. 1911.

Bowman, A. and Thomas, D. *The Vindolanda Writing Tablets (Tabulae Vindolandenses II)*. London: British Museum Press. 1994.

Caesar = *The Conquest of Gaul*, trans. S. A. Handford, revised by J. F. Gardner. London and New York: Penguin Books. 1982.

Capitularia regum Francorum, vol. II, ed. A. Boretius and V. Krause. 1897.

Carolingian Chronicles: Royal Frankish Annals and Nithard's Histories, trans. B. H. Scholtz and B. Rogers. Ann Arbor: University of Michigan Press. 1970.

Cassius Dio, *Roman History*, trans. E. Cary. 9 vols (Loeb Classical Library). Cambridge, MA: Harvard University Press. 1914–27.

Codex Exoniensis. A Collection of Anglo-Saxon Poetry, from a Manuscript in the Library of the Dean and Chapter of Exeter, ed. and trans. B. Thorpe. London: William Pickering for the Society of Antiquaries of London. 1842.

Einhard, *The Life of Charlemagne*, trans. S. E. Turner. New York: Harper & Brothers. 1880.

Flavius Josephus, *Antiquities of the Jews*, trans. William Whiston. 1895.

Florence of Worcester, *The Chronicle of Florence of Worcester*, trans. T. Forester. London: Henry T. Bohn. 1854.

Geoffrey of Monmouth, *History of the Kings of Britain*, trans. A. Thompson, rev. J. A. Giles. Cambridge, ON: In Parentheses Publications. 1999.

Gildas, *The Works of Gildas and Nennius*, trans. J. A. Giles. London: James Bohn. 1841.

Heimskringla, by Snorri Sturluson, vol. 1, trans. A. Finlay and A. Faulkes. Viking Society for Northern Research. University College London. 2011.

Henry of Huntingdon = *The Chronicle of Henry of Huntingdon*, trans. T. Forester. London: Henry G. Bohn. 1853.

Herodotus, *The Histories*, trans. R. Waterfield. Oxford and New York: Oxford University Press. 1998.

Hesiod, *Works and Days*, in *Hesiod, Homeric Hymns, Epic Cycle, Homerica*, trans. H. G. Evelyn-White. Loeb Classical Library. London: Heinemann. 1914.

Historia Brittonum, translated in *Six Old English Chronicles*, ed. J. A. Giles. London: Henry G. Bohn. 1848.

Inscriptiones Latinae Selectae, ed. H. Dessau. Berlin: Weidmann. 1892–1916.

Isidore, *The Etymologies of Isidore of Seville*, ed. and trans. S.A. Barney, W. J. Lewis, J. A. Beach and O. Bergho. Cambridge: Cambridge University Press. 2006.

Jordanes, *The Origins and Deeds of the Goths*, trans. C. C. Mierow. Princeton, NJ: Princeton University Press. 1908.

Keynes, S. and Lapidge, M. (trans.) *Alfred the Great: Asser's Life of King Alfred and other Contemporary Sources*. Harmondsworth: Penguin Books. 1983.

Laws = The Laws of the Earliest English Kings, ed. and trans. F. L. Attenborough. Cambridge: Cambridge University Press. 1922.

Lucretius, *De Rerum Natura*, trans. W. E. Leonard. New York: E. P. Dutton. 1916.

Murray, A. C. (ed. and trans.) *From Roman to Merovingian Gaul: A Reader*. Toronto, ON: Higher Education University of Toronto Press. 2008.

Notitia Dignitatum or Register of Dignitaries, trans. W. Fairley. Translations and Reprints from Original Sources of European History 6 (4). Philadelphia: University of Pennsylvania Press. 1900.

Old English Chronicles, ed. and trans. J. A. Giles. London: George Bell & Sons. 1906.

Patrick, *Confessio*, trans. P. McCarthy. Dublin: Royal Irish Academy. 2003.

Pliny the Elder, *The Natural History*, trans. J. Bostock and H. T. Riley. London: Taylor and Francis. 1855.

The Poetic Edda, trans. C. Larrington. Oxford World's Classics (2nd ed.). Oxford: Oxford University Press. 2014.

Posidonius, Vol. 1: *The Fragments*, ed. L. Edelstein and I. Kidd (Cambridge Classical Texts and Commentaries 13) (2nd ed.). Cambridge and New York: Cambridge University Press. 1989.

Procopius, *History of the Wars*, with an English translation by H. B. Dewing. Loeb Classical Library. London: William Heinemann; Cambridge, MA: Harvard University Press. 1962.

The Prose Edda, by Snorri Sturluson, trans. A. G. Brodeur. New York: The American Scandinavian Foundation. 1916.

Ptolemy, Claudius. *The Geography*. No reliable complete English translation is in print. That used is trans. E. L. Stevenson. New York: New York Public Library. 1932.

Rigveda, The Hymns of the, trans. Ralph T. H. Griffith (2nd ed.). Kotagiri (Nilgiri). 1896.

The Roman Inscriptions of Britain, ed. R. G. Collingwood and R. P. Wright. Oxford: Clarendon Press. 1965.

Saga of the Volsungs, ed. and trans. R. G. Finch. London and Edinburgh: Thomas Nelson. 1965.

Sawyer, P. H. *Anglo-Saxon Charters: An Annotated List and Bibliography*. London: University College London. 1968. Continued online and with full text as The Electronic Sawyer: http://www.esawyer.org.uk.

Strabo, *Geography*, trans. H. L. Jones. Loeb Classical Library III. 1924.

Sven Aggesen, *Brevis historia regum Dacie, c. 1*, in *Scriptores minores historiæ Danicæ: Medii Ævi*, ed. M. Cl. Gertz, vol. 1. Copenhagen: C. E. C. Gad. 1917.

Tacitus, *Agricola and Germania*, trans. H. Mattingly 1948, rev. J. B. Rives. London: Penguin Books. 2009.

Tacitus, *Annals*, trans. C. Damon. London and New York: Penguin Group. 2012.

Tacitus, *The Histories*, trans. K. Wellesley, rev. R. Ash. London and New York: Penguin Group. 2009.

Thietmar of Merseburg, *Ottonian Germany. The Chronicon of Thietmar of Merseburg*, trans. and annotated by D. A. Warner. Manchester and New York: Manchester University Press 2001.

Velleius Paterculus, *Compendium of Roman History*, trans. F. W. Shipley. Loeb Classical Library. Cambridge, MA: Harvard University Press. 1924.

Vita Sancti Wilfridi auctore Edmero = The Life of Saint Wilfrid by Edmer, ed. and trans. B. J. Muir and A. J. Turner (Exeter Medieval Texts and Studies). Exeter: University of Exeter Press. 1998.

Widsith, ed. K. Malone, rev. ed. Copenhagen: Rosenkilde and Bagger. 1962.

Widukind of Corvey. *Deeds of the Saxons*, ed. and trans. B. S. Bachrach and D. S. Bachrach. Washington DC: The Catholic University of America Press. 2014.

William of Malmesbury, *The Deeds of the Bishops of England (Gesta Pontificum Anglorum)*, trans. D. Preest. Woodbridge, Suffolk and Rochester, NY: Boydell Press. 2002.

Secondary Sources

Adams, M. 2013. *The King in the North: The Life and Times of Oswald of Northumbria*. London: Head of Zeus.

Adams, N. 2010. Rethinking the Sutton Hoo shoulder clasps and armour, in *Intelligible Beauty: Recent Research on Byzantine Jewellery* (British Museum Research Publication 178), C. Entwistle and N. Adams (eds), 83–112. London: British Museum.

Aikio, A. 2006. On Germanic-Saami contacts and Saami prehistory, *Suomalais-Ugrilaisen Seuren Aikakauskirja/Journal de la Société Finno-Ougrienne*, 91: 9–55.

Aikio, A. 2012. An essay on Saami ethnolinguistic prehistory, in *A Linguistic Map of Prehistoric Northern Europe* (Suomalais-Ugrilaisen Seuran Toimituksia [Mémoires de la Société Finno-Ougrienne] 266), R. Grünthal and P. Kallio (eds), 63–117. Helsinki: Société Finno-Ougrienne.

Allentoft, M. E. et al. 2015. Population genomics of Bronze Age Eurasia, *Nature*, 522: 167–72.

Andersen, H. 1996. *Reconstructing Prehistorical Dialects: Initial Vowels in Slavic and Baltic* (Trends in Linguistics: Studies & Monographs 91). Berlin and New York: Mouton de Gruyter.

Andrzejowski, J. 2010. The Przeworsk culture. A brief story (for the foreigners), in *Worlds Apart? Contacts across the Baltic Sea in the Iron Age*, U. Lund Hansen and A. Bitner-Wróblewska (eds), 1–52. Copenhagen: Det Kongelige Nordiske Oldkriftsekskab; Warsaw: Państwowe Muzeum Archeologiczne.

Anlezark, D. 2002. Sceaf, Japheth and the origins of the Anglo-Saxons, *Anglo-Saxon England*, 31: 13–46.

Anthony, D. W. 2007. *The Horse, the Wheel and Language: How Bronze Age Riders from the Eurasian Steppes Shaped the Modern World*. Princeton, NJ and Oxford: Princeton University Press.

Anthony, D. W. 2008. A new approach to language and archaeology: The Usatovo Culture and the separation of Pre-Germanic, *Journal of Indo-European Studies*, 36 (1–2): 1–51.

Anthony, D. W. and Ringe, D. 2015. The Indo-European homeland from linguistic and archaeological perspectives, *Annual Review of Linguistics*, 1: 199–219.

Arnold, B. 1990. The past as propaganda: Totalitarian archaeology in Nazi Germany, *Archaeology*, 64 (244): 464–78.

Arnold, B. 1992. The past as propaganda: How Hitler's archaeologists distorted European prehistory to justify racist and territorial goals, *Archaeology* (New York), 45 (4): 30–37.

Aston, M. 2000. *Mick's Archaeology*. Stroud, Gloucestershire: Tempus.

Aurell, M. 2007. *The Plantagenet Empire, 1154–1224*, trans. D. Crouch. Harlow: Pearson Education.

Babik, Z. 2001. *Najstarsza warstwa nazewnicza na ziemiach polskich*. Crakow: Universitas Kraków.

Backhouse, J. 1981. *The Lindisfarne Gospels*. London: Phaidon.

Bagnasco, G. et al. 2017. Tarquinia and the north. Considerations on some archaeological evidence of the 9th–3rd century BC, in *Inter-regional Contacts during the First Millenium B.C. in Europe: Proceedings from the session organized during the 19th meeting of European Association of Archaeologists, held in Pilsen (5th–9th September 2013)*, M. Trefný and B. Jennings (eds), *ArchaeoMedia* (6 September), 46–91.

Bakka, E. 1981. Scandinavian-type gold bracteates in Kentish and continental grave finds, in *Angles, Saxons and Jutes*, V. I. Evison (ed.), 11–38. Oxford: Clarendon Press; New York: Oxford University Press.

Barber, K. E. et al. 2004. Late Holocene climatic history of northern Germany and Denmark: Peat macrofossil investigations at Dosenmoor, Schleswig-Holstein, and Svanemose, Jutland, *Boreas*, 33 (2): 132–44.

Barjamovic, G. 2011. *A Historical Geography of Anatolia in the Old Assyrian Colony Period* (Carsten Niebuhr Institute Publications 38). Copenhagen: Museum Tusculanum Press.

Batini, C. et al. 2015. Large-scale recent expansion of European patrilineages shown by population resequencing, *Nature Communications*, 6: 7152.

Bazelmans, J. 2009. The early-medieval use of ethnic names from classical antiquity: The case of the Frisians, in *Ethnic Constructs in Antiquity: The Role of Power and Tradition*, T. Derks and N. Royman (eds), 321–37. Amsterdam: Amsterdam University Press.

Behre, K.-E. 2004. Coastal development, sea-level change and settlement history during the later Holocene in the Clay District of Lower Saxony (Niedersachsen), northern Germany, *Quaternary International*, 112: 37–53.

Biddle, M. and Hill, D. 1971. Late Saxon planned towns, *Antiquaries Journal*, 51: 70–85.

Bill, J. 2008. Viking ships and the sea, chapter 11 in *The Viking World*, S. Brink and N. Price (eds), 170–80. London and New York: Routledge.

Birmingham Museums Trust. 2014. *The Staffordshire Hoard*. Birmingham: Birmingham Museums Trust.

Blackmore, L. 2002. The origins and growth of Lundenwic, a mart of many nations, in Hårdh and Larsson (eds) 2002: 273–301.

Blair, J. 2005. *The Church in Anglo-Saxon Society*. Oxford and New York: Oxford University Press.

Blair, P. H. 1970. *The World of Bede*. Cambridge and New York: Cambridge University Press.

Bochnak, T. 2006. Les Celtes et ses voisins septentrionaux, in *Celtes et Gaulois, l'Archéologie face à l'Histoire, 3: Les Civilisés et les Barbares (du ve au iie siècle avant J.-C.). Actes de la table ronde de Budapest, 17–18 juin 2005*, M. Szabó (dir.), 159–83. Glux-en-Glenne: Bibracte, Centre archéologique européen.

Bochnak, T. 2011. The eastern Celts in the north, in *The Eastern Celts. The Communities between the Alps and the Black Sea*, M. Guštin and M. Jevtić (eds), 13–17. Ljubljana: Narodni muzej Slovenije.

Bochnak, T. and Harasim, P. 2012. Interregional and multidirectional contacts of local elites: A case of scabbards with crossbars decorated with three or more s-figures in *Northern Poland, People at the Crossroads of Space and Time (Footmarks of Societies in Ancient Europe) II, Archaeologia Baltica*, 18: 59–82.

Boscher, L. C. 2016. Reconstructing the Arsenical Copper Production Process in Early Bronze Age Southwest Asia. PhD thesis submitted to University College London.

Bradley, R. et al. 2016. *The Later Prehistory of North-West Europe: The Evidence of Development-Led Fieldwork*. Oxford and New York: Oxford University Press.

Bramanti, B. et al. 2009. Genetic discontinuity between local hunter-gatherers and Central Europe's first farmers, *Science*, 326 (5949): 137–40.

Brandt, J. and Rauchfuß, B. (eds). 2014. *Das Jastorf-Konzept und die vorrömische Eisenzeit im nördlichen Mitteleuropa. Beiträge der Internationalen Tagung zum einhundertjährigen Jubiläum der Veröffentlichung der Ältesten Urnenfriedhöfe bei Uelzen und Lüneburg durch Gustav Schwantes 18.–22.05.2011 in Bad Bevensen*. Hamburg: Archäologisches Museum.

Breay, C. and Meehan, B. (eds). 2015. *The St Cuthbert Gospel: Studies on the Insular Manuscript of the Gospel of John*. London: British Library.

Breeze, A. 2008. Where was Gildas born?, *Northern History*, 45: 347–50.

Breeze, A. 2013. Gildas and the schools of Cirencester, *The Antiquaries Journal*, 90: 131–38.

Brink, S. 2008. Who were the Vikings?, in *The Viking World*, S. Brink and N. Price (eds), 4–7. London and New York: Routledge.

Brookes, S. 2007. Boat-rivets in graves in pre-Viking Kent: Reassessing Anglo-Saxon boat-burial traditions, *Medieval Archaeology*, 51: 1–18.

Brooks, N. 1971. The development of military obligations in eighth- and ninth-century England, in *England Before the Conquest: Studies in Primary Sources Presented to Dorothy Whitelock*, P. Clemoes and K. Hughes (eds), 69–84. Cambridge: Cambridge University Press.

Browne, G. F. 1908. *Alcuin*

of York. London: Society for Promoting Christian Knowledge.

Bruce-Mitford, R. L. 2005. *The Corpus of Late Celtic Hanging-Bowls*. Oxford and New York: Oxford University Press.

Cameron, A. 1985. *Procopius and the Sixth Century*. Berkeley: University of California Press; London: Duckworth.

Campbell, J. 2000. *The Anglo-Saxon State*. London and New York: Hambledon & London.

Capelli, C. et al. 2003. A Y chromosome census of the British Isles, *Current Biology*, 13: 979–84.

Caruth, J. and Goffin, R. 2012. *Land South of Hartismere High School, Eye, Suffolk. Post-Excavation Assessment Report*. Ipswich: Suffolk County Council Archaeological Service.

Carver, M. O. H. 2000. *Sutton Hoo: Burial Ground of Kings?* London: British Museum Press: Philadelphia: University of Philadelphia Press.

Carver, M., Hills, C. and Scheschkewitz, J. 2009. *Wasperton. A Roman, British and Anglo-Saxon Cemetery in Central England*. Woodbridge, Suffolk: The Boydell Press.

Chadwick Hawkes, S. 1982. The archaeology of conversion: Cemeteries, in *The Anglo-Saxons*, J. Campbell (ed.), 48–49. Oxford: Phaidon.

Charles-Edwards, T. M. 2013. *Wales and the Britons 350–1064*. Oxford: Oxford University Press.

Chase, C. (ed.) 1981. *The Dating of Beowulf*. Toronto and London: University of Toronto Press.

Christensen, T. 2015. *Lejre bag Myten: De arkæologiske udgravninger*. Højbjerg: Jysk Arkæologisk Selskab for the Roskilde Museum.

Clark, J. G. D. 1966. Invasion

hypothesis in British archaeology, *Antiquity*, 40 (159): 172–89.

Cline, E. H. 2014. *1177 B.C.: The Year Civilization Collapsed*. Princeton, NJ and Oxford: Princeton University Press.

Cramp, L. J. E. et al. 2014. Neolithic dairy farming at the extreme of agriculture in northern Europe, *Proceedings of the Royal Society B: Biological Sciences*, 281(1791): 20140819.

Crick, J. C. 2004. Monmouth, Geoffrey of (d. 1154/5), *ODNB*.

Croft, R. A., Gaffney, C. F. and Gater, J. A. 1993. Athelney, *Somerset Archaeology and Natural History*, 137: 142–43.

Cruciani, F. et al. 2010. Human Y chromosome haplogroup R-V88: A paternal genetic record of early mid Holocene trans-Saharan connections and the spread of Chadic languages, *European Journal of Human Genetics*, 18: 800–07.

Crystal, D. 2003. *The Cambridge Encyclopedia of the English Language* (2nd ed.). Cambridge and New York: Cambridge University Press.

Curtis, L. P. 1971. *Apes and Angels: The Irishman in Victorian Caricature*. Newton Abbot: David & Charles; Washington DC, Smithsonian Institution Press.

Cwaliński, M. 2014. The influx of amber to the circum-Adriatic areas during the Bronze Age. Proposition of an interpretative model, *Fontes Archaeologici Posnanienses*, 50 (2): 183–99.

Czebreszuk, J. 2008. The northern section of the first amber trail. An outline of significance for civilization development, *Amber in Archaeology, Proceedings of the Fifth International Conference on Amber in Archaeology, Belgrade 2006*, 100–9. Belgrade: National Museum.

Czebreszuk, J. 2013. Mysterious raw material from the far north: Amber in Mycenaean culture, in *Counterpoint: Essays in Archaeology and Heritage Studies in Honour of Professor Kristian Kristiansen* (BAR International Series 2508), S. Bergerbrant and S. Sabatini (eds), 557–63. Oxford: Archaeopress.

Dales, D. 2013. *Alcuin, Theology and Thought*. Cambridge: James Clark & Co.

Davis, C. R. 2006. An ethnic dating of Beowulf, *Anglo-Saxon England*, 35: 111–30.

De la Bédoyère, G. 2013. *Roman Britain: A New History*, revised ed. London and New York: Thames & Hudson.

De Nie, M. 2004. *The Eternal Paddy: Irish Identity and the British Press, 1798–1882*. Madison, WI and London: University of Wisconsin Press.

Desrosiers, P. M. (ed.). 2012. *The Emergence of Pressure Blade Making: From Origin to Modern Experimentation*. New York and London: Springer.

Ditchfield, P. H. 1901. *English Villages*. London: Methuen & Co; New York: James Pott & Co.

Downham, C. 2007. *Viking Kings of Britain and Ireland: The Dynasty of Ívarr to A.D. 1014*. Edinburgh: Dunedin Academic Press.

Drauschke, J. 2007. 'Byzantine' and 'oriental' imports in the Merovingian Empire from the second half of the fifth to the beginning of the eighth century, in *Incipient Globalization? Long-Distance Contacts in the Sixth Century* (BAR International Series 1644), A. Harris (ed.), 53–73. Oxford: Archaeopress.

Dzięgielewski, K. 2010. Expansion of the Pomeranian culture in Poland during the early Iron Age: Remarks on the mechanism and

possible causes, in *Migration in Bronze and Early Iron Age Europe*, K. Dzięgielewski, M. S. Przybyła, A. Gawlik (eds), 173–95. Crakow: Księgarnia Akademicka.

Eaton, K. et al. 2015. *Museum of London Report on the DNA Analyses of Four Roman Individuals*. Available from the Museum of London.

Ferguson, R. 2009. *The Hammer and the Cross: A New History of the Vikings*. London and New York: Allen Lane/Penguin Books.

Field, D. 1998. Round barrows and the harmonious landscape: Placing Early Bronze Age burial monuments in South-East England, *Oxford Journal of Archaeology*, 17 (3): 309–26.

Finberg, H. P. R. 1961. *The Early Charters of the West Midlands*. Leicester: Leicester University Press.

Fischer, D. H. 1989. *Albion's Seed: Four British Folkways in America*. Oxford and New York: Oxford University Press.

Fischer, S. 2004. Alemannia and the North – early runic contexts apart (400–800), in *Alamannien und der Norden*, H.-P. Naumann (ed.), 266–317. Berlin and New York: Walter de Gruyter.

Fischer, S. 2005. *Roman Imperialism and Runic Literacy. The Westernization of Northern Europe (150–800 AD)*. Aun 33. Uppsala: Uppsala University, Deparment of Archaeology and Ancient History.

Flierman, R. 2017. *Saxon Identities, AD 150–900*. London and New York: Bloomsbury Academic.

Fornander, E. 2011. Consuming and Communicating Identities: Dietary Diversity and Interaction in Middle Neolithic Sweden. PhD thesis in Archaeological Science, Stockholm University.

Fraser, J. E. 2009. *From Caledonia to Pictland: Scotland to 795* (The New Edinburgh History of Scotland 1). Edinburgh: Edinburgh University Press.

Freeborn, D. 1992. *From Old English to Standard English: A Course Book in Language Variations Across Time*. London: MacMillan.

Frei, K. M. et al. 2015. Tracing the dynamic life story of a Bronze Age female, *Scientific Reports*, 5: 10431.

Frei, K. M. et al. 2017. A matter of months: High precision migration chronology of a Bronze Age female, *PLoS ONE* 12 (6): e0178834.

Fu, Q. et al. 2016. The genetic history of Ice Age Europe, *Nature*, 534: 200–205.

Furholt, M. 2014. Upending a 'totality': Re-evaluating Corded Ware variability in Late Neolithic Europe, *Proceedings of the Prehistoric Society*, 80: 67–86.

Galinsky, K. J. et al. 2016. Population structure of UK Biobank and ancient Eurasians reveals adaptation at genes influencing blood pressure, *American Journal of Human Genetics*, 99 (5): 1130–39.

Geary, P. J. and Veeramah, K. 2016. Mapping European population movement through genomic research, *Medieval Worlds*, 4: 65–78.

Gelling, M. 1973. Further thoughts on pagan place-names, in *Otium et Negotium: Studies in Onomatology and Library Science Presented to Olof von Feilitzen*, F. Sandgren (ed.), 109–28. Stockholm: P. A. Norstedt & Sons.

Gerrard, C. with Aston, M. 2007. *The Shapwick Project, Somerset: A Rural Landscape Explored* (The Society for Medieval Archaeology Monograph 25). Abingdon: Routledge.

Gibbs, K. and Jordan, P. 2013.

Bridging the boreal forest: Siberian archaeology and the emergence of pottery among prehistoric hunter-gatherers of Northern Eurasia, *Sibirica*, 12 (1): 1–38.

Gilchrist, R. and Green, C. 2015. *Glastonbury Abbey: Archaeological Investigations 1904-79*. London: Society of Antiquaries of London.

Gladkih, M. I., Kornietz, N. L. and Soffer, O. 1984. Mammoth-bone dwellings on the Russian plain, *Scientific American* (November): 164–75.

Godfrey, J. 1979. The defeated Anglo-Saxons take service with the Eastern Emperor, in *Proceedings of the Battle Conference on Anglo-Norman Studies I*, R. A. Brown (ed.), 63–74. Ipswich: The Boydell Press; Totova, NJ: Rowman & Littlefield.

Goldhahn, J. 2009. Bredarör on Kivik: A monumental cairn and the history of its interpretation, *Antiquity*, 83 (320): 359–71.

Goldsworthy, A. 2014. *Augustus: From Revolutionary to Emperor*. London: Weidenfeld & Nicolson.

Gough, M. 1973. *The Origins of Christian Art*. London: Thames & Hudson; New York: Praeger.

Gray, H. L. 1915. *English Field Systems*. Cambridge, MA: Harvard University Press.

Green, D. H. 1998. *Language and History in the Early Germanic World*. Cambridge, New York and Melbourne: Cambridge University Press.

Green, M. 1991. *The Sun-Gods of Ancient Europe*. London: Batsford.

Greenfield, H. J. 2010. The secondary products revolution: The past, the present and the future, *World Archaeology*, 42 (1): 29–54.

Günther, T. et al. 2018. Population genomics of

Mesolithic Scandinavia: Investigating early postglacial migration routes and high-latitude adaptation, *PLoS Biology*, 16(1): e2003703.

Gwynn, R. 1985. England's 'First Refugees', *History Today*, 35 (5).

Haak, W. et al. 2008. Ancient DNA, Strontium isotopes, and osteological analyses shed light on social and kinship organization of the Later Stone Age, *Proceedings of the National Academy of Sciences of the United States of America*, 105 (47): 18226–231.

Haak, W. et al. 2015. Massive migration from the steppe is a source of Indo-European languages, *Nature*, 522: 207–11.

Hall, J. M. 2002. *Hellenicity: Between Ethnicity and Culture*. Chicago and London: University of Chicago Press.

Hamerow, H. 2002. *Early Medieval Settlements: The Archaeology of Rural Communities in North-West Europe 400-900* (Medieval History and Archaeology). Oxford and New York: Oxford University Press.

Hamerow, H. 2012. *Rural Settlements and Society in Anglo-Saxon England*. Oxford and New York: Oxford University Press.

Hamerow, H., Ferguson, C. and Naylor, J. 2013. The Origins of Wessex Pilot Project, *Oxoniensia*, 78: 49–69.

Hannon, G. E. et al. 2008. The Bronze Age landscape of the Bjäre peninsula, southern Sweden, and its relationship to burial mounds, *Journal of Archaeological Science*, 35 (3): 623–32.

Hårdh, B. and Larsson, L. (eds). 2002. *Central Places in the Migration and the Merovingian Periods: Papers from the 52nd Sachsensymposium, Lund, August 2001* (Acta Archaeologica Lundensia Series 39). Stockholm: Almqvist & Wiksell.

Hare, M. 2014. Hemming's Crosses, in *Towns and Topography: Essays in Memory of David H. Hill*, G. R. Owen-Crocker and S. D. Thompson (eds), 26–36. Oxford and Philadelphia: Oxbow Books.

Härke, H. 2007. Invisible Britons, Gallo-Romans and Russians: Perspectives on culture change, chapter 5 in *Britons in Anglo-Saxon England*, N. Higham (ed.), 57–67. Woodbridge: Boydell Press.

Härke, H. 2011. Anglo-Saxon immigration and ethnogenesis, *Medieval Archaeology*, 55: 1–28.

Harrington, S. and Welch, M. 2014. *The Early Anglo-Saxon Kingdoms of Southern Britain AD 450–650: Beneath the Tribal Hidage*. Oxford and Philadelphia: Oxbow Books.

Harrison, R. and Heyd, V. 2007. The transformation of Europe in the third millennium BC: The example of 'Le Petit-Chasseur I + III' (Sion, Valais, Switzerland), *Praehistorische Zeitschrift*, 82 (2): 129–214.

Haslam, J. 1987. Market and fortress in England in the reign of Offa, *World Archaeology*, 19 (1): 76–93.

Haslam, J. 2014. The Late Saxon burhs of Somerset, in *Towns and Topography: Essays in Memory of David. H. Hill*, G. R. Owen-Crocker and S. D. Thompson (eds), 46–67. Oxford and Philadelphia: Oxbow Books.

Heather, P. 2009. *Empires and Barbarians: Migration, Development and the Birth of Europe*. London: Macmillan.

Heather, P. and Matthews, J. 1991. *The Goths in the Fourth Century*. Liverpool: Liverpool University Press.

Heighway, C. 1984. Saxon Gloucester, in *Anglo-Saxon Towns in Southern England*, J. Haslam, (ed.), 359–83.

Chichester: Phillimore & Co. Ltd.

Henn, B. H. et al. 2012. Genomic ancestry of North Africans supports back-to-Africa migrations, *PLoS Genetics*, 8 (1): e1002397.

Henson, D. 2006. *The Origins of the Anglo-Saxons*. Ely: Anglo-Saxon Books.

Hey, D. 2000. *Family Names and Family History*. London and New York: Hambledon Continuum.

Heyd, V. 2017. Kossinna's smile, *Antiquity*, 91 (356): 348–59.

Higham, H. J. 1992. *Rome, Britain and the Anglo-Saxons*. Guildford: Seaby.

Higham, N. J., and Ryan, M. J. 2013. *The Anglo-Saxon World*. New Haven and London: Yale University Press.

Hill, D. and Rumble, A. R. (eds). 1996. *The Defence of Wessex: The Burghal Hidage and Anglo-Saxon Fortifications*. Manchester and New York: Manchester University Press.

Hills, C. and Lucy, S. 2013. *Spong Hill IX: Chronology and Synthesis*. Cambridge: McDonald Institute for Archaeological Research.

Hines, J. and Ijssennagger, N. (eds). 2017. *Frisians and their North Sea Neighbours from the Fifth Century to the Viking Age*. Woodbridge: Boydell & Brewer.

Hirst, S. et al. 2004. *The Prittlewell Prince*. London: Museum of London Archaeology Service.

Hooke, D. 1985. *The Anglo-Saxon Landscape: The Kingdom of the Hwicce*. Manchester: Manchester University Press; New York: Palgrave.

Hope-Taylor, B. 1977. *Yeavering: An Anglo-British Centre of Early Northumbria* (DoE Archaeological Report 7). London: HMSO.

Hornblower, S., Spawforth, A.

and Eidinow, E. (eds). 2012. *The Oxford Classical Dictionary* (4th ed.) Oxford: Oxford University Press.

Iakovleva, L. and Djindjian, F. 2005. New data on mammoth bone settlements of Eastern Europe in the light of the new excavations of the Gontsy site (Ukraine), *Quaternary International*, 126–28: 195–207.

Iverson, R. and Kroonen, G. 2017. Talking Neolithic: Linguistic and archaeological perspectives on how Indo-European was implemented in Southern Scandinavia, *American Journal of Archaeology*, 121 (4): 511–25.

Jobling, M. et al. 2014. *Human Evolutionary Genetics* (2nd ed.) New York and Abingdon: Garland Science.

Johannsen, J. W. 2010. The wheeled vehicles of the Bronze Age on Scandinavian rock-carvings, *Acta Archaeologica*, 81: 150–250.

John, E. 1996. *Reassessing Anglo-Saxon England*. Manchester and New York: Manchester University Press.

Jones, E. et al. 2015. Upper Palaeolithic genomes reveal deep roots of modern Eurasians, *Nature Communications*, 6: 8912.

Jones, E. et al. 2017. The Neolithic Transition in the Baltic was not driven by admixture with early European farmers, *Current Biology*, 27: 1–7.

Jordan, P. 2010. Understanding the spread of innovations in prehistoric social networks: New insights into the origins and dispersal of early pottery in Northern Eurasia, in *Transference: Interdisciplinary Communications 2008/2009*, W. Østreng (ed.) (internet publication). Oslo: Centre for Advanced Study.

Jovaisa, E. 2001. The Balts and the amber, in *Baltic Amber: Proceedings of the International Interdisciplinary Conference: Baltic Amber in Natural Sciences, Archaeology and Applied Arts, 13–18 September 2001, Vilnius, Palana, Nida*, A. Butrimas (ed.), 149–56. Vilnius: Vilnius Academy of Fine Arts Press.

Juras, A. et al. 2014. Ancient DNA reveals matrilineal continuity in present-day Poland over the last two millennia, *PloS ONE*, 9 (10): e110839.

Kaliff, A. 2001. *Gothic Connections: Contacts between Eastern Scandinavia and the Southern Baltic Coast 1000 BC–500 AD* (Occasional Papers in Archaeology 26). Uppsala: Uppsala University.

Kallio, P. 2012. The prehistoric Germanic loanword strata in Finnic, in *A Linguistic Map of Prehistoric Northern Europe* (Suomalais-Ugrilaisen Seuran Toimituksia [Mémoires de la Société Finno-Ougrienne] 266), R. Grünthal and P. Kallio (eds), 225–38. Helsinki: Société Finno-Ougrienne.

Kallio, P. 2015. The language contact situation in prehistoric Northeastern Europe, in *The Linguistic Roots of Europe: Origin and Development of European Languages* (Copenhagen Studies in Indo-European 6), R. Mailhammer, T. Vennemann and B. A. Olsen (eds), 77–102. Copenhagen: Museum Tusculanum Press.

Kaul, F. 1998. Ships on Bronzes. *A Study in Bronze Age Religion and Iconography*. Copenhagen: National Museum Studies in Archaeology and History, 3.

Kaul, F. 2014. Mythological aspects of Nordic Bronze Age religion, chapter 9 in *The Handbook of Religions in Ancient Europe*, L. B. Christiansen,

O. Hammer and D. A. Warburton (eds), 70–76. Abingdon and New York: Routledge.

Kershaw, J. and Røyrvik, E. C. 2016. The 'People of the British Isles' project and Viking settlement in England, *Antiquity*, 90 (354): 1670–80.

Kivisild, T. 2017. The study of human Y chromosome variation through ancient DNA, *Human Genetics*, online: 4 March 2017.

Kokowski, A. 2013. The Goths in ca. 311 AD, in *Wulfila 311–2011: International Symposium. Uppsala University June 15–18, 2011* (Acta Bibliothecae R. Universitatis Upsaliensis, vol. XLVIII, Occasional Papers in Archaeology 57), A. Kaliff and L. Munkhammar (eds), 71–96. Uppsala: Uppsala University.

Krahe, H. 1963. *Die Struktur der alteuropäischen Hydronomie*. Wiesbaden: Akademie der Wissenschaften und der Literatur.

Kremenetski, C. V. 2003. Steppe and forest-steppe belt of Eurasia: Holocene environmental history, chapter 2 in *Prehistoric Steppe Adaptation and the Horse*, M. Levine, C. Renfrew and K. Boyle (eds), 11–27. Cambridge: McDonald Institute for Archaeological Research.

Kremenetski, C. V., Chichagova, O. A. and Shishlina, N. I. 1999. Palaeoecological evidence for Holocene vegetation, climate and land-use change in the low Don basin and Kalmuk area, southern Russia, *Vegetation History and Archaeobotany*, 8 (4): 233–46.

Kristiansen, K. 1989. Prehistoric migrations – the case of the Single Grave and Corded Ware cultures, *Journal of Danish Archaeology*, 8: 211–25.

Kristiansen, K. 1998. *Europe*

before History (New Studies in Archaeology). Cambridge and New York: Cambridge University Press.

Kristiansen, K. 2005. What language did Neolithic pots speak? Colin Renfrew's European farming-language-dispersal model challenged, *Antiquity*, 79 (305): 694–95.

Kristiansen, K. 2017. Interpreting Bronze Age trade and migration, chapter 10 in *Human Mobility and Technological Transfer in the Prehistoric Mediterranean*, E. Kiriatzi and C. Knappett (eds), 154–80. Cambridge and New York: Cambridge University Press.

Kristiansen, K. et al. 2017. Re-theorising mobility and the formation of culture and language among the Corded Ware Culture in Europe, *Antiquity*, 91 (356): 334–47.

Kristiansen, K. and Larsson, T. B. 2005. *The Rise of Bronze Age Society: Travels, Transmissions and Transformations*. Cambridge and New York: Cambridge University Press.

Kristinsson, A. 2010. *Expansions: Competition and Conquest in Europe Since the Bronze Age*. Reykjavik: Reykjavik Academy.

Kroonen, G. 2012. Non-Indo-European root nouns in Germanic evidence in support of the Agricultural Substrate Hypothesis, in *A Linguistic Map of Prehistoric Northern Europe* (Suomalais-Ugrilaisen Seuran Toimituksia [Mémoires de la Société Finno-Ougrienne] 266), R. Grünthal and P. Kallio (eds), 239–60. Helsinki: Société Finno-Ougrienne.

Kuzmin, Y. V. and Keates, S. G. 2016. Siberia and neighboring regions in the Last Glacial Maximum: Did people occupy northern Eurasia at that time?, *Archaeological and Anthropological Sciences*, online 21 May 2016.

Lapidge, M. et al. 1999. *The Blackwell Encyclopedia of Anglo-Saxon England*. Oxford and Malden, MA: Blackwell Publishers.

Larichev, V., Khol'ushkin, U. and Laricheva, I. 1990. The Upper Paleolithic of Northern Asia: Achievements, problems, and perspectives. II. Central and Eastern Siberia, *Journal of World Prehistory*, 4(3): 347–85.

Larsson, Å. M. 2009. Breaking and Making Bodies and Pots: Material and Ritual Practices in Sweden in the Third Millennium BC. Dissertation, Uppsala University.

Lazaridis, I. et al. 2014. Ancient human genomes suggest three ancestral populations for present-day Europeans, *Nature*, 513: 409–13.

Lazaridis, I. et al. 2016. Genomic insights into the origin of farming in the ancient Near East, *Nature*, 536: 419–24.

Lbova, L. V. and Volkov, P. V. 2015. Microscopic analysis of the anthropomorphic figurines from Malta (technology of formation, detalization and decoration), *Stratum plus* (1): 161–68.

Leahy, K. and Bland, R. 2014. *The Staffordshire Hoard* (2nd ed.). London: The British Museum.

Leslie, S. 2015. The fine-scale genetic structure of the British population, *Nature*, 519: 309–14.

Lindow, J. 2002. Myth read as history: Odin in Snorri Sturluson's *Ynglinga Saga*, chapter 7 in *Myth: A New Symposium*, G. A. Schrempp and W. F. Hansen (eds), 107–23. Bloomington and Chesham: Indiana University Press.

Ling, J. 2012. War canoes or social units? Human representation in rock-art ships, *European Journal of Archaeology*, 15 (3): 465–85.

Ling, J. et al. 2014. Moving metals II: Provenancing Scandinavian Bronze Age artefacts by lead isotope and elemental analyses, *Journal of Archaeological Science*, 41: 106–32.

Ling, J. and Stos-Gale, Z. 2015. Representations of oxhide ingots in Scandinavian rock art: The sketchbook of a Bronze Age traveller?, *Antiquity*, 89 (343): 191–209.

Lipson, M. 2017. Parallel ancient genomic transects reveal complex population history of early European farmers, *Nature*, 551: 368–72.

Ljungkvist, J. 2008. Valsgärde. Valsgärde – development and change of a burial ground for 1300 years, in *Valsgärde Studies: The Place and its People, Past and Present*, S. Norr (ed.), 13–55. Uppsala: Uppsala University.

Ljungkvist, J. 2010. Influences from the empire: Byzantine-related objects in Sweden and Scandinavia – 560/570–750/800 AD, in *Byzanz – das Römerreich im Mittelalter Teil 3 Peripherie und Nachbarschaft*, F. Daim and J. Drauschke (eds), 419–41. Mainz: Verlag des Römisch-Germanischen Zentralmuseums.

Lomax, S. 2013. *Nottingham: The Buried Past of a City Revealed*. Barnsley: Pen and Sword Archaeology.

Looijenga, T. 2003. *Texts and Contexts of the Oldest Runic Inscriptions*. Leiden and Boston: Brill.

Lõugas, L., Kriiska, A. and Maldre, L. 2007. New dates for the Late Neolithic Corded Ware Culture burials and early husbandry in the East Baltic region, *Archaeofauna*, 16: 21–31.

McGrail, S. 2004. *Boats of the World: From the Stone Age to Medieval Times* (2nd ed.). Oxford and New York: Oxford University Press.

McKenzie, H. G. 2010. Review of early hunter-gatherer pottery in Eastern Siberia, in *Ceramics before Farming: The Dispersal of Pottery among Prehistoric Eurasian Hunter-Gatherers*, P. Jordan and M. Zvelebil (eds), 166–207. Walnut Creek, CA: Left Coast Press.

McKinley, J. I., Schuster, J. and Millard, A. 2013. Dead-sea connections: A Bronze Age and Iron Age ritual site on the Isle of Thanet, chapter 6 in *Celtic from the West 2: Rethinking the Bronze Age and the Arrival of Indo-European in Atlantic Europe*, J. T. Koch and B. Cunliffe (eds), 157–83. Oxford and Oakville, CT: Oxbow Books.

Maitland, F. W. 1897. *Domesday Book and Beyond: Three Essays in the Early History of England*. Cambridge: Cambridge University Press; Boston: Little, Brown & Co.

Makhortyk, S. V. 2008. On the question of Cimmerian imports and imitations in Central Europe, in *Import and Imitation in Archaeology*, P. F. Biehl and Y. Ya. Rassamakin (eds), 167–86. Langenweißbach: Beier & Beran.

Mallory, J. P. 1989. *In Search of the Indo-Europeans: Language, Archaeology and Myth*. London and New York: Thames & Hudson.

Mallory, J. P. 2013. The Indo-Europeanization of Atlantic Europe, chapter 1 in *Celtic from the West 2: Rethinking the Bronze Age and the Arrival of Indo-European in Atlantic Europe*, J. T. Koch and B. Cunliffe (eds), 17–39. Oxford and Oakville, CT: Oxbow Books.

Mallory, J. P. and Adams, D. Q. (eds). 1997. *Encyclopedia of Indo-European Culture*. London and

Chicago: Fitzroy Dearborn Publishers.

Mallory, J. P. and Adams, D. Q. 2006. *Oxford Introduction to Proto-Indo-European and the Proto-Indo-European World*. Oxford and New York: Oxford University Press.

Malmstrom, H. et al. 2009. Ancient DNA reveals lack of continuity between Neolithic hunter-gatherers and contemporary Scandinavians, *Current Biology*, 19: 1–5.

Manco, J. 1995. Iron Acton: A Saxon nucleated settlement, *Bristol and Gloucestershire Archaeological Society*, 113: 89–95.

Manco, J. 1998. Saxon Bath: The legacy of Rome and the Saxon rebirth, *Bath History*, 7: 27–54.

Manco, J. 2015, *Ancestral Journeys: The Peopling of Europe from the First Venturers to the Vikings* (2nd ed.). London and New York: Thames & Hudson.

Manco, J. 2015. *Blood of the Celts: The New Ancestral Story*. London and New York: Thames & Hudson.

Maran, J. 2013. Bright as the sun: The appropriation of amber objects in Mycenaean Greece, chapter 11 in *Mobility, Meaning and Transformations of Things: Shifting Contexts of Material Culture Through Time and Space*, H. P. Hahn and H. Weis (eds), 147–69. Oxford: Oxbow; Oakville, CT: David Brown Book Co.

Martens, J. 2010. Pre-Roman Iron Age settlements in southern Scandinavia, in *Berliner Archäologische Forschungen*, 8, M. Meyer (ed.), 229–50.

Martens, J. 2014. Jastorf and Jutland (On the northern extent of the so-called Jastorf Culture), in Brandt and Rauchfuß (eds) 2014, 245–66.

Martínez Pizarro, J. 1996. Kings in adversity: A note on Alfred and the cakes, *Neophilologus*, 80 (2): 319–26.

Martiniano, R. et al. 2016. Genomic signals of migration and continuity in Britain before the Anglo-Saxons, *Nature Communications*, 7: 10326.

Mathieson, I. et al. 2015. Genome-wide patterns of selection in 230 ancient Eurasians, *Nature*, 528: 499–503.

Mathieson, I. et al. 2018. The genomic history of southeastern Europe, *Nature*, 555: 197–203.

Melheim, L. 2012. Towards a new understanding of Late Neolithic Norway – the role of metal and metal working, in *Becoming European*, C. Prescott and H. Glørstad (eds), 70–81. Oxford and Oakville, CT: Oxbow Books.

Melheim, L. and Prescott, C. 2016. Exploring new territories – expanding frontiers: Bowmen and prospectors on the Scandinavian Peninsula in the 3rd millennium BC, chapter 10 in *Comparative Perspectives on Past Colonisation, Maritime Interaction and Cultural Integration*, L. Melheim, H. Glørstad and Z. T. Glørstad (eds), 189–217. Sheffield: Equinox Publishing.

Michalowski, A. 2014. Elements of the Jastorf culture in Wielkopolska. Import of ideas or migration of peoples?, in Brandt and Rauchfuß (eds) 2014, 287–301.

Mittnik, A. et. al. 2018. The genetic history of Northern Europe, *Nature Communications*, 9: 442.

Moffat, A. and Wilson, J. 2011. *The Scots: A Genetic Journey*. Edinburgh: Birlinn.

Montgomery, J. et al. 2005. Continuity or colonization in Anglo-Saxon England? Isotope evidence for mobility, subsistence practice, and status at West Heslerton, *American Journal of Physical Anthropology*, 126: 123–38.

Moreno-Mayar, J. V. et al. 2018. Terminal Pleistocene Alaskan genome reveals first founding population of Native Americans, *Nature*, 553: 203–7.

Morgunova, N. L. and Turetskij, M. A. 2016. Archaeological and natural scientific studies of Pit-Grave Culture barrows in the Volga-Ural interfluve, *Estonian Journal of Archaeology*, 20 (2): 128–49.

Mörner, N.-A. and Lind, B. G. 2015. Long-distance travel and trading in the Bronze Age: The East Mediterranean-Scandinavia case, *Archaeological Discovery*, 3: 129–39.

Mukherjee, A. J. et al. 2008. The Qatna lion: scientific confirmation of Baltic amber in late Bronze Age Syria, *Antiquity*, 82: 49–59.

Müller, J. et al. 2009. A revision of Corded Ware settlement pattern – new results from the Central European low mountain range, *Proceedings of the Prehistoric Society*, 75: 125–42.

Müller, M. 1888. *Biographies of Words and the Home of the Aryas*. London and New York: Longman's, Green & Co.

Müller, R. 2000. Jastorf-Kultur, *Reallexikon der Germanischen Altertumskunde* (2nd ed.), vol. 16. Berlin/New York: Walter de Gruyter.

Murdoch, A. 2006. *Rome's Greatest Defeat: Massacre in the Teutoburg Forest*. Stroud, Gloucestershire: Sutton Publishing.

Murray, T. 2007. *Milestones in Archaeology: A Chronological Encyclopedia*. Santa Barbara, CA and Oxford: ABC CLIO.

Murillo-Barroso, M. and Montero-Ruiz, I. 2012. Amber sources and trade in the prehistory of the Iberian Peninsula, *European Journal of Archaeology*, 15 (2): 187–216

Neidorf, L. 2013. The dating of Widsið and the study of Germanic antiquity, *Neophilologus*, 97: 165–83.

Neidorf, L. 2013. Scribal errors of proper names in the Beowulf manuscript, *Anglo-Saxon England*, 42: 249–69.

Neidorf, L. (ed.) 2014. *The Dating of Beowulf: A Reassessment*. Cambridge: D. S. Brewer.

Neidorf, L. 2015. Cain, Cam, Jutes, giants, and the textual criticism of Beowulf, *Studies in Philology*, 112 (4): 599–632.

Neveux, F. 2008. *A Brief History of the Normans: The Conquests that Changed the Face of Europe*, trans. H. Curtis. London: Constable & Robinson; Philadelphia: Running Press.

Nieuwhof, A. 2013. Anglo-Saxon immigration or continuity? Ezinge and the coastal area of the northern Netherlands in the Migration Period, *Journal of Archaeology in the Low Countries*, 4 (2): 53–83.

Niles, J. D. (ed.), 2007. *Beowulf and Lejre*. Arizona Studies in the Middle Ages and the Renaissance 22. Tempe, AZ: ACMRS.

Norquist, K. et al. 2012. Early copper use in Neolithic Northeastern Europe: an overview, *Estonian Journal of Archaeology*, 16 (1): 3–25.

Ó Carragáin, É. 2007. Christian inculturation in eighth-century Northumbria: The Bewcastle and Ruthwell Crosses, *Colloquium*, 4. New Haven: Yale Institute of Sacred Music.

Olausson, D. 2015. Burial in the Swedish-Norwegian Battle Axe Culture: Questioning the myth of homogeneity, in *Neolithic Diversities: Perspectives from a Conference in Lund, Sweden*, K. Brink, S. Hydén, K. Jennbert, L. Larsson, and D. Olausson (eds), 98–106. Lund: Lund University.

Olsen, S. L. 2006. Early horse domestication on the Eurasian steppe, chapter 17 in *Documenting Domestication: New Genetic and Archaeological Paradigms*, M. Zeder, D. G. Bradley, E. Emshwiller and B. D. Smith (eds), 245–69. Berkeley, CA and London: University of California Press.

Ormrod, W. M. 2013. Medieval immigrants: Moving to England in the Middle Ages, *BBC History Magazine*. And see the online database: https://www.englandsimmigrants.com.

Pare, C. F. E. 2000. Bronze and the Bronze Age, in *Metals Make the World Go Round: The Supply and Circulation of Metals in Bronze Age Europe. Proceedings of a Conference Held at the University of Birmingham in June 1997*, C. F. E. Pare (ed.), 1–32. Oxford: Oxbow Books.

Parpola, A. 2008. Proto-Indo-European speakers of the Late Tripolye culture as the inventors of wheeled vehicles: Linguistic and archaeological considerations, in *Proceedings of the 19th Annual UCLA Indo-European Conference* (The Journal of Indo-European Studies Monograph Series 54), K. Jones-Bley, M. E. Huld, A. Della Volpe and M. Robbins Dexter (eds), 1–59. Washington, DC: Institute for the Study of Man.

Parpola, A. 2012. Formation of the Indo-European and Uralic (Finno-Ugric) language families in the light of archaeology: Revised and integrated 'total' correlations, in *A Linguistic Map of Prehistoric Northern Europe* (Suomalais-Ugrilaisen Seuran Toimituksia [Mémoires de la Société Finno-Ougrienne] 266), R. Grünthal and P. Kallio (eds), 119–84. Helsinki: Société Finno-Ougrienne.

Parsons, D. and Sutherland, D. 2013. *The Anglo-Saxon Church of All Saints, Brixworth, Northamptonshire: Survey, Excavation and Analysis 1972–2010*. Oxford: Oxbow Books.

Pelteret, D. A. E. 1985. Slavery in Anglo-Saxon England, chapter 9 in *The Anglo-Saxons: Synthesis and Achievement*, J. D. Woods and D. A.E. Pelteret (eds), 117–33. Waterloo, ON: Wilfrid Laurier University Press; Atlantic Highlands, NJ: Humanities Press.

Perdikaris, S. 2004. Pre-Roman Iron Age Scandinavia, in *Ancient Europe 8000 BC–AD 1000: Encyclopedia of the Barbarian World*, vol. 2, P. Bogucki and P. J. Crabtree (eds), 269–75. Farmington, MI and London: Charles Scribner's & Sons.

Pereltsvaig, A. and Lewis, M. 2015. *The Indo-European Controversy: Facts and Fallacies in Historical Linguistics*. Cambridge: Cambridge University Press.

Pernicka, E. and Anthony, D. W. 2010. The invention of copper metallurgy and the Copper Age of Old Europe, in *The Lost World of Old Europe – the Danube Valley 5000–3500 BC*, D. W. Anthony and J. Y. Chi (eds), 163–177. Princeton, NJ and Oxford: Princeton University Press.

Piotrowska, D. 1998. Biskupin 1933–1996: Archaeology, politics and nationalism, *Archaeologia Polona*, 35–36 (1997–98): 255–85.

Pitulko, V. V. et al. 2004. The Yana RHS site: Humans in the Arctic before the last glacial maximum, *Science*, 303: 52–56.

Pitulko, V. V. et al. 2012. The oldest art of the Eurasian Arctic: Personal ornaments and symbolic objects from Yana RHS, Arctic Siberia, *Antiquity*, 86 (333): 642–59.

Pitulko, V. V. et al. 2016. Early human presence in the Arctic: Evidence from 45,000-year-old mammoth remains, *Science*, 351 (6270): 260–63.

Pohl, W. 1997. Ethnic names and identities in the British Isles: A comparative perspective, in *The Anglo-Saxons from the Migration Period to the Eighth Century: An Ethnographic Perspective*, J. Hines (ed.), 7–64. Woodbridge and Rochester, NY: Boydell Press.

Pokutta, D. A. 2014. Journey to murder: Atypical graves of the immigrants in the Early Bronze Age Europe, *Sprawozdania Archeologiczne*, 66: 91–100.

Pratchett, T. 1997. *Jingo*. London: Victor Gollancz.

Pratchett, T. 2014. *A Slip of the Keyboard: Collected Non-Fiction*. London: Corgi Books; New York: Doubleday.

Prescott, C. 2006. Copper production in Bronze Age Norway?, in *Historien i Forhistorien. Festskrift til Einar Østmo på 60-årsdagen* (Skrifter no. 4, Kulturhistorisk Museum), H. Glørstad, B. Skar and D. Skre (eds), 183–90. Oslo: Universitetet i Oslo.

Price, T. D. 2015. *Ancient Scandinavia: An Archaeological History from the First Humans to the Vikings*. Oxford and New York: Oxford University Press.

Quintana-Murci, L. and Fellous, M. 2001. The human Y chromosome: The biological role of a 'functional wasteland', *Journal of Biomedicine and Biotechnology*, 1 (1): 18–24.

Raghavan, M. et al. 2014. Upper Palaeolithic Siberian genome reveals dual ancestry of Native Americans, *Nature*, 505: 87–91.

Ramqvist, P. H. 1992. Building traditions during the Iron Age, in *Contacts across the Baltic Sea during the Late Iron Age 5th–12th centuries: Baltic Sea Conference, Lund October 25–27, 1991*, B. Hårdh and B. Wyszomirska-Werbart (eds), 63–75. Lund: University of Lund.

Ray, K. and Bapty, I. 2016. *Offa's Dyke: Landscape & Hegemony in Eighth-Century Britain*. Oxford: Windgather Press.

Redfern, R. C. et al. 2016. Going south of the river: A multidisciplinary analysis of ancestry, mobility and diet in a population from Roman Southwark, London, *Journal of Archaeological Science*, 74: 11–22.

Ringe, D. 2006. *From Proto-Indo-European to Proto-Germanic: A Linguistic History of English Vol. 1*. Oxford: Oxford University Press. Kindle ed.

Ringe, D. and Taylor, A. 2014. *The Development of Old English: A Linguistic History of English Vol. II*. Oxford: Oxford University Press.

Ringe, D., Warnow, T. and Taylor, A. 2002. Indo-European and computational cladistics, *Transactions of the Philological Society*, 100: 59–129.

Rives, J. B. 2012. Germania, chapter 3 in *A Companion to Tacitus*, V. E. Pagán (ed.), Chichester and Malden, MA: Wiley-Blackwell.

Rivet, A. L. F. and Smith, C. 1979. *The Place-Names of Roman Britain*. London: Batsford; Princeton, NJ: Princeton University Press.

Rix, R. 2014. *The Barbarian North in Medieval Imagination: Ethnicity, Legend, and Literature*. New York and Abingdon, Oxon: Routledge.

Roberts, B. W., Thornton, C. P. and Pigott, V. C. 2009. Development of metallurgy in Eurasia, *Antiquity*, 83: 1012–22.

Roberts, J. (ed.). 2007. *Oxford Dictionary of the Classical World*. Oxford and New York: Oxford University Press.

Robertson, J. S. 2012. How the Germanic Futhark came from the Roman alphabet, *Futhark: International Journal of Runic Studies*, 2: 7–25.

Roller, D. W. 2006. *Through the Pillars of Herakles: Greco-Roman Exploration of the Atlantic*. New York and London: Routledge.

Rose, C. B. 2014. *The Archaeology of Greek and Roman Troy*. New York: Cambridge University Press.

Russo, D. G. 1998. *Town Origins and Development in Early England c. 400–950 AD*. Westport, CT and London: Greenwood Press.

Salmons, J. 2012. *A History of German*. Oxford: Oxford University Press.

Sarauw, T. 2006. Bejsebakken: a Bell Beaker site in northern Jutland, in *People, Material Culture and Environment in the North: Proceedings of the 22nd Nordic Archaeological Conference, University of Oulu, 18–23 August 2004* (Studia Humaniora Ouluensia 1), V.-P. Herva (ed.), 238–47. Oulu, Finland: Humanisten tiedekunta, Oulun ylipisto.

Schiffels, S. et al. 2016. Iron Age and Anglo-Saxon genomes from East England reveal British migration history, *Nature Communications*, 7: 10408.

Schrader, O. 1883. *Sprachvergleichung und Urgeschichte. Linguistisch-historische Beiträge zur Erforschung des indogermanischen Altertums*. Jena. The 2nd ed. was translated into English by F. B. Jevons as *Prehistoric*

Antiquities of the Aryan Peoples, London: Charles Griffin & Co. 1890.

Schrijver, P. 2014. Language Contact and the Origins of the Germanic Languages. New York and Abingdon, Oxon: Routledge.

Schröder, E. 1999. Walburg, die Sibyll, Archiv für Religionswissenschaft, 19: 196–200.

Schuenemann, V. J. et al. 2017. Ancient Egyptian mummy genomes suggest an increase of Sub-Saharan African ancestry in Post-Roman periods, Nature Communications, 8: 15694.

Scull, C. 2002. Ipswich: Development and contexts of an urban precursor in the seventh century, in B. Hårdh and L. Larsson (eds) 2002, 303–15.

Scull, C., Minter, F. and Plouviez, J. 2016. Social and economic complexity in early medieval England: A central place complex of the East Anglian kingdom at Rendlesham, Suffolk, Antiquity, 90 (354): 1594–612.

Seeley, J. R. 1883. The Expansion of England: Two Courses of Lectures. London: Macmillan.

Sheppard, A. 2004. Families of the King: Writing Identity in the Anglo-Saxon Chronicle. Toronto, ON, Buffalo, NJ and London: University of Toronto Press.

Sherlock, S. and Simmons, M. 2008. A seventh-century royal cemetery at Street House, north-east Yorkshire, England, Antiquity, 82 (316).

Sherlock, S. J. and Welch, M. G. 1992. An Anglo-Saxon Cemetery at Norton, Cleveland. Report No. 82. York: Council for British Archaeology.

Shishlina, N. 2013. The steppe and the Caucasus during the Bronze Age: Mutual relationships and mutual

enrichments, in Counterpoint: Essays in Archaeology and Heritage Studies in Honour of Professor Kristian Kristiansen (BAR International Series 2508), S. Bergerbrant and S. Sabatini (eds), 53–60. Oxford: Archaeopress.

Sims-Williams, P. 1988. St Wilfred and two charters dated AD 676 and 680, Journal of Ecclesiastical History, 39 (2): 163–83.

Sims-Williams, P. 1990. Religion and Literature in Western England 600–800. Cambridge and New York: Cambridge University Press.

Sims-Williams, P. 2006. Ancient Celtic Place-Names in Europe and Asia Minor (Publications of the Philological Society, 39). Oxford and Boston: Blackwell Publishing.

Smith, A. D. 1986. The Ethnic Origins of Nations. Oxford and New York: Blackwell.

Smith, E., Hutton, G. and Cook, O. 1979. English Parish Churches. New York and London: Thames & Hudson.

Sørensen, M. 2013. The first eastern migrations of people and knowledge into Scandinavia: Evidence from studies of Mesolithic technology, 9th–8th millennium BC, Norwegian Archaeological Review, 46(1): 19–56.

Soulat, J. 2009. La pénétration des groupes Saxons et Anglo-Saxons dans Le Ponthieu entre la fin du IVe et le milieu du VIe siecle, Revue Archaeologique de Picardie, 1 (2): 27–34.

Spall, C. and Toop, N. 2008. Before Eoforwic: New light on York in the 6th–7th centuries, Medieval Archaeology, 52: 1–25.

Springer, M. 2003. Location in space and time, in The Continental Saxons from the Migration Period to the Tenth

Century: An Ethnographic Perspective, D. H. Green and F. Siegmund (eds), 11–36. Woodbridge: Boydell Press.

Spurkland, T. 2010. The Older Fuþark and Roman script literacy, Futhark: International Journal of Runic Studies, 1: 65–84.

Stenton, F. M. 1970. Medeshamstede and its colonies, in Preparatory to Anglo-Saxon England, Being the Collected Papers of Frank Merry Stenton, D. M. Stenton (ed.), 179–92. Oxford: Oxford University Press.

Stoodley, N. 2002. The origins of Hamwic and its central role in the seventh century as revealed by recent archaeological discoveries, in Hårdh and Larsson (eds) 2002, 317–31.

Szécsényi-Nagy, A. et al. 2015. Tracing the genetic origin of Europe's first farmers reveals insights into their social organization, Proceedings of the Royal Society B: Biological Sciences, 282 (1805): 20150339.

Talbert, R. J. A. (ed.). 2000. Barrington Atlas of the Greek and Roman World. 2 vols. Princeton, NJ and Oxford: Princeton University Press.

Teasdale, D. et al. 2017. The York Gospels: A one thousand year biological palimpsest, Royal Society Open Science, 4:170998.

Teska, M. 2014. The Oksywie Culture on the right-bank Lower Vistula, Archaeologia Lituana, 15: 23–30.

Theune-Großkopf, B. 2008. Warrior and musician: The lyre from Grave 58 at Trossingen and its owner, in Challenges and Objectives in Music Archaeology (Studien zur Musikarchäologie VI, Orient-Archäologie 22), A. A. Both, R. Eichmann, E. Hickmann and L.-C. Koch (eds), 217–27. Rahden: Leidorf.

Thirsk, J. 1964. The common fields, *Past & Present*, 29 (1): 3–25.

Thomas, C. 1981. *Christianity in Roman Britain to AD 500*. Berkeley and Los Angeles: University of California Press; London: Batsford.

Thornton, C. P. 2009. The emergence of complex metallurgy on the Iranian Plateau: Escaping the Levantine paradigm, *Journal of World Prehistory*, 22 (3): 301–27.

Todd, M. 2004. *The Early Germans* (The Peoples of Europe) (2nd ed.). Maldon, MA, Oxford and Carlton, Victoria: Wiley-Blackwell.

Tolkien, J. R. R. 1937. Beowulf: The monsters and the critics, *Proceedings of the British Academy*, 22: 245–95.

Tolkien, J. R. R. 1953. The homecoming of Beorhtnoth Beorhthelm's son, *Essays and Studies by Members of the English Association*, 6: 1–18.

Tolkien, J. R. R. 1981. *The Letters of J. R. R. Tolkien*, ed. H. Carpenter. Boston: Houghton Mifflin; London: George Allen & Unwin.

Toorians, L. 2006. Betuwe en Hessen, Bataven en Chatten, *Naamkunde*, 36: 179–90.

Tristram, H. 2007. Why don't the English speak Welsh?, chapter 15 in *Britons in Anglo-Saxon England*, N. Higham (ed.), 192–214. Woodbridge: Boydell Press.

Tucker, S. 2011. *Battles that Changed History: An Encyclopedia of World Conflict*. Santa Barbara, CA: ABC-CLIO.

Ulmschneider, K. 2002. Central places and metal-detector finds: What are the English 'Productive Sites'? in Hårdh and Larsson (eds) 2002, 333–39.

Vandkilde, H. 2005. A review of the early Late Neolithic period in Denmark: Practice, identity and connectivity, online at: http://www.jna.uni-kiel.de/index.php/jna/article/view/13. Last accessed 3 May 2018.

Vandkilde, H. 2011. Cultural perspectives on the beginnings of the Nordic Bronze Age, *Offa*, 67/68: 51–77.

Varberg, J. et al. 2015. Between Egypt, Mesopotamia and Scandinavia: Late Bronze Age glass beads found in Denmark, *Journal of Archaeological Science*, 54: 168–81.

Varberg, J. et al. 2016. Mesopotamian glass from Late Bronze Age Egypt, Romania, Germany, and Denmark, *Journal of Archaeological Science*, 74: 184–94.

Vasilieva, I. N. 2011. The early neolithic pottery of the Volga-Ural region (based on the materials of the Elshanka culture), *Archaeology, Ethnology and Anthropology of Eurasia*, 39 (2): 70–81.

Weale, M. E. et al. 2002. Y chromosome evidence for Anglo-Saxon mass migration, *Molecular Biology and Evolution*, 19: 1008–21.

Webster, L. 2011. The Prittlewell (Essex) burial: A comparison with other Anglo-Saxon princely graves, in *Transformations in North-Western Europe (AD 300–1000): Proceedings of the 60th Sachsensymposion 19.–23. September 2009 Maastricht (Neue Studien zur Sachsenforschung 3)*, T. A. S. M. Panhuysen and B. Ludowici (eds), 266–72. Hanover: Konrad Theiss.

Webster, L. 2012. *The Franks Casket*. London: British Museum Press.

Wicker, N. L. 2015. Bracteate inscriptions and context analysis in the light of alternatives to Hauck's iconographic interpretations, *Futhark: International Journal of Runic Studies*, 5 (2014, publ. 2015): 25–43.

Wightman, E. M. 1985. *Gallia Belgica*. Berkeley and Los Angeles: University of California Press; London: Batsford.

Williams, G. 2011. *Treasures from Sutton Hoo*. London: The British Museum Press.

Williams, H. 2015. Beowulf and archaeology: Megaliths imagined and encountered in Early Medieval Europe, in *The Lives of Prehistoric Monuments in Iron Age, Roman and Medieval Europe*, M. Diaz-Guardamino Uribe, L. García Sanjuán and D. Wheatley (eds), 77–97. Oxford: Oxford University Press.

Włodarczak, P. 2009. Radiocarbon and dendrochronological dates of the Corded Ware culture, *Radiocarbon*, 51 (2): 737–49.

Włodarczak, P. 2014. The traits of Early-Bronze Pontic cultures in the development of Old Upland Corded Ware (Małopolska group) and Złota culture communities, in *Reception Zones of 'Early Bronze Age' Pontic Culture Traditions: Baltic Basin – Baltic and Black Sea Drainage Borderlands, 4/3 Mil. to First Half 2 Mil. BC* (Baltic-Pontic Studies 19), A. Kosko et al. (eds), 7–52. Poznań: Adam Mickiewicz University.

Woidich, M. 2014. The Western Globular Amphora Culture: A new model for its emergence and expansion, *eTopoi: Journal for Ancient Studies*, 3: 67–85.

Wood, I. 1991. The Franks and Sutton Hoo, chapter 1 in *People and Places in Northern Europe, 500–1600: Essays in Honour of Peter Hayes Sawyer*,

I. Wood and N. Lund (eds), 1–14. Woodbridge, Suffolk and Rochester, NY: Boydell Press.

Woodward, A. and Hunter, J. et al. 2015. *Ritual in Early Bronze Age Grave Goods*. Oxford and Philadelphia: Oxbow.

Woolf, A. 2007. Apartheid and economics in Anglo-Saxon England, chapter 10 in *Britons in Anglo-Saxon England*, N. Higham (ed.), 115–29. Woodbridge: Boydell Press.

Wozniak, Z., Grygiel, M., Machajewski, H. and Michalowski, A. 2013. *The Jastorf Culture in Poland* (BAR International Series 2579). Oxford: Archaeopress.

Wu, X. et al. 2012. Early pottery at 20,000 years ago in Xianrendong Cave, China, *Science*, 336 (6089): 1696–700.

Yener, K. A. et al. 2015. New tin mines and production sites near Kültepe in Turkey: A third-millennium BC

highland production model, *Antiquity*, 89 (345): 596–612.

Yorke, B. A. E. 1982. The foundation of the Old Minster and the status of Winchester in the seventh and eighth centuries, *Proceedings of the Hampshire Field Club and Archaeological Society*, 38: 75–84.

Yorke, B. 1990. *Kings and Kingdoms of Early Anglo-Saxon England*. London and New York: Routledge.

Acknowledgments

This book has benefited from the kindness of archaeologists who have passed their papers and ideas on to me: Heinrich Härke and Catherine Hills have been enlightening on the Anglo-Saxons, while Alan Reilly generously shared with me his suggestion of a link between pressure-blade making and incomers into Europe from Siberia. Enthusiast Harry Amphlett has been an unfailing source of encouragement to pursue the Anglo-Saxons, pointing me to many useful publications. Michał Milewski has kindly advised me on Polish history, as well as making publicly available his research on Y-DNA R1a.

Sources of Illustrations

Index